The Springer Series on Death and Suicide

ROBERT KASTENBAUM, Ph.D., Series Editor

Brian L. Mishara PhD, is Professor in the Psychology Department and researcher in the Laboratory for Research on Human and Social Ecology (LAREHS) at the University of Québec at Montréal. His numerous publications in English and French in the areas of suicidology and gerontology include research on the effectiveness of suicide prevention hotlines, theories of the development of suicidality, and the recent books: *Le Vieillissement* (Aging) (with R. Riedel, Presses Universitaires de France); and *Drugs and Aging* (with W. A. McKim, Butterworth). Besides his university activities, Professor Mishara is a founder of Suicide Action Montréal, the Montréal regional suicide prevention center, and the Québec Association of Suicidology. He is past president of the Canadian Association for Suicide Prevention, was co-organizer of the 1993 Congress of the International Association for Suicide Prevention, and is the recipient for 1994–1995 of the Bora Laskin Canadian National Fellowship on Human Rights Research for his work on human rights issues regarding the involvement of physicians and family members in assisted suicide and euthanasia.

The Impact
OF Suicide

Brian L. Mishara, PhD

Editor

 Springer Series on Death and Suicide

To
Réjean Marier and Sara

Springer Publishing Company, Inc.
536 Broadway
New York, NY 10012-3955

Cover design by Tom Yabut
Production Editor: Pam Ritzer

95 96 97 98 99 / 5 4 3 2 1

Library of Congress Cataloging-in-Publication Data

The impact of suicide / Brian L. Mishara, Editor
    p. cm.—(Springer series on death and suicide) ISBN 0-8261-8870-2
    Includes bibliographical references index.
    1. Suicide. 2. Suicide—Social aspects. I. Mishara, Brian L.
II. Series.
    HV6545.I393   1995
    362.2'8—dc20   95-7293
                                                            CIP

Printed in the United States of America

Contents

Contributors

Alan Berman, PhD
National Center for the Study and
   Prevention of Suicide
Washington School of Psychiatry
Washington, DC

Unni Bille-Brahe, MA
Unit for Suicidological Research
Odense University
Odense, Denmark

Marc P.H.D. Cleiren, PhD
Rijks University
Leiden, The Netherlands

**Anthony T. Davis, MB, BS,
   FRANZCP**
Department of Psychiatry
University of Adelaide
Adelaide, Australia

René F. W. Diekstra, PhD
Rijks University
Leiden, The Netherlands

Ronald J. Dyck, PhD
Alberta Health (Mental Health
   Division)
Edmonton, Alberta
Canada

Dr. Sándor Fekete
Department of Psychiatry
University of Pécs
Hungary

Robert D. Goldney, MD
Department of Psychiatry
University of Adelaide
Adelaide, Australia

Børge Jensen, MS
Unit for Suicidological Research
Odense University
Odense, Denmark

Gert Jessen, MA
Unit for Suicidological Research
Odense University
Odense, Denmark

Robert Kastenbaum, PhD
Arizona State University
Tempe, Arizona

Michael J. Kral, PhD
Department of Psychology
Windsor University
Windsor, Ontario
Canada

David Lester, PhD
Center for the Study of Suicide
Blackwood, NJ

Keltie Paul, MA
Some Other Solutions Society for
   Crisis Prevention
Fort McMurray, Alberta
Canada

Carole Renaud, MA
Québec City Suicide Prevention
   Centre
Québec, Québec
Canada

Mounir H. Samy, MD
Montréal Children's Hospital
Montréal, Québec
Canada

Dr. Armin Schmidtke
Clinical Psychology
University of Würzburg
Würzburg, Germany

Bryan Tanney, MD
Calgary General Hospital
Calgary, Alberta
Canada

M. Tiggemann
Department of Psychiatry
University of Adelaide
Adelaide, Australia

Michel Tousignant, PhD
Psychology Department and
   Laboratory for Research on
   Human and Social Ecology
Université du Québec a Montréal
Montréal, Québec
Canada

A. H. Winefield
Department of Psychiatry
University of Adelaide
Adelaide, Australia

H. R. Winefield
Department of Psychiatry
University of Adelaide
Adelaide, Australia

Bijou Yang
Drexel University
Philadelphia, PA

Chapter 1

Beyond Suicide: The Impact on Family and Friends, Helpers, Individuals, and Society

Brian L. Mishara

Suicide occurs in every country in the world and has existed throughout known history. Despite significant progress in understanding suicide, the identification of high-risk groups and the development of a variety of prevention and intervention programs for suicidal individuals, there has been significantly less concern for the impact of suicide. Completed suicides, suicide attempts, and suicidal ideation have profound effects upon family, friends, and helpers. Suicide influences the fabric of society and cultural differences influence the nature of the repercussions of suicidal ideation behavior. Individuals who have considered killing themselves, as well as those who attempted suicide without a fatal outcome, may also experience the impact of their suicidal behavior upon their lives. This book brings together for the first time a variety of perspectives on how completed suicides, suicidal behaviors, and suicidal ideation may affect family and friends, helpers, individuals, and society.

The chapters in this book have been developed primarily out of papers presented at the XVII biannual meeting of the International Association for

Suicide Prevention in June of 1993, which was a joint meeting with the Canadian Association for Suicide Prevention, the Quebec Association of Suicidology, and Suicide-Action Montréal. The principal theme of that meeting was "The Impact of Suicide," and this book includes many of the key presentations related to the conference theme. These chapters represent only a small portion of the presentations at this meeting, but we feel that they represent the major perspectives and topics related to the main conference theme.

One of the most obvious and poignant topics concerning the impact of suicide is the effect of a death by suicide upon family and friends. For each person who dies by suicide there are several family members and a number of friends and acquaintances who are profoundly affected by the loss. Loss of a loved one invariably produces significant bereavement reactions which have been well documented in the research literature. In this book, the discussion of bereavement after suicide begins with an in-depth review (Chapter 2) in which Cleiren and Diekstra examine how bereavement after suicide may be different from other types of deaths and what factors may affect the nature of the bereavement process after suicide. Although research data may be extremely useful in understanding suicidal bereavement, there also exists as well rich clinical experiences which may clarify the nature of how family and friends consider and deal with suicidal loss. This chapter is followed by an essay by Mounir Samy (Chapter 3) from a psychoanalytic perspective, which provides an analysis of responses to the question "Why did he/she kill him/herself?"

Throughout this book we have tried to present not only explanations of the impact of suicide but also examples and discussion of how the negative consequences of suicide may be diminished. Chapter 4, by Renaud, reports on examples of the many bereavement group to help those who have experienced a loss through suicide. Turning to the community level, some communities have developed "postvention protocols" which provide for an emergency response team to react immediately after a suicide or a serious suicide attempt. Chapter 5, by Paul, presents the details of how such a postvention protocol developed in one community and discusses its implementation.

It has been well documented that the majority of persons who attempt suicide communicate their intentions by discussing their desire to end their lives with friends and family members. Hearing that a friend or family member is contemplating suicide certainly has some impact and often these acquaintances seek help to deal with the potentially suicidal person. In Chapter 6 Mishara discusses typical reactions to suicidal threats and offers information on how friends and family members may learn to better help persons who express suicidal ideation.

Most people who are troubled and suicidal seek some form of help from professional therapists, community agencies, or telephone hotlines. Despite a high level of skill and training, those who work in helping suicidal individuals have a risk of eventually experiencing a loss or multiple losses by suicide. Examples of the experience of such losses and how therapists may deal with them are presented by Berman, in Chapter 7, with vivid descriptions of two suicidal deaths and how two different therapists handled the situation. This chapter is followed by a detailed review by Tanney (Chapter 8) on how caregivers may better develop their abilities to deal with a loss by suicide.

When we consider the impact of suicide on individuals, the topic includes the influence of suicidal ideation and suicide attempts upon the life of an individual. This section begins with Chapter 9, by Goldney, Winefield, Tiggemann, and Winefield, which looks at what happens in the future to persons who considered suicide at some time in their lives. Chapter 10, by Davis, looks more directly at the effect upon an individual following a suicide attempt.

One of the most controversial issues in suicide prevention is the effect of mass media reports on suicide. Studies suggest that the impact of certain mass media reports may be an increase in suicidal behavior. Chapter 11, by Fekete and Schmidtke, reviews studies on the effect of mass media reports on suicide and present data from their investigations in Hungary and Germany.

Bille-Brahe, Jessen, and Jensen present an analysis in Chapter 12 of the difficulties involved in assessing to what extent persons who attempt suicide may attempt again.

The nature of the impact of any event or group of events is influenced by the socio-cultural context. Also, powerful events, such as suicides, have an important impact upon society. The final section of this book discusses the impact of suicide and society from several different perspectives. Kastenbaum, in Chapter 13, presents an incisive analysis of how suicide is an important component of the "death system" which exists in any society. In Chapter 14, Tousignant reviews studies on how the impact of suicide varies across different cultures. Then Kral and Dyck present an information processing model of the relationship between culture and suicide (Chapter 15). Finally, Chapter 16, by Lester and Yang, presents an overview of various ways in which suicide may have an important impact upon society.

This book presents contemporary analyses of the impact of different forms of suicidal behavior, from completed suicides to suicide attempts and suicidal ideation. The chapters take different perspectives including research literature reviews and presentation of new data as well as clinical investigations and descriptions of treatment programs and intervention recommendations. This is an area of interest in suicidology which is growing rapidly and it is obvious that much more work needs to be done on this topic. Some subjects, such as the process of bereavement after a loss by suicide, have been the subject of numerous research studies and clinical investigations. However, most of the other topics addressed in this book have been the subject of relatively few studies at this time. It is hoped that this book may inspire more investigations on the impact of suicide by those who find the presentations in these chapters to be far from complete. In the meantime, the presentations in this book may be useful for researchers, clinicians, and helpers, as well as any individuals concerned with the impact of suicide in its many manifestations.

Part I

The Impact of Suicide on Family and Friends

Chapter 2

After the Loss: Bereavement after Suicide and Other Types of Death

Marc P.H.D. Cleiren and René F.W. Diekstra

> So many types of grief
> I don't mention them.
> But one, to renunciate and separate.
> And not the cutting is so painful
> but being cut off.
>
> **'Sotto Voce'—Vasalis, 1954, fragment**

The most immediate impact of suicide is upon family and friends. The impact is most evident in the bereavement reaction after a death by suicide. This chapter reviews theoretical and empirical studies on how bereavement after suicide differs from bereavement reactions to other types of death. This chapter also reviews factors affecting bereavement, studies on how people cope with a death by suicide as well as assessments and interventions for persons bereaved by suicide. [Ed.]

Suicide is a mode of death that is mostly experienced as a brutal dissolution of life, and a violent disunion of existing relationships. What influence has this on the process of bereavement? Is suicide a more traumatic type of death? Also, does this influence the frequency and intensity of physical and mental health problems?

The purpose of this chapter is to outline the shape of grief and the problems associated with suicide bereavement in the family, and focus on how these compare with bereavement from other causes of death. We will present a theoretical framework that may help to disentangle and explain the main empirical findings in this field.

ADAPTATION: HEALTH AFTER THE LOSS

First of all, it is important to know to what extent bereavement is disruptive to physical and mental health. An initial step in many population studies is often to estimate the percentage of the bereaved population that experience problems after the loss. One difficulty is the diversity in criteria for adaptation. Some studies use the respondent's own judgment about adjustment (Zisook, 1987). Others employ bereavement scales (Zisook & Lyons, 1988), or use expert judgments of the level of well-being of the survivor (e.g., Parkes & Weiss, 1983). A related problem is the diversity and obscurity of the criteria for judging functioning as "poor." Thus the percentages of dysfunction reported in studies may reflect different and incomparable criteria. Fortunately, in the last decade, the use of validated general depression criteria as outcome measures has increased (e.g., Lund et al. 1986; Stroebe et al., 1988; van der Wal, 1988). In a number of studies, efforts have been made to determine the number of people who do not, or who only partially, recover after bereavement. In general population studies, the estimates of the percentage of persons having severe difficulties in adjustment one to four years after bereavement, range from 18% to 34% (*cf.* Cleiren, 1993). Severe depressive symptomatology and psychiatric disturbances are, however, much rarer (in our own studies only 2% after the first year).

THE ABSENCE OF PHASES

Longitudinal studies have shown that there generally is a quick recovery of mental health and decrease of complaints related to bereavement during the first period. Relatively little change occurs after the first year (Cleiren, 1993; Farberow, Gallagher-Thompson, Gilewski, & Thompson, 1992; Zisook & Schuchter, 1986; Lehman, Wortman, & Williams, 1987). Furthermore, it seems that persons who are initially effective in coping with the loss remain effective in the long run (Cleiren, 1993; Farberow, Gallagher-Thompson, Gilewski, & Thompson, 1992; Johnson, Lund, & Dimond, 1986).

In the past, several theories of grief have been proposed based upon a concept of "stages" or "phases" in grief. (Bowlby, 1969; Kübler-Ross, 1982; Parkes, 1970). Most propose a linear process, where the bereaved changes from numbing, disbelief, shock, anger, depression, to recovery. In the last decades, serious doubts have been raised about the validity of the stage or phase models (Shackleton, 1984; Wortman & Silver, 1989). In virtually none of the empirical research has there been found evidence for the existence of distinct stages (e.g., Barrett & Schneweiss, 1980/1981; Zisook, 1987). Almost all the longitudinal studies mentioned above found that the diversity of grief symptoms decreases more or less quickly over time, with some symptoms disappearing faster than others. Since it has been found that the emotions and behaviors in grief could overlap, change in order, be absent, or recur, we conclude that grief is marked by a large variety of emotional states that may or may not occur and recur over time. The concept of distinct stages in adaptation after bereavement thus seems untenable.

Today, more authors have adopted "component" models (e.g., Bugen, 1977; Parkes, 1983, 1988) in which the time element is less compelling, or "task" models which concentrate on the fact that the bereaved is an actor in the adaptation to the loss, and deals with the tasks the loss poses (Schuchter, 1986; Spiegel, 1973; van der Wal, 1988; Weiss, 1988; Worden, 1982).

In the following sections, we will describe a model that combines the component and task frameworks with a stress-approach (Cleiren, 1993; Horowitz, 1979; Lazarus, 1966; Lazarus & Launier, 1978). A model is presented in the context of findings from empirical studies, in particular the Leiden Bereavement Study (Cleiren, 1991, 1993; Cleiren, Diekstra, Kerkhof, & van der Wal, 1994; Cleiren, van der Wal, & Diekstra, 1988a,b; van der Wal, 1988). In a longitudinal, prospective time sample survey study, we examined the consequences of a loss after suicide (n = 91), traffic fatality (n = 93), or long-term illness (n = 15) for next of kin. First-degree family members (73 bereaved spouses, 68 parents, 86 siblings, and 9 adults who lost a parent) were interviewed at four and fourteen months after the loss.

LOSS, RESOURCES, AND ADAPTATION

The consequences of a loss in our lives may be demonstrated by seeing ourselves as a ship captain in a stormy sea. The sea would be the metaphor for the world with its ever changing events and turmoil, with bereavement as the strong wind that sweeps up the water into roaring waves. Our ship is our body and on board we have the knowledge, skills, and abilities we possess about how to deal with the surrounding sea. Part of these may be swept away by the storm, or we may be so blinded by it that we cannot find the way on our own ship, and use our own machinery. We are, at the same time, the captain—who determines the goal of the journey, oversees the possibilities of the ship, and chooses the actions to get to his destination. As captains have multiple destinations and goals, from the basic need to keep the ship afloat and survive, to reaching the farthest goals or destinations.

In calm weather, we may have relatively little difficulty to keep ourselves on course, but when in heavy storms, we have to fight to be not helplessly adrift, tossed wherever the currents and waves push us. Our well-being is dependent on the conditions of the ship *and* the sea *and* the captain. A rough sea, with many currents, strong winds, and sudden events, makes the journey tough. A small, feeble ship, with few abilities, will be in danger of destruction more easily. With less capacity to deal with the waves, an inexperienced captain is less likely to keep the ship on course or take the right protective measures.

In other words: events (such as changes in our environment, losses we suffer) test our equipment and our skills (the resources available to us) to keep on the course of our goals and ideals.

Following this analogy, we can break down the consequences of bereavement into an assessment of the following aspects:

- *The magnitude of the loss:* To what parts of our ship does the damage extend? What areas or components of life suffered a loss? In particular, we want to distinguish between a partial loss of instrumental and adaptational resources, a loss of roles and goals in life, a loss of faith in the reliability and stability of the world, and a loss of parts of our self.
- *The strength and availability of instrumental resources:* Does one have on board what it takes to deal with the changes brought about by the loss? Here we find the availability of material and social resources to deal with the practical and emotional implications of the loss, our existing skills to deal with our environment.
- *The strength and characteristics of adaptational resources:* Where and how do we steer the ship? What course do we, explicitly or implicitly, take to keep afloat, and repair the damages? In other words, how well is one able to use instrumental resources to deal with the loss, and what strategies does one use to reduce its impact? Adaptational resources are defined by several related cognitive and behavioral processes. Attributional activity determines how one perceives the meaning of

the loss, and the reasons for it (who or what is to blame). Adaptational self-efficacy pertains to the confidence in one's ability to make the arrangements necessary to reduce impact. This precedes and determines the coping efforts the person undertakes in terms of problem focused/emotion focused coping, anger, and acquisition of new skills and resources.

The loss-resource model proposes a specific dynamic relationship between these elements. Figure 2.1 presents the relationship between loss and adaptation graphically.

The impact of the loss we may see as the incongruity or tension between the magnitude of the loss, and the availability of resources to deal with it. In other words, the impact of the loss determines the number and significance of tasks the bereaved encounters. For instance, the death of a good friend may mean a loss of the support that friend gave. The *impact* of this aspect of the loss depends, however, on the availability of other sources of social support.

There are many characteristics of the loss that are unique to the lost relationship. There remains, as it were, a net loss, for which existing resources cannot cover. Adaptational strategies are necessary to deal with these.

To lessen the pain and improve well-being, it is necessary to reorient

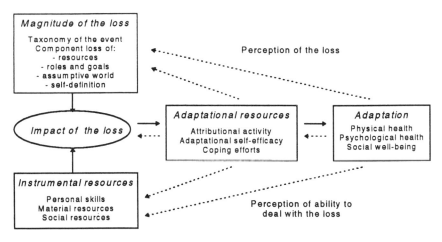

FIGURE 2.1 A loss-resource model of adaptation after bereavement.

our view of the world, as well as our actions. The extent to which one is able to make these necessary adaptations ultimately determines the quality of adaptation. This is illustrated by Parkes & Weiss (1983) studies of widowhood, in which they found that widows in the initial period after the loss were unable to use their social resources, regardless of social class and income. Bereaved with a combination of rich instrumental resources, like money and skills, and poor adaptational resources (e.g., little belief in their ability to change the situation, or rigidity) are likely still to have poor outcomes. Strong adaptational resources may permit bereaved with little instrumental resources to quickly acquire these, thus having a better perspective for recovery. Our level of adaptation, in terms of health and social well-being, is thus moderated by the way we try to reduce the impact of the loss on our life.

On the other hand, our adaptational resources and our level of adaptation also inversely influence the way we perceive the loss and our ability to deal with it. This is reflected in the dotted arrows, pointing from right to left in Fig. 2.1. Attributions of the loss, and confidence in our skills determine the perceived magnitude of the loss. Likewise, we must not only consider health to be affected by bereavement, but it also impacts on the bereaved's ability to cope (Rutter, 1985). Illness may reprieve the bereaved from the use of resources. Depression undermines adaptational resources (pessimism about one's ability to adapt) and distorts the perception of the availability of instrumental resources.

Using the background of this model, we will, in the following sections, outline the dynamics of bereavement and the risk factors for problems in adaptation. We will do this on the basis of our own and other empirical studies, and focus in particular on the differences between suicide bereavement and other losses.

THE MAGNITUDE OF THE LOSS

Bereavement encompasses a large variety of component losses that extend to different areas of the bereaved's life. To assess the magnitude of the loss we must look at the joint effect of all these components. This aspect is reflected in the relationship between bereaved and deceased, with fixed characteristics such as the kinship relationship and individually varying ones such as frequency of contact, intimacy, ambivalence, and proximity in the relation. The taxonomy of the loss event is another aspect to be considered in examining its extent. Expected, peaceful, natural death may differ from unexpected, violent, unnatural death in the themes the bereaved must deal with.

The Taxonomy of the Event

In both clinical lore and theory, sudden and violent losses have been regarded as more debilitating than an expected, natural losses. In particular, suicide bereavement has been assumed detrimental to the health of the bereaved. However, many controlled studies, using systematic comparative observation, have shown that bereavement after different modes of death is marked more by similarities than by differences (Cleiren, 1991, 1993; Demi, 1984; Farberow et al. 1987, 1992; McIntosh & Kelly, 1992; Miles & Demi, 1988; Shepard & Barraclough, 1974; van der Wal, 1988). Moreover, no substantial long-term health differences are found between sudden, expected, accidental, or suicide deaths. Although initial shock appears to be somewhat greater in the case of unexpected death, even this is only marginal. Virtually all studies have shown that, when differences occur, they are related to the *themes* of preoccupation and rumination (which we will consider later), but rarely to the *intensity*. In other words, the overall level of *adaptation* in terms of preoccupation, depression, and health problems, differs only marginally between modes of death.

Still, there are differences related to the mode of death that determine to a certain extent the type of problems facing the bereaved. Each mode of death we may consider as comprising a combination of psychologically relevant dimensions, each of which may play a relatively independent role in adaptation to loss:

- Expectedness (expected versus unexpected)
- Naturalness (natural versus unnatural)
- Violence (low versus high)
- Perpetration (self versus other, or unknown)

Each cause of death can be ranged along these dimensions with, for instance, bereavement after a fatal traffic accident often being unexpected, unnatural, caused by the deceased, or another person, and untimely (see Table 2.1).

Bereavement after a prolonged illness is more often characterized as expected, natural, and ambiguous perpetration. However, if the illness is a infectious disease, as is the case with AIDS, the perpetrator is also another person. We will discuss some of the evidence for the role of each of these dimensions in the next sections.

Expectedness of Death

Studies examining the influence of forewarning of death have more often been conducted among bereaved from natural death, and less on

TABLE 2.1   Dimensions of Some Causes of Death

Mode of Death	Expectedness	Violence	Naturalness	Perpetrator
Suicide	low/high	low/high	unnatural	deceased
Traffic fatality	low	high	unnatural	deceased/other
Homicide	low	high	unnatural	other
Sudden illness	low	low	natural	unclear
Prolonged illness	high	low	natural	unclear
HIV-AIDS	high	low	natural	other

unnatural ones such as suicide death. The majority of studies show that fore-warning of death has no, or very little, impact on the adaptation after bereavement (Bornstein et al., 1973; Cleiren, van der Wal, & Diekstra, 1988; Gerber et al., 1975; Hill et al., 1988; Maddison & Walker, 1967; Roach & Kitson, 1989), but others find a worse outcome after unexpected death in younger bereaved (Ball, 1977/1978; Carey, 1977; Parkes & Weiss, 1983). It may be in older samples that death, even sudden death, will not be entirely unexpected (Parkes, 1975). Cleiren et al. (1988) found that the extent to which the bereaved had given up hope for recovery of the patient during the last month of his life was associated with adaptation to the loss. When the factor of giving up hope was controlled statistically, it appeared that the duration of forewarning did not predict adaptation to the loss at all. Giving up hope may be seen as a cognitive preparation for the loss. Although forewarning in principle *enables* the bereaved to cognitively prepare for a possible loss, anticipation and (cognitive) preparation is something quite different.

This same process was observed in bereaved after suicide. A limited psychological autopsy was conducted on 44 of the suicide-bereaved families in our own study (Cleiren, 1991, 1993) to assess the history of the deceased. It turned out that in 36 (82%) there had been a long history of severe depression and often hospitalization related to this. Twenty-one families (48%) reported earlier suicidal attempts by the deceased, and in 5 cases (11%) the suicide was actually literally announced in advance by the deceased. In 7 suicides (16%) the main motive for the suicide seemed to be an unbearable physical suffering, which most often was accompanied by depression as well. In at least two cases, euthanasia had been requested but rejected, so that the deceased had decided to take matters into their own hands. Only 5 suicides (11%) did not directly fit into the above categories. The common characteristics of these (as also apparent from some letters of farewell) included masked depression, financial debts, and psychoactive drug addiction. In about half of the suicide-bereaved, the suicide was more or less expected: *When I got the phone call that he had done it, my first thought was: so this is it.*

Natural versus Unnatural Death

A cause of death is formally qualified as "natural" death when not attributed to suicide, homicide or accidental death. This categorization is used
by coroners in the U.S. and is widely accepted in the world. Nonetheless,
the definition is somewhat deceptive: death in a natural disaster would not
be a natural death. Kitson et al. (1989) in their review of the literature, state
that initial responses are the same for both natural and unnatural death
causes, but that some of the particular characteristics correlated with suicide and homicide may debilitate longer-term adjustment.

Unnatural causes of death are more often unexpected and untimely
than natural deaths. A human actor is usually involved in bringing about
the death, purposely or accidentally. One of the differences with a natural
death is that the police are involved (Shneidman, 1993). The investigation,
especially in the case of uncertainty about suicide or murder, may be
lengthy. When not conducted carefully, this may be a source of intense
additional stress for the bereaved (Barraclough & Shepherd, 1976, 1977;
van der Wal & Cleiren, 1990).

Violent Death

An unnatural death is often a violent death. The suicide-bereaved may be
confronted with a severely damaged or mutilated body of the deceased.
Identification by family members is often necessary, and this may in itself
be a traumatic experience. The unexpected confrontation of the finder with
the body, especially if this is a family member, may constitute an even
greater shock (van der Wal, 1988; van der Wal & Cleiren, 1990).

The bereaved may be traumatized, in particular, when they have
witnessed the death or its direct consequences. Witnessing the death of a
family member from close distance (e.g., in a fatal accident, or in the case
of suicide), or finding the body of the deceased, which is quite common in
suicide bereavement, are likely to result in strong post-traumatic stress
reactions and problems in adaptation (McIntosh, 1987). Dunne (1992) found
that a high percentage of the suicide bereaved applying for help belonged
to this group.

Perpetration of the Death

Whereas in illness death, there is no clear perpetrator, in unnatural death
there mostly is. In the case of suicide it is the deceased him or herself. In
the case of a murder, someone else was the actor, while accidents may be
either or both. In the case of an unnatural death, there may be a police investigation, and in the case of some accidents (for example, drunk driving) or
unclear circumstances of the death (suspected homicide, one-car-one-driver

accidents), long-lasting and wearisome criminal procedures may take place. Dissatisfaction with a verdict, and the question whether or not to start an appeal procedure may prolong the distress (van der Wal & Cleiren, 1990). Preoccupation with the question of who or what was ultimately responsible for the death is common, especially among bereaved after suicide (van der Wal, 1988; Cleiren, 1993; Cleiren et al., 1994). Since this is, however, essentially an attributional activity, we will discuss this later in the context of adaptational strategies.

COMPONENTS OF THE LOSS

The psychosocial situation in which a loss takes place determines to a substantial degree which aspects the bereaved has to cope with. There is a growing consensus that the kinship relationship to the deceased is of major importance in evaluating the impact, and understanding the reactions of the bereaved. The kinship relationship is a denominator for many types of roles and other resources that are lost, and is a major indicator of the magnitude of the loss.

All available comparative studies indicate that loss of a child is the most devastating of bereavements. Cleiren (1988, 1993), Sanders (1979/ 1980), Levav (1982), Miles and Demi (1983/1984, 1991/1992), McIntosh and Kelly (1992), Osterweis et al. (1984), and Zisook and Lyons (1988) found that intensity of grief was greatest in parental bereavement. Parents who lose a child, regardless of its age, show more depression, anger, guilt, and despair than those who lose a spouse or parent. Mothers are particularly at risk: many experience an overwhelming feeling of loss of control over the world and their lives.

The loss of a spouse substantially differs from other family relationships in a multitude of roles, goals, and social characteristics. The importance of the spouse as a provider of security and support, the frequent operation of the couple as a social unit, and the intricate entanglements of daily life are, to some extent, unique or apply more strongly to the spousal relationship. The sex difference in functioning among spouses appears to be the reverse of that in the other kinship groups. In our own study (Cleiren, 1993; Cleiren et al., 1994), we found that, in most kinship groups, the women suffer from more loss reactions and health complaints than do men. Only among the widowed do we find that widowers and widows are affected about equally. In terms of social functioning, the widowers do worse than widows.

An explanation for the above differences may be found by looking at the loss components they entail. In the following sections we will discuss the differences found between family members and different modes of death from this perspective.

Loss of Roles and Goals

In close relationships, when people live together, daily roles (in particular marital, and parental roles) are partly or entirely disrupted as a consequence of a loss. Meaningful activities the bereaved performed for the deceased, as well as functions the deceased had in the life of the bereaved, are lost. A death in families with intricate networks of relationships will be likely to upset and shift the roles of their members. Death of the oldest child in a family may, for instance, put a younger child in a more responsible position.

In particular in cohabitational partner relationships, the loss of roles is an issue. Most couples build up and develop an extensive set of (sex)-specific roles. Women, even when employed, still more often develop home-making, social abilities, and networking, while men have developed the latter skills less. Sex-specificity in adaptation appears clearly in the empirical research on bereavement (Stroebe & Stroebe, 1983).

In suicide bereavement, as in cases of a longer-term illness, caregiver roles tend to disappear. In many suicide-bereaved families, long-lasting psychological or psychiatric problems of the deceased put a heavy burden on the family. Their story about the time before the loss shows a pattern similar to the case of terminal illness: a past of hope for recovery, recurrent fears of the loss. The caregiver role was often frustrated, and reduced to the role of worrying bystander. Related to this, we find feelings of relief in suicide bereavement virtually as strong as in bereavement after long-term illness (Cleiren, 1991, 1993; McIntosh & Kelly, 1992). These feelings are mostly related to death bringing an end to long-lasting suffering and an unbearable or hopeless situation, rather than relief about the loss itself, or the way it happened.

In suicide-bereaved families, we find patterns of emotional relationships with the deceased before the loss that are markedly different from those in other bereaved (Cleiren, 1993). The suicide bereaved tend to look back on the relationship with the deceased as being less intimate, less satisfactory, and more ambivalent, whereas they viewed the deceased as having been more dependent on them. The image of the pre-loss relationship is often one of a frustrated, self-protecting emotional withdrawal from the unpredictable and/or difficult psycho-emotional situation, with less frequent contacts with the later deceased.

As a rule, openly problematic or ambivalent relationships do not seem to give rise to a problematic bereavement process and, to the contrary, often appear to mark a more independent self-definition in the bereaved. This we find more often in suicide bereavement (Cleiren, 1991, 1993). The perception of the deceased having been difficult, inaccessible, and hostile, creates an emotional and physical distance that may serve protective qualities in the bereaved. In particular, when suicide victims have a long psychiatric history, we find bereaved reporting a withdrawal from (helper) roles, a definition of the deceased as having been incurably ill, and a resignation from shared life goals.

Loss of Resources

Bereavement may also imply a loss of the very material and social resources one would normally need and use to deal with the consequences of the loss.

Loss of Material Resources

Several authors found that socioeconomic status is influenced by bereavement. Babri and Kitson (1988), Balkwell (1981), Berardo (1970), Cleiren (1993), Hyman (1983), McCrae and Costa (1988), Morgan (1989), and Weiss (1984) found that widowhood in men as well as women was associated with a drop in family income, although for widowers this loss is smaller than for widows. In a comparative longitudinal survey in the United States, Morgan (1989) found that 40% of widows and 26% of the divorced fell in the "poverty" category within 5 years after the loss.

Loss of Social Resources

McCrae and Costa (1988) found that in the long-term, the social networks of widows were a little smaller than those of matched married women. However, in widowhood, men appear to have relatively more problems to continue social relationships than women, probably because they suffer a loss of social support in two ways:

First, in the marital relationship, the woman is generally the most important provider of emotional and practical support to the man, but married women more often find their sources of support in (female) friendship relationships. In addition to many men, their wife appears to be the "gateway" to the social friendship network. Thus widowers may find themselves cut off from support that they often need in the stressful period after the loss.

Second, loss of social resources is found in both widows and widowers, in particular in the younger and middle-age groups. Often the intimate friendship network consists mainly of other couples. Many bereaved spouses report that being single after the loss, in meeting with befriended couples, they are perceived by the same-sex member of that couple as a threat to the relationship, and friendship bonds may break down because of this.

Rudestam (1992) points to the "contagion of stress" effect: loss of a relative is typically a life event that afflicts those who are emotionally close. This may diminish the available support for each of the members of the network. In marital relationships after the loss of a child this is particularly clear. The roller-coaster ride that both spouses take on the waves of emotions and events after the loss make it more difficult to reach each other. Many marriages are disrupted in the first years after the loss.

Another type of social loss may occur when the bereaved is stigmatized or being blamed by their social environment for the loss and/or the circumstances preceding it. There are indications that suicide bereaved are more vulnerable. Many studies report suicide bereaved experiencing blame for what happened in their environment. However, studies have shown that there is not more social isolation in suicide bereaved in comparison with other causes (Cleiren, 1993; Demi, 1984; Farberow et al., 1992), although initially there may be more blame (Ness & Pfeffer, 1990) and less emotional support for feelings of depression and grief in comparison with natural death survivors (Farberow et al., 1992; Range & Calhoun, 1990). Isolation from significant others is relatively rare. One problem that is sometimes reported is difficulty in discussing the suicide with the family, but is sometimes also labeled as desirable. As a widow in our own studies put it: *We don't talk about it in our family. We have peace now.*

People who are bereaved after other modes of death also tend to suffer negative reactions from their social environment. There are indications that in the suicide bereaved the same reaction (e.g., others avoiding talking about the subject, or pretending not to see the bereaved) is more likely to be interpreted as a sign of blame, rather than a sign of incapability on the part of the social environment (Cleiren, 1993).

In religious communities, a suicide may still sometimes be viewed as a death-sin and lead to disapproval and isolation of the bereaved. An explicit negative attitude by important members of that community, and a hesitation on the part of the deceased to seek support from that community may result. In our own study, in rare instances, the bereaved encountered overt condemning statements by the clergy that the deceased would not be accepted by God, and would go to hell.

Loss of the Assumptive World

One basic survival quality is our ability to organize our world, both on the outside, by moving about, and influencing it with our actions, and internally by organizing the information coming to us through our senses into meaningful "schemas." What we literally do is "make sense" of our life: we ascribe meaning to what is happening to us, so that we, on the basis of this knowledge, steer ourselves through the seas and storms toward our goal with as little damage as possible. In our life, we learn, build up a more and more differentiated image of the world, including abilities, skills, conceptions of "how things work", "what is important", and also *who* is important. Parkes (1988) proposed the term "assumptive world" for this set of beliefs and cognitions.

Bereavement is likely to upset at least part of these assumptions, and may undermine beliefs of controllability and trust. For instance, Stroebe et al. (1988) found that the bereaved, in comparison with a matched control group, had an increased belief that events are controlled by chance. Our studies have shown that feelings of meaninglessness and strong reactions to the loss are associated with a general loss of control (Cleiren, 1993; van der Wal, 1988).

One might expect that the violence or suddenness of the loss may render the bereaved insecure about what may happen to others and oneself: *If he can die just like that, without any warning, then I may too.* Still, most comparative studies do not find an important general influence of these factors in terms of loss of control or disorientation. However, when the characteristics of the bereaved and his situation closely resembled those of the deceased (which is often the case in siblings), and when the bereaved identifies with the deceased, the trust in a "safe world" may be strongly affected. His fears are often specifically related to the cause of death. In case of an illness, the sibling (or other family member) may be afraid to run a hereditary risk of dying from the same disease. In the case of death by accident, apprehension for risky situations is found. In the suicide bereaved, it is a common fear that they may resort to suicide, often by the same method as the deceased, should problems occur.

Existential and religious beliefs are sometimes put to the test or undermined by the loss, but a general breakdown is rare. In particular, in the case of suicide, the act may conflict strongly with religious convictions, and questions about the fate of the deceased may play a role. In our own study, this was sometimes reported. The mother of a man who shot himself worried: *I hope he has asked forgiveness of God before he committed suicide.*

Loss of Self-Definition

Perhaps the strongest link to long-term problems is the extent to which one's definition of self is affected by the loss. In fact, this implies that we define the lost person as an "extended part of self," essential to our own ability to function or lead a satisfactory life. Whether this type of loss occurs is largely dependent on how one's self-concept is organized in the first place. It is the combination of losses of the assumptive world, roles and goals, and at the same time being unable to restructure or repair these, declaring oneself to be impoverished and handicapped. This is often reflected in expressions such as *I will never be able to love someone again. A part of me died with him;* or *Now my life has no sense any more.*

Experiencing bereavement during adolescence may result in the loss of an important role model. Adolescents may experience fears about their own demise, mixed with feelings of longing to die and join with the lost person. They may also develop a pessimistic belief system and severe problems in building their identity (Valente & Saunders, 1993; Valente, Saunders, & Street, 1988). However, research has not come up with clear differences in outcome for adolescents.

INSTRUMENTAL RESOURCES

Given the magnitude and number of component losses the death entails, the bereaved are situated against a background of instrumental resources that, when present, can be used to mitigate the effects of the loss. Psychomotor, cognitive, and social skills, material resources like money and goods, are some of the instruments that can be used to manipulate and master the new situation.

A fact that sometimes is overlooked is that bereavement may also lead to the availability of *new* resources, that were not previously accessible. The time freed by the death of a husband who needed a great deal of care may enable the widow to give attention to activities previously given up, or the development of new interests. Likewise, with the death of a dominant or belligerent spouse, many widowed discover personal skills they were not aware of (Cleiren, 1993).

Income and Socioeconomic Status

In the general population (Kessler et al., 1985; Schwab & Schwab, 1978) it has been consistently shown that existing low-income, low-level education, and low level of skills are related to more mental and physical health problems. Bereavement studies including non-bereaved control groups (Gallagher et al., 1983; Morgan, 1976; Sanders, 1979/1980) typically find that low-income and low-socioeconomic status (SES) are associated with more sadness and depressed mood, boredom, and loneliness in both bereaved and controls, but they fail to find an excess risk for the widowed.

There is a mutual causal relationship between SES and other resources. We may consider SES the ultimate product of the aggregated adaptational and instrumental resources, as well as determining the possibilities and constraints of the development of these.

Social Support

Availability of practical, informational, and emotional support is also important. The number of supporting relationships is less important than its quality (Brown & Harris, 1978; Holahan & Moos, 1986; Stroebe & Stroebe, 1987) and fit with the needs of the bereaved (Kitson et al., 1989; Maddison & Walker, 1967).

Those who are bereaved by illness who were caregivers for the deceased may suffer from a reduced social network. Intensive and lengthy care may lead to social withdrawal and social isolation. This in turn may lead to a lack of social support in the time after bereavement (Cleiren et al., 1988; Fulton & Gottesman, 1980; Sanders 1982/1983).

Social support imposes different rules for men and women (Stroebe & Stroebe, 1987). In our society physical supportive contact, for example, is less likely to be given to men than to women, and women more often than men seem to be mediators in supportive social networks. In this perspective, the sex of the bereaved can also be considered as one of the aspects defining the resources after bereavement.

We must be aware, however, that resources of social support are not independent of the personal characteristics of the bereaved. Typically, people organize and maintain their social networks themselves. Good quality support is as much dependent on the environment as it is on personal skill and health factors (Lopata, 1988). Depressed persons tend to demand more emotional and informational support than non-depressed, (Coyne, Aldwin, & Lazarus, 1981), but are less likely to recognize help offered to them (Lakey & Cassady, 1990).

ADAPTATIONAL RESOURCES AND STRATEGIES

Besides instrumental resources, we use more pronounced *adaptational* resources. These are the faculties that we use to cognitively and behaviorally reconstruct and master our world in the context of new experiences.

The bereaved must integrate the loss experience into the assumptive world (attributional activity), that is, to develop an image of what has happened, the reasons for what happened, and evaluate the damage.

The bereaved takes a course to mitigate the effects and to deal with the practical problems and emotions associated with the loss (coping efforts). The direction and taxonomy of the adaptive strategy depends on the trust in one's abilities to perform the neccessary actions (adaptational self-efficacy).

Coping efforts include acquisition and mastery of new, previously unknown instrumental skills and/or strategies to regulate affect, such as denial and avoidance. Self-blame and anger can be seen as attributions of the loss, but will be discussed here in the context of coping efforts. We will, in the same context, look at suicidal tendencies following the loss.

Attributional Activity and Meaning of the Loss

In many studies, it is reported that resolving the 'meaninglessness' of the loss is essential for recovery (e.g., Parkes & Weiss, 1983). Feelings of meaninglessness are related not only to the earlier described taxonomy of the event itself, but also strongly to the preexisting situation and the extent to which the deceased was central in the life of the bereaved. That the death upsets the order of the world as we perceive it is strongly demonstrated in parents who lose a son or daughter. Regardless at what age, they often refer to the "injustice" of it, and insist that they had rather traded places: the normal state of things is that they should die before their child.

Whether or not the loss is considered timely by the bereaved is, of course, to some extent related to the mode of death and the age of the deceased. The death of a young child will virtually always be considered as untimely, as is accidental death. However, the timeliness is, in fact, an evaluation of what happened in the context of the life perspective of the deceased. We thus find that the death of a suffering baby, however painful, may be experienced as timely in the perspective for a severely handicapped miserable life. For the same reason, we find that even the suicide death of a younger person with a long history of severe mental problems and depression is quite often regarded as timely by the bereaved.

In the case of suicide, it has been argued that finding meaning in the loss is extremely difficult. This has only been partially confirmed in empirical studies. The question *Why did it have to happen to me* was often present in bereaved, but not more so than after other modes of death (Cleiren, 1993; Lehman, Wortman, & Williams, 1987). It appeared from our own studies that the reasons for the suicide to occur were often retrospectively quite clearly detected by the bereaved. Two "historical backgrounds" of suicide were prevalent in the stories of suicide-bereaved families.

The first was *extreme psychological suffering* with a long history of severe depression. This was very common in our study. A clear depressive-psychiatric history was reported by most suicide bereaved. This was often accompanied by a feeling of powerlessness or helplessness with regard to helping the deceased.

The second attribution was *the prospect or presence of extreme physical suffering*. In some (2) cases, the medical staff had refused dying patients—who had a prospect of even more suffering in the future—the possibility of euthanasia. The deceased had thereupon decided to take the decision to end suffering in his own hands. For most bereaved, this type of situation appeared to be somewhat easier to accept than when psychological suffering was involved. The reason for this was mostly that they judged it to be a more or less conscious and deliberate decision "for the best."

Some bereaved people stated that the suicide was announced in advance by the deceased. The fact that they had not believed this, was for some bereaved a source of guilt, but there were also others that persisted in their opinion that the completed suicide was . . . *just a way to draw attention*. In our own studies (Cleiren et al., 1988a,b; Cleiren, 1993; Cleiren et al., 1994) we found many signs of cognitive restructuring between both interviews, which were to some extent specific to the mode of death. Illness and suicide bereaved alike tend to define their own ability to prevent the death as limited. In the latter, thoughts as *It was his/her own decision; There is nothing that I, nor anybody else could have done to prevent it; He/she was ill;* and *I have done everything in my power to prevent it* were generally related to better outcomes and less preoccupation with the loss in the longer run.

Adaptational Self-Efficacy

Bereavement research has rarely included measures of self-efficacy. In bereavement research we mostly find this area under less specific associated terms such as: helplessness, ego-strength, locus of control, and attribution of control. Hansson & Remondet (1988) state that the sense of personal control is the integrating theme in the factors that influence adaptation after a loss.

Bandura (1977) defines self-efficacy as "The confidence one has that one is able to produce the actions that are needed to produce a certain outcome." Self-efficacy in dealing with the post-loss situation may be considered an important adaptational resource, since the confidence that one can deal with a problem (one's self-efficacy) is the precursor of coping effort.

The bereaved's self-efficacy or perceived control in a specific domain determines to a substantial degree whether or not coping efforts take place, and which shape they take (cf. Bandura, 1994). In the adaptation to loss, new resources may be needed that never were available to the bereaved in the first place: the widower may have to learn to cook and care for the children. If, therefore, the bereaved has little trust in the capacity to *acquire* the needed skills, it is very likely that no effort will be undertaken to take that course. That does not mean that the goal is unreachable: the widower may alternatively hire someone to cook and provide child care. In other words, depending on their self-efficacy in specific domains, the bereaved may take different paths and use different resources to adapt to the situation.

Recent re-analysis of the data in the Leiden Bereavement Study (Cleiren, 1993) showed that the confidence of the bereaved that they would be able to deal with the loss (adaptational self-efficacy) was one of the major indicators of adaptation. Confidence in this ability was related to a low level of depression at both four and fourteen months after the loss. Moreover, it appeared strongly to predict the development of depression over time, regardless of the initial level. To a somewhat lesser extent, we found the same to be true for the intensity of difficulty with detachment.

The educational level of the bereaved is not only related to the level of instrumental skills, but the associated abilities also act as an adaptational resource through experience and self-efficacy in obtaining new skills. Higher educated widows are found to make better use of their resources. They are more likely to restructure their identity (Lopata, 1973) and engage more often in social interactions (Kivett, 1978).

Coping Efforts

Efforts to reduce the impact of the loss may be a mixture of proactive (adapting the situation to one's needs and goals) and reactive actions (relinquishing or lowering one's goals to reduce stress), depending on the self-efficacy judgments the bereaved makes.

Gass and Chang (1989) found that better psychosocial functioning was associated with low threat appraisal (little fear for other bereavement-related losses and problems that exceed one's power), more problem-focused coping (engagement in managing or altering the situation that causes distress) and less use of emotion-focused coping (engagement in regulating the emotional response to the problem). Other studies (Cleiren, 1993; Johnson, Lund, & Dimond, 1986; Stroebe et al., 1988) have found similar results.

Anger

Anger is a response that has sometimes been described as a normal reaction in the period after the loss (e.g., Kübler-Ross, 1982; Tekavic-Grad & Zavasnik, 1992). From most empirical studies, however, it appears that strong feelings of anger are more a specific way of coping with the loss. When prevalent in the early period of bereavement, anger is indicative for a longer term problematic adaptation (e.g., Cleiren, 1993; Osterweis, Salomon, & Green, 1984; Parkes & Weiss, 1983).

Anger, in general, may be seen as instrumental in an attempt to change the situation or to avoid the looming damage (Lazarus, 1966). In bereavement, where the damage has been done already, it may operate as a dysfunctional reaction to retrieve an irretrievable loss (Bowlby, 1980). Comparative bereavement studies show no higher prevalence of anger among suicide bereaved. The object of anger may, however, be specific to the circumstances of a suicidal death.

The bereaved sometimes perceive the suicide victim as having been pushed to the act by people in the environment, including psychotherapists or others at mental institutions where the deceased was treated. Anger may also be directed toward the community at large, that 'did not care', or toward the unjust world, that had brought extreme misfortune to the deceased.

Anger toward the committer of suicide is sometimes found, and may be long-lasting and distressing. In our research (Cleiren, 1993) this was demonstrated in the reaction of a son whose father shot himself: *When I saw how my mother suffered after his death, I thought: I'd like to get him back and then kill him.* A man whose son committed suicide by an overdose of medicine during the vacation of his parents, commented, *When they phoned us at the camping site in Spain, I was furious: just when I had time to spend with my wife, he wants to be in the picture again.*

Self-Blame and Guilt

Guilt we may see as anger directed toward the self. Feelings of guilt originate in not being able to comply with the standards or goals one explicitly or implicitly sets for oneself. When these standards extend to the standards of the social environment, this leads to feelings of shame. A generalized tendency to feel guilty is part of the definition of depression, and may thus be counter to psychological well-being. In the context of loss, however, we will examine guilt as an adaptational strategy.

Bereaved individuals may blame themselves for not having prevented the death, or intervened at an earlier stage. When the bereaved perceive themselves as responsible for the well-being of the deceased, the question of one's own role in the loss is, to some extent, an inescapable or natural one in the search for meaning of what has happened. This is corroborated by the finding that guilt is stronger in bereaved parents than in other family members (Cleiren, 1993; Miles & Demi, 1991/1992). It is often related to them experiencing it as a failure in rearing their child, of not recognizing signals or attending to their child's illness or, in the case of suicide, the psychological problems of their child.

Most comparative studies *do not* find the suicide bereaved to feel more guilty (Barrett & Scott, 1987; Cleiren, 1993; McIntosh & Kelly, 1992; McIntosh & Milne, 1986; Vargas et al., 1984).

On the other hand, several studies (Cleiren, 1993; Henslin, 1970; van der Wal, 1988; Wallace, 1973) found that preoccupation with the *question* of responsibility is more prevalent among those bereaved from suicide. The subject of their questions is often the *proximate* blame for what happened: their inability to prevent the suicide itself. This can be clearly distinguished from a more generalized *ultimate* responsibility for the death: considering one's actions to be *the reason* why the deceased died. A woman who had taken care of her severely ill father wondered whether her fatigue had been the reason that he had committed suicide.

The ultimate responsibility for any death is often much harder, or even impossible, to retrace, and may be attributed to entirely different sources. Taking the ultimate blame for the death appears to be as rare in suicide bereaved as in other bereaved (Cleiren, 1993, Cleiren et al. 1994; McIntosh & Kelly, 1992). When present, strong self-blame is related to more ruminations about the loss and depression in the longer run.

The majority of the suicide bereaved came to the conclusion that there had been a limit to their power to protect the deceased from him or herself, and concluded that the ultimate responsibility for the event was with the deceased. Sometimes it appears to be quite clear that the suicidal family member pushed away the family members, and that the latter after the death felt guilty to have submitted to that. One woman reported that the last contact with her severely ill sister had been the latter saying, "Bugger off." One day later, she jumped out of the hospital window, dying instantly.

Feelings of guilt are, in some suicide bereaved, intense and pervasive and clearly related to problems of physical and mental functioning. This was well reflected in "Notes regarding the last days of J.L.," that was written by her brother Christian after her suicide, a subject in our study. He was moderately depressed, and continued to feel severely guilty throughout the entire research period. This put his relationship with his wife under severe pressure. Fourteen months after the death, she wanted

to divorce him because of his "self-destructive" tendencies. The episode
quoted here, he wrote a few weeks after his sister's suicide, and its setting
is more than a month before it.

> J. is back with us after a failed vacation.
> For me an important period.
> She irritated with her "annoyance" about a vacation
>   with trivialities!! But she was ILL.!
> We did not see HOW severe it was.
> I wasn't myself! I raged and shouted!
> Linda [Christian's wife] said later: "But that wasn't
>   Christian.—
>   That was someone else!!!"
> How hard I was on her!!! The blackest page of my
>   life!
> I have hurt her, wounded, but did not realize how
>   terribly ill and *deeply unhappy and lonely she was.*
> I swore, I raged, I said terrible things—(called her
>   .... just name it) and let myself go in a terrible
>   way (in particular with regard to the church). *That
>   was the worst thing!*
> After that, her situation deteriorated!
> In my opinion, this was too much for her.
>   I AM DEEPLY ASHAMED!
> Instead of a source of warmth, I was a refrigerator.
>   How is it possible! I don't understand anything!
> The only excuse: I was desperate—I wanted to shake
>   her to awake. I believe, know for certain that I
>   meant well.
>   NO ONE WANTED JOANNA TO DIE!!!!!!!!
> More and more I realized that I was making a big
>   mistake—
> BUT UNCONSCIOUSLY!!!
> In all telephone calls, it appeared HOW depressed
>   she was.

The underlying message is not only one of anger and frustration with himself, but it also implies a paradox: *Without knowing or wanting it I can destroy someone I love.* This ambiguity may effectively inhibit the bereaved in their relationships and in recovery, and in itself lead to withdrawal and depression.

Suicide as Problem Solving

During the first weeks of bereavement, most epidemiological studies find an increased suicide risk, with widowed men initially being more at risk than women (Bojanovsky & Bojanovsky, 1976; Gove, 1972; MacMahon & Pugh 1965). Bunch (1972) found that among the bereaved who committed suicide, previous psychiatric breakdown was more frequently found than among the other bereaved.

A unique characteristic of problematic grief after suicide is the strong model-function of this mode of death as a form of problem solving for the bereaved (an adaptational strategy). Suicide is demonstrated to the bereaved to be a possible solution to the unbearable suffering that results form the loss. There is evidence for a cross-generational "suicidal coping" history in the suicide bereaved. Of the 44 families included in our own studies (Cleiren, 1991, 1993), in 4 families (11%), previous completed suicides in the family were reported, and 8 families (19%) reported attempts of close family members. In all, at least 30% of the suicide-bereaved families reported a history of suicide attempts and completed suicide in other family members than the deceased. To a number of families, suicide was thus not an unknown phenomenon.

Within some suicide-bereaved families, we also observed a more general tendency to choose partners who were also vulnerable to depression and suicidal ideation. Some spousal relationships had originated in psychiatric hospitals where the suicide and the bereaved had met, and sometimes several suicides had occurred in the past within the family.

ASSESSING THE RISK
OF PROBLEMATIC ADAPTATION

Death of a family member is generally an event with a large impact, but for whom is it a devastating experience that needs professional care? The majority of the bereaved seem to do quite well in terms of adaptation. Still, there is a substantial number who evidence long-lasting effects.

As we saw, empirical data provide support for the dynamics of the model we proposed in the beginning of this chapter. In order to assess the prognostics for recovery in a bereaved person, by ticking each of the concepts listed in the loss-resource model (Fig. 2.1), and by following its dynamics, we can obtain a precise image of the expected long-term outcome of the loss.

In Table 2.2, we have summarized the main early indicators for longer-term problems in adaptation. An intake evaluation of a bereaved

TABLE 2.2 Major Risk-Indicators for Poor Long-Term Physical and Psychological Health in Bereavement

In terms of the magnitude of the loss:
* *Kinship relationship*
  In particular, couples who lose a child are at risk for severe depressive and relational problems. The kinship groups most at risk for problems after bereavement are (in descending order of risk) mothers, followed at some distance by widowers, fathers, widows, and sisters of the deceased.
* *Intimacy of the relationship*

In terms of instrumental resources:
* *Bad health before the loss*
* *Little practical and informational resources*
  Lacking skills and support in dealing with the demands of daily life put spouses in particular at greater risk.

In terms of adaptational adequacy:
* *Feelings of despair*
* *Strong reactions of anger and guilt*
* *Little confidence in one's ability to deal with the loss*

In terms of early reactions to the loss:
* *Strong post-traumatic stress reactions and difficulty with detachment from the deceased*
  This type of reaction in the early months after the loss is a strong indication of future problems in adaptation, rather than a sign of adequately "working through" the loss.

---

person applying for help should, besides the assessment of risk factors listed in the table, preferably comprise an assessment of the life history and current and pre-existing (psycho)pathology, as well as the current level of suicidal ideation. Clinicians and others involved in the care of patients who committed suicide should take into account not only the parent or spouse, but also siblings and children of the deceased; they should be monitored for the risk factors mentioned here. The centrality of the relationship with the deceased before the loss is related to a greater magnitude of the loss, and stronger reactions of shock and difficulty with detachment. When the deceased had a pivotal position in life and strong identity, the bereaved's adaptation requires extensive rearrangements both in daily life and in the "assumptive world."

Absence of sufficient instrumental resources, such as emotional, practical, and informational social support, practical skills, and material resources, increases the impact of the loss upon life. Physical and psychological health also act as pre- and post-loss resources: bereaved in poor health have fewer possibilities of restructuring their life.

The course recovery takes seems particularly dependent upon adaptational resources. Self-efficacy beliefs, the attribution of the death (guilt), and the attitudes of the bereaved toward the loss (in particular anger) are important predictors of longer-term outcome.

Some aspects are in themselves not, or only marginally related to adaptation. People bereaved after natural, expected deaths run virtually the same risk of developing health problems in the longer term after the loss as bereaved after violent and suicide deaths, although witnessing (the consequences of) a violent death may lead to an increased level of post-traumatic stress problems

The level of social well-being in bereavement seems hardly to be related to the magnitude of the loss at all. In general, social resources are a more or less stable background not fundamentally changed by bereavement. Although the suicide bereaved are more prone to experience negative social reactions, these generally do not lead to a breakdown of their social support network.

DIFFERENT INTERVENTIONS
FOR THE SUICIDE BEREAVED?

What may therapists expect when the suicide bereaved come knocking on their door for help? It is unlikely that the symptomatology of problematic adaptation in suicide bereavement differs from that of other types of bereavement. From most studies of clinical and self-help samples (e.g., Battle, 1984; Dunne, 1992; Farberow, 1992; Wrobleski & McIntosh; 1987) it is clear that the symptomatology of problematic adaptation after a loss through suicide is diverse. Characteristically, a mixture of inability to find meaning in the loss, high depression, agitation, strong feelings of guilt and anger, and perturbation by blame of others are found to play major roles in bereaved who seek help.

Although this symptom complex is sometimes claimed to be unique to suicide bereavement (Hauser, 1987; Ness & Pfeffer, 1990), this must be seriously doubted. The same symptom complex of problematic adaptation is described in studies of such diverse help-seeking groups as homicide survivors (Getzel & Masters, 1984), parents who lost a child through fatal illness (Johansen, 1988), holocaust survivors (Cohen, 1991), unemployed (Keefe, 1984), family members of drunk-driver victims (Kowaz, Roesch, & Friezen, 1990), parents losing a baby to Sudden Infant Death Syndrome (Lowman, 1979), survivors of AIDS victims (Murphy & Perry, 1988), family members of victims of Alzheimer's disease (Rabins, 1984), wives of victims of a stroke (Smith, 1977), and farmers who had to give up their farm (Farmer, 1986).

To find out what an intervention with bereaved should encompass, we may again turn to the loss-resource model. Interventions should be tailored, in the first place, to what component losses were suffered, and what instrumental and adaptational resources are missing. A thorough assessment of these is a fundamental prerequisite to be able to provide the bereaved with the necessary equipment to recover. In this light, we should also determine our choice of methods of intervention.

Research shows that problems in bereavement are likely to have their roots in times preceding the loss, and many problematic grievers will probably be better off with a psychotherapeutic intervention centering on the rebuilding of instrumental and adaptational skills rather than support groups.

Self-help groups of fellow sufferers are likely to provide the bereaved with possibilities for social exchange and acceptance of their experiences, as well as new social resources (i.e., the members of the group). But without professional and change-oriented guidance, they generally do not lead to an improvement of adaptational skills. We should avoid putting suicide survivors with severe adaptational deficits in non-directive sharing settings. In that type of group, the suicide as a model for problem-solving may become a self-perpetuating idea for solving the pain of bereavement.

Although, from a clinical point of view, there are few indications that suicide survivors form an unique group with regard to their level of adaptation, this implies that treatment of severely affected suicide bereaved should be identical.

In group settings, the themes related to unnatural and violent deaths, such as suicide, accidental death, and homicide, are so specific, that in mixed groups there would be few joint themes and mutual recognition. Also, an implicit hierarchy of "who has suffered the worst loss" may influence the group process. When we look at specific themes of shame and guilt about the loss, in comparison with natural modes of death, there is a chance that the suicide bereaved will be more hesitant to join a mixed survivor group. For these reasons, mode-specific groups are to be preferred over mixed modes of death. Topics may focus on dealing with the specific dimensions for each mode of death (the expectedness, naturalness, violence, and the perpetrator). Differential practical skills may be required in the suicide bereaved (how to deal with the police, and the reactions of the environment), in accidental or homicide death (how to deal with a criminal procedure, court hearings, confrontation with the perpetrator, desire of retaliation and conviction of the latter), and illness death (how to restore social contacts lost during the illness period).

On the other hand, we have seen that kinship may even be a more important denominator for the impact and meaning of bereavement, and could even be a more important grouping criterion than cause of death. In particular, the grief of siblings of the deceased tends to be overshadowed by that of parents and spouses. The loss of a brother or sister has entirely different consequences and meaning, than spousal or parental loss. Only recently, the important influence of sibling loss on one's life has received specific attention (Cleiren, 1993; Valente & Saunders, 1993; Valente, Saunders, & Street, 1988; Gaffney, Jones, & Dunne-Maxim, 1992).

A problem in getting specific bereavement groups off the ground is that, in smaller towns or less densely populated rural areas, it may be difficult to fill survivor groups with suicide as the specific target loss. In that case, mixed groups may be considered, if they accentuate the development and use of adaptational resources rather than social sharing. Otherwise, individual counseling, or one-on-one telephone sessions with fellow sufferers, are a possibility.

In view of the empirical evidence (cf. Farberow, 1992) we may assume that, in case of a group approach, professionally guided groups with an intake procedure screening for personality and psychopathology are to be preferred to non-guided ones.

CONCLUSION

We are weavers on the patchwork of our own life. The fabric we weave consists of smaller and larger patches of the important and less important people in our lives, our relationships, beliefs, and capacities. The loss of someone close leaves a smaller or greater hole in the fabric: the threads of the cloth do not connect any more, and all the threads by which we were attached end in the emptiness. We feel the pain of the loss when we follow the fiber to the point where it ends. Whether the patch was torn out, cut out, or worn out, may make a difference in the painfulness of the event but, ultimately, the size of the hole remains the same.

What does the weaver do with the severed life? We find a smaller gap easier to mend. The bigger the hole, the more dead ends. We may try to avoid the hole, not think of it, not move, withdraw to a small corner of the cloth. Then there is no pain, and no motion, depression, and no life. We may hem up along the borders of the gap, and move cautiously around it. With that, if we hurriedly repair, and leave parts of ourself in it, we may lock up some of our own capacities to function and feel love.

In order to restore the fabric, and close the gap, we have to make connections over that unstructured abyss. We have to have courage and trust to start out doing that, we need stamina and material to help us. The fabric will never look the same again, of course, but we can move around freely at least. If the weaver is negative about his ability to repair, and undertakes no action, the hole remains open and painful, and it may, by wear and tear, become larger.

It is especially important to recognize that those bereaved who suffer a combination of a substantial loss, little material resources, weak personal and social skills, and little belief in their own abilities to deal with it, are a risk group. They tend to isolate from others and the fabric of their social and personal life tears further, making them suffer, in fact, more and more losses.

Fortunately, the violence or abruptness of suicide as a mode of death does not predestine the prospects of recovery in the bereaved. The fact that most bereaved are capable of making a difference by using and rebuilding resources, and applying adequate adaptational strategies, outlines both the goal and the basis for therapeutic interventions in suicide bereavement.

REFERENCES

Babri, K. B., & Kitson, G. C. (1988). *Who's worse off? Economic problems and mental health consequences for widowed and divorced women.* Case Western University, unpublished.

Balkwell, C. (1981). Transition to widowhood. *Family Relations, 30*, 117.

Ball, J. F. (1976/1977). Widow's grief: The impact of age and mode of death. *Omega, 7*(4), 307–333.

Bandura, A. (1977). Self-efficacy: Toward a unifying theory of behavioral change. *Psychological Review, 84*, 191–215.

Bandura, A. (1994). *Self-efficacy: The exercise of control.* New York: Freeman.

Barraclough, B. M., & Shepherd, D. M. (1976). Public interest: Private grief. *British Journal of Psychiatry, 129*, 109–113.

Barraclough, B. M., & Shepherd, D. M. (1977). The immediate and enduring effects of the inquest on relatives of suicides. *British Journal of Psychiatry, 131*, 400–404.

Barrett, C. J., & Schneweis, K. M. (1980/1981). An empirical search for the stages of widowhood *Omega, 11*(2), 97–104.

Barrett, C. J., & Scott, T. B. (1990). Suicide bereavement and recovery patterns compared with nonsuicide bereavement patterns. *Suicide and Life Threatening Behavior, 20*(1), 1–15.

Barrett, T. W., & Scott, T. B. (1987). *Suicide versus other bereavement recovery patterns.* Paper presented at the combined meeting of the American Association of Suicidology and the International Association for Suicide Prevention, San Francisco.

Battle, A. O. (1984). Group therapy for survivors of suicide. *Crisis, 5*(1), 45–58.

Berardo, F. M. (1970). Survivorship and social isolation: The case of the aged widower. *Family Coordinator, 19*, 11–25.

Bornstein, P. E., Clayton, P. J., Halikas, J. A., et al. (1973). The depression of widowhood after thirteen months. *British Journal of Psychiatry, 122*, 561–566.

Bowlby, J. (1969). *Attachment and loss. Vol. 1: Attachment.* New York: Basic Books.

Bowlby, J. (1980). *Attachment and loss. Vol. 3: Loss, sadness and depression.* New York: Basic Books.

Brown, G. W., & Harris, T. (1978). *Social origins of depression: A study of psychiatric disorder in women.* New York: Free Press.

Bugen, L. A. (1977). Human grief: A model for prediction and intervention. *Journal of Orthopsychiatry, 47*, 196–206.

Carey, R. G. (1977). The widowed: A year later. *Journal of Counseling Psychology, 24*(2), 125–131.

Cleiren, M. P. H. D. (1991). *Adaptation after bereavement: A comparative study of the aftermath of death from suicide, traffic accident and illness for next of kin.* Leiden: DSWO Press.

Cleiren, M. P. H. D. (1993). *Bereavement and adaptation: A comparative study of the aftermath of death.* Washington, DC: Hemisphere Publishing.

Cleiren, M. P. H. D., Diekstra, R. F. W., Kerkhof, A. J. F. M., & van der Wal, J. (1994). The role of kinship and mode of death in bereavement: Focussing on "who" rather than "how." *Crisis, 15*(1), 22–35.

Cleiren, M. P. H. D., van der Wal, J., & Diekstra, R. F. W. (1988a). Death after a long-term disease: Anticipation and outcome in the bereaved. Part I. *Pharos International, 54*(3), 112–114.

Cleiren, M. P. H. D., van der Wal, J., & Diekstra, R. F. W. (1988b). Death after a long-term disease: Anticipation and outcome in the bereaved. Part II. *Pharos International, 54*(4), 136–139.

Cohen, B. B. (1991). Holocaust survivors and the crisis of aging. *Families in Society, 72*(4), 226–231.

Coyne, J. C., Aldwin, C., & Lazarus, R. (1981). Depression and coping in stressful episodes. *Journal of Abnormal Psychology, 90*(5), 439–447.

Demi, A. S. (1984). Social adjustment of widows after a sudden death: Suicide and non-suicide survivors compared. *Death Education, 8*, 91–111.

Demi, A. S., & Miles, M. S. (1988). Suicide bereaved parents: Emotional distress and physical health problems. *Death Studies, 12*(4), 297–307.

Dunne, E. (1992). Psychoeducational intervention strategies for survivors of suicide. *Crisis, 13*(1), 35–40.

Farberow, N. L. (1992). The Los Angeles Survivors-After-Suicide program: An evaluation. *Crisis, 13*(1), 23–34.

Farberow, N. L., Gallagher, D. E., Gilewski, M. J., & Thompson, L. W. (1987). An examination of the early impact of bereavement on psychological distress in survivors of suicide. *Gerontologist, 27*, 592–598.

Farberow, N. L., Gallagher, D. E., Gilewski, M. J., & Thompson, L. W. (1992). Changes in grief and mental health of bereaved spouses of older suicides. *Journal of Gerontology, 47*(6), 357–366.

Farmer, V. (1986). Broken heartland. *Psychology Today, 20*(4), 54–57, 60–62.

Fulton, R., & Gottesman, D. J. (1980). Anticipatory grief: a psychosocial concept reconsidered. *British Journal of Psychiatry, 137*, 45–54.

Gallagher D. E., Breckenridge, J. N., Thompson, L. W., & Peterson, J. A. (1983). Effects of bereavement on indicators of mental health in elderly widows and widowers. *Journal of Gerontology, 8*(5), 565–571.

Gass, K. A., & Chang, A. S. (1989). Appraisals of bereavement, coping, resources, and psychological health dysfunction in widows and widowers. *Nursing Research, 38*(1), 31–36.

Gerber, I., Rusalem, R., Hannon, N., Battin, D., & Arkin, A. (1975). Anticipatory grief and aged widows and widowers. *Journal of Gerontology, 30*, 225–229.

Getzel, S., & Masters, R. (1984). Serving families who survive homicide victims. *Social Casework, 65*(3), 138–144.

Hansson, R. O., & Remondet, J. H. (1988). Old age and widowhood: Issues of personal control and independance. *Journal of Social Issues, 44*(3), 159–174.

Hauser, M. J. (1987). Special aspects of grief after suicide. In E. J. Dunne, J. L. MacIntosh, & K. Dunne-Maxim (Eds.), *Suicide and its aftermath: Understanding and counseling the survivors* (pp. 73–84). New York: Norton.

Henslin, J. M. (1970). Guilt and guilt neutralization: Response and adjustment to suicide. In J. D. Douglas (Ed.), *Deviance and responsability: The social construction of moral meanings*. New York: Basic Books.

Hill, C. D., Thompson, L. W., & Gallagher, D. (1988). The role of anticipatory bereavement in older women's adjustment to widowhood. *Gerontologist, 28*(6), 792–796.

Holahan, C. J., & Moos, R. H. (1986). Personality, coping and family resources in stress resistance: A longitudinal analysis. *Journal of Personality and Social Psychology, 51*, 389–395.

Horowitz, M. J., Wilner, N., & Alvarez, W. (1979). Impact of Event Scale: A measure of subjective stress. *Psychosomatic Medicine, 41*, 209–218.

Hyman, H. H. (1983). *Of time and widowhood: Nationwide studies of enduring effects.* Durham, NC: Duke University Press.

Johansen, B. B. (1988). Parental grief over the death of a child. *Loss, Grief and Care, 2*(3–4), 143–153.

Johnson, R. J., Lund, D. A., & Dimond, M. F. (1986). Stress, self esteem, and coping during bereavement among the elderly. *Social Psychology Quarterly, 49*, 273–279.

Keefe, T. (1984). The stresses of unemployment. *Social Work, 29*(3), 264–268.

Kessler, R. C., Price, R. H., & Wortman, C. B. (1985). Social factors in psychopathology: Stress, social support and coping processes. *Annual Review of Psychology, 36*, 531–572.

Kitson, G. C., Babri, K. B., Roach, M. J., Placidi, K. S. (1989). Adjustment to widowhood and divorce. *Journal of Family Issues, 10*(1), 5–32.

Kivett, V. R. (1978). Loneliness and the rural widow. *Family Coordinator, 27*(4), 249–258.

Kowaz, A. M., Roesch, R., & Friesen, W. J. (1990). Personal needs and social goals: Issues in professional involvement with victims' self-help groups. *Canadian Journal of Community Mental Health, 9*(1), 63–73.

Kübler-Ross, E. (Ed.) (1982). *Reif werden zum Tode.* Gütersloher Verlagshaus Mohn.

Lakey, B., & Cassady, P. B. (1990). Cognitive processes in perceived social support. *Journal of Personality and Social Psychology, 59*(2), 337–343.

Lazarus, R. S. (1966). *Psychological stress and the coping process.* New York: McGraw-Hill.

Lazarus, R. S., & Folkman, S. (1984). *Stress, appraisal and coping.* New York: Springer Publishing.

Lazarus, R. S., & Launier, R. (1978). Stress-related transactions between person and environment. In L. A. Pervin & L. Lewis (Eds.), *Perspectives in interactional psychology.* New York: Plenum Press.

Lehman, L. R., Wortman, C. B., & Williams, A. F. (1987). Long-term effects of losing a spouse or child in a motor vehicle crash. *Journal of Personality and Social Psychology, 52,* 218–231.

Levav, I. (1982). Mortality and psychopathology following the death of an adult child: An epidemiological review. *Israel Journal of Psychiatry & Related Sciences, 19*(1), 23–38.

Lopata, H. Z. (1973). Living through widowhood. *Psychology Today, 7,* 87–92.

Lopata, H. Z. (1988). Support systems of American widowhood. *Journal of Social Issues, 44*(3), 113–128.

Lowman, J. (1979). Grief intervention and Sudden Infant Death Syndrome. *American Journal of Community Psychology, 7*(6), 665–677.

Lund, D. A., Caserta, M. S., & Dimond, M. F. (1986). Gender differences through two years of bereavement among the elderly. *Gerontologist, 26*(3), 314–320.

Maddison, D. C., & Walker, W. L. (1967). Factors affecting the outcome of conjugal bereavement. *British Journal of Psychiatry, 113,* 1057–1067.

McCrae, R. R., & Costa, P. T. (1988). Psychological resilience among widowed men and women: A 10-year follow-up study of a national sample. *Journal of Social Issues, 44*(3), 129–142.

McIntosh, J. L. (1987). Survivors family relationships: Literature review. In E. J. Dunne, J. L. MacIntosh, & K. Dunne-Maxim (Eds.), *Suicide and its aftermath: Understanding and counseling the survivors* (pp. 73-84) New York: Norton.

McIntosh, J. L., & Kelly, L. D. (1992). Survivors' reactions: Suicide vs. other causes. *Crisis, 13*(2), 82–93.

McIntosh, J. L., & Milne, K. L. (1986, April). *Survivor's reactions: Suicide versus other causes.* Paper presented at the meeting of the American Association of Suicidology, Atlanta.

Miles, M. S., & Demi, A. S. (1983/1984). Toward the development of a theory on bereavement guilt: Sources of guilt in bereaved parents. *Omega, 14,* 299–314.

Miles, M. S., & Demi, A. S. (1991/1992). A comparison of guilt in bereaved parents whose children died by suicide, accident, or chronic disease. *Omega Journal of Death and Dying, 24*(3), 203–215.

Morgan, L. A. (1976). A re-examination of widowhood and morale. *Journal of Gerontology, 31,* 687–695.

Morgan, L. A. (1989). Economic well-being following marital termination: A comparison of widowed and divorced women. *Journal of Family Issues, 10,* 86–101.

Murphy, P., & Perry, K. (1988). Hidden grievers. Special Issue: AIDS: Principles, practices, and politics. *Death Studies, 12*(5–6), 451–462.

Ness, D. E., & Pfeffer, C. R. (1990) Sequelae of bereavement resulting from suicide. *American Journal of Psychiatry, 147*(3), 279–285.

Osterweis, M., Salomon, F., & Green, M. (Eds.). (1984). *Bereavement. Reactions, consequences and care*. Washington, DC: National Academy Press.

Parkes, C. M. (1970). The first year of bereavement. *Psychiatry, 33,* 444–467.

Parkes, C. M. (1975a). Determinants of outcome following bereavement. *Omega, 6*(4), 303–323.

Parkes, C. M. (1975b). Unexpected and untimely bereavement: A statistical study of young Boston widows and widowers. In B. Schoenberg, A. C. Carr, A. H. Kutcher, et al. (Eds.), *Anticipatory grief*. New York: Columbia University Press.

Parkes, C. M. (1988). Bereavement as a psychosocial transition: Processes of adaptation to change. *Journal of Social Issues, 44*(3), 53–65.

Parkes, C. M., & Weiss, R. S. (1983). *Recovery from bereavement*. New York: Basic Books.

Parkes, K. R. (1986). Coping in stressful episodes: The role of individual differences, environmental factors, and situational characteristics. *Journal of Personality and Social Psychology, 51*(6), 1277–1292.

Rabins, P. V. (1984). Management of dementia in the family context. *Psychosomatics, 25*(5), 369–375.

Range, L. M., & Calhoun, L. G. (1990). Responses following suicide and other types of death: The perspective of the bereaved. *Omega Journal of Death and Dying, 21*(4), 311–320.

Range, L.M., & Niss, N. M. (1990). Long-term bereavement from suicide, homicide, accidents, and natural deaths. *Death Studies, 14*(5), 423–433.

Roach, M. J., & Kitson, G. C. (1989). The impact of forewarning on adjustment in widowhood and divorce. In D. A. Lund (Ed.), *Older bereaved spouses: Research with practical implications*. New York: Hemisphere.

Rudestam, K. E. (1992). Research contributions to understanding the suicide survivor. *Crisis, 13*(1), 41–46.

Sanders, C. M. (1979/1980). A comparison of adult bereavement in the death of a spouse, child, and parent. *Omega, 10,* 303–322.

Sanders, C. M. (1981/1983). Effects of sudden vs. chronic illness death on bereavement outcome. *Omega, 13,* 227–241.

Schneidman, E. (1993). *Suicide as psychache: A clinical approach to self-destructive behavior*. Northvale, NJ: Jason Aronson.

Schuchter, S. R. (1986). *Dimensions of grief*. San Francisco/London: Jossey-Bass.

Schwab, J. J., & Schwab, M. E. (1978). *Sociocultural roots of mental illness: An epidemiologic survey*. New York: Plenum.

Shackleton, C. H. (1984). The psychology of grief. *Advances in Behaviour Research and Therapy: An international review, 6,* 153–205.

Shepherd, D., & Barraclough, B. M. (1974). The aftermath of suicide. *British Medical Journal, 2,* 600–603.

Smith, C. W. (1977). Releasing pressure caps: Using TA with women whose husbands have had strokes. *Transactional Analysis Journal, 7*(1), 55–57.

Spiegel, Y. (1973). *Der Prozess des Trauerns: Analyse und Beratung.* Kaiser: Grunewald.

Stein, Z., & Susser, M. W. (1969). Widowhood and mental illness. *British Journal of Preventive and Social Medicine, 23,* 106–110.

Stroebe, M. S., & Stroebe, W. (1983). Who suffers more? Sex differences in health risks of the widowed. *Psychological Bulletin, 93*(2), 279–301.

Stroebe, M. S., Stroebe, W., & Hansson, R. O. (1988). Bereavement research: An historical introduction. *Journal of Social Issues, 44*(3), 1–18.

Stroebe, W., & Stroebe, M. S. (1987). *Bereavement and health. The psychological and physical consequences of partner loss.* Cambridge: Cambridge University Press.

Tekavic-Grad, O., & Zavasnik, A. (1992). Anger as a natural part of suicide bereavement. *Crisis, 13*(2), 65–69.

Valente, S. M., & Saunders, J. M. (1993). Adolescent grief after suicide. *Crisis, 14*(1), 16–20.

Valente, S. M., Saunders, J. M., & Street, R. (1988). Adolescent bereavement following suicide: An examination of relevant literature. *Journal of Counseling and Development, 67*(3), 174–177.

van der Wal, J. (1988). *De nasleep van suicides en dodelijke verkeersongevallen. Een onderzoek naar de psychische en sociale gevolgen voor nabestaanden.* Leiden: DSWO-press.

van der Wal, J., & Cleiren, M. P. H. D. (1990). *Politie en nabestaanden. Een handreiking voor het werk van de politie in rouwsituaties.* Schiedam: Report for the Ministry of the Interior.

Vargas, L. A., Loya, F., & Vargas, J. (1984). Grief across modes of death in three ethnic groups. Paper presented at the 9nd Annual Convention of the American Psychological Association, Toronto, Canada.

Vasalis, M. (1954). Sotto Voce. In *Vergezichten en gezichten.*

Wallace, S. E. (1973). *After suicide.* New York: John Wiley.

Weiss, J. M. (1984). Behavioral and psychological influences on gastrointestinal pathology: Experimental techniques and findings. In W. D. Gentry (Ed.), *Handbook of behavioral medicine.* New York: Guilford.

Weiss, R. S. (1988). Loss and recovery. *Journal of Social Issues, 44*(3), 37–52.

Worden, J. W. (1982). *Grief counseling and grief therapy.* London & New York: Tavistock Publications.

Wortman, C. B., & Silver, R. C. (1989). The myths of coping with loss. *Journal of Consulting and Clinical Psychology, 57,* 349–357.

Zisook, S. (Ed.). (1987). *Biopsychosocial aspects of bereavement.* Washington, DC: American Psychiatric Press.

Zisook, S., & Lyons, L. (1988). Grief and relationsip to the deceased. *International Journal of Family Psychiatry, 9,* 135–146.

Zisook, S., & Shuchter, S. R. (1986). The first four years of widowhood. *Psychiatric Annals, 16*(5), 288–294.

Zisook, S., Schuchter, S.R., & Lyons, L. E. (1988a). Grief and relationship to the deceased. *International Journal of Family Psychiatry, 9*(2), 135–146.

Zisook, S., Schuchter, S. R., & Lyons, L. E. (1988b). Predictors of psychological reactions during the early stages of widowhood. *Psychiatric Clinics of North America, 10*(3), 355–368.

Chapter 3

Parental Unresolved Ambivalence and Adolescent Suicide: A Psychoanalytic Perspective

Mounir H. Samy

For those who experience a loss by suicide, understanding the dynamics of the suicidal death is an important preoccupation which affects the impact of the event upon their lives. One of the most important intellectual currents in understanding suicide is the psychoanalytic perspective. This chapter presents a psychoanalytic view on the dynamics of suicide in a family which may have important implications before a suicide as well as afterwards in the family's attempt to understand what has occured. [Ed.]

INTRODUCTION

One of the hardest duties of a therapist is to meet with bereaved parents following the suicide of their child. Not infrequently a parent decides to enter into psychoanalysis one or more years later. What happens then, contrary to one's expectation, is not a journey into the past and present relationship with the lost child. Rather, there occurs a regression during which the parent becomes himself/herself an expendable child in conflict with his/her parents.

Some issues are transgenerational and especially so if not brought to conscious awareness and resolution. Conflicts over parenting, if unresolved, get transmitted down from the parent to the child who later becomes a parent placed with the demands of parenting. One drastic impact of the suicide of a child or adolescent is the crushing painful unravelling of these long hidden dynamics.

Suicide attempts, if met with successful crisis intervention which has included the whole family, should hopefully have the same impact. An important work of secondary prevention then becomes possible if parents are helped to acknowledge their ambivalence and mixed conflicted feelings about their child.

This chapter explores the role of this unresolved parental ambivalence which is often brought to the surface during a suicidal crisis and how this ambivalence relates to suicidality in the child. It is hoped that this may give us an additional valuable dynamic tool in our attempts to prevent an escalation in the severity of repeated attempts, a completed suicide, or help in reducing the negative impact of a suicide on family members.

I will first address the role of aggression in the family and the individual dynamics of adolescent suicide. In exploring these dynamics, this chapter will speak more of aggression than of violence. The most violent part of aggression is often the suicide itself.

This chapter will then try to situate these dynamics within the developmental tasks of adolescents, namely, the advent of genital sexuality, separation–individuation, and the adolescent oedipus. Finally, it will touch on the question of the suicide option since the suicidal acting-out cannot be explained only by the presence of an unconscious conflict; it is also the result of regression to a concrete form of thinking. The manifest failure of symbol formation in these adolescents is also related to the question of unresolved aggression.

FAMILY AND INDIVIDUAL DYNAMICS

To say it simply, suicide in children and adolescents is most frequently a response to a perceived psychological abandonment. The child stops feeling that he is desired or in any way important to the lives of his parents.

This final abandonment feeling draws its importance from the fact that it is only the current repetition of multiple earlier experiences of rejection in the family. I would like to suggest that the child's feelings of rejection and abandonment are the result of parental ambivalence which has never been metabolized or metaphorized and which is often unacknowl-edged—a conflict of love and hate which has never been resolved and which manifests as an overt, or covert, poorly mastered aggression.

Parental ambivalence may antedate the birth of the child. According to Feder (1980), "management of parental ambivalence prior to conception has an impact on the life of the developing child." Aggression, rather than being acknowledged and safely integrated into the total relationship, may be denied, expressed as its opposite, or unconsciously expressed through symptoms of open or disguised rejection. Messages of hatred, incestuous activity or dynamics, and death fantasies toward the child are common manifestations of repressed parental ambivalence.

Feder (1980) describes "the newborn child's position as a displacer, interrupter of a supposedly idyllic marriage, demanding narcissistic rival and destroyer of the mother's beauty, calmness and freedom" (p. 172). This is often denied and presented as the opposite with an idealization of the child and an exultation of maternity which may accentuate parental guilt and further repression of ambivalence.

It is not, of course, the presence of aggression in itself which is patho-logical or problematic. Aggression is an essential component of many of our drives. It is rather the amount of aggression or its pathological expres-sion which is problematic. Winnicott (1949) reminds us that a good enough mother must be able to hate her child.

We will retain here Laplanche and Pontalis' definition of violence as a destructive motor action (Laplanche & Pontalis, 1973). Violence is there-fore a form of aggression that combines the use of physical force. Violence in the family is the most drastic example of ambivalence, rejection, and at times a direct message of an infanticidal wish. A statistical and dynamic link between violence in the family and suicide is made by many authors (Orbach, 1988; Paulson et al., 1978; Richman, 1971).

By his suicide the child complies to what he perceives as a parental wish. The suicidal drama produces not so much guilt for the unconscious wish of the child to murder the parent but rather a reaction of abandon-ment on the part of the child to the parent's unconscious wish for the child's death (Litman, 1967).

We can also add that the child identifies with the aggressor while find-ing a vehicle of expression for his own accumulated rage. The problem with violence, like for any acting-out, is that it fails to resolve psychological problems. Violence is thus closely linked to despair and helplessness which are the immediate determinants of suicide. However, not all suicidogenic families are violent. In many families hatred and aggression may be hid-den or disguised but nevertheless powerful determinants of self-destruc-tiveness.

We owe to Sabbath the valuable description of "the expendable child"(Sabbath, 1969). The child lives in a rejecting family atmosphere filled with destructive messages. The couple has marital conflicts and the relation toward the child is ambivalent from birth. "The problem is that I was born," said one of my young patients. He did not feel essential to the life of his parents or to the family. "I never felt I was important to my mother's happiness," said a 16-year-old suicidal girl. The adolescent is thus convinced that his disappearance would solve all family problems. Everybody will be happier without him. He is expendable to his family. Unconsciously, however, he believes that in his death he will finally win parental affection.

These children receive all kinds of destructive messages—which Rosenbaum calls Suicidogenic Messages (Rosenbaum & Richman, 1970): "Go break your neck in two." "The only problem is that you didn't succeed in your attempt." A father gave a gun as a birthday gift to his suicidal adolescent. A thirteen-year-old girl wrote in her suicidal note that she wanted red roses on her grave. She missed her suicide attempt and was hospitalized in the intensive care unit. The day after, the parents came to visit her with a big bouquet of red roses (Samy, 1989). However, the most powerful of all suicidogenic messages is the suicide itself of one of the parents. Alex's mother told him as she was leaving home with the car keys in her hands: "You'll join me in heaven" and killed herself in a car crash. Yasmina's mother killed herself after two hours when she couldn't find her daughter who had run away.

Psychological abandonment may yet take other forms. Zilbrog (1937) described adolescent suicide as an identification with the (both physically and psychologically) absent father. The maternal presence may deny the child an emotional existence. The mother here is robotized: she provides mechanical, instrumental care without any emotional or psychological resonance and the child is treated like "an inanimate object" (Tustin, 1991). The child is not granted a mind of his/her own. These mothers have been severely deprived or depressed themselves. Finally, aggression and consequent psychological abandonment may result from the internalization of a trauma. Incest is on the top of the list of childhood traumas associated later with suicide and suicide attempts. Childhood incestuous traumas acquire a special meaning at the advent of puberty. Compounded with the trauma itself is the destructive effect of the presence of a secret both at the level of the individual and family dynamics.

The consequences of parental ambivalence on the psychological life of the child are multiple and complex. Ambivalence toward the adolescent leads to the adolescent having ambivalence toward himself (self-hatred) in addition to ambivalence toward his parents. Similarly, these parents are ambivalent about themselves as individuals and in their parental role are often ambivalent about their own parents. The child becomes today's recipient of an anger which actually belongs to the parents' past.

The adolescent who commits suicide doesn't only kill himself and symbolically the loved but also hated internal object. He also kills the family as a group and as an indivisible unit. Menninger (1938) ascribes three unconscious wishes to the suicidal individual: *to kill, to be killed*, and *to die*.

This highlights, I think, the importance of shared unconscious conflicts and fantasies of members of a group as an important aspect of the holding environment within which the child may develop. If the shared unconscious fantasies are of a destructive nature, they fail to function as a holding environment.

In these families the open acknowledgement of feelings of aggression and hatred is not possible. They are therefore unconscious and repressed. "Acknowledgement of hatred would kill and recognition of a disinterest would starve" (Shapiro & Freedman, 1988). Consequently, these families are enmeshed while keeping a façade of care.

PARENTAL AGGRESSION AND THE EMOTIONAL LIFE OF THE CHILD

Family Symbiosis and Sado-Masochistic Relations

Toolan (1962) remarked that the more a child feels rejected and unloved by his parents the more he needs them. Such a child become insecurely attached. A major conflict develops around his dependency needs. He can neither individuate safely nor depend safely.

The families of the suicidal child are described by Richman as closed-in symbiotic families with a strong restriction on the experience of individuality (Richman, 1978). Changes (the adolescent changes triggered by puberty being an example) are not tolerated. Conflicts are not resolved. There are longstanding marital problems. In these families the adolescent is the recipient of aggression and violence but is not allowed himself any aggression or rebelliousness. The result is a sado-masochistic model of relation. The child becomes the scapegoat of his family and this gives him an important status as he keeps the family together and maintains homeostasis. These adolescents are often afraid to grow up. At any rate, they are little-prepared for the demands of adult reality. They are unable to tolerate and survive failures. Any personal failure causes an important regression and a wish for reunification with the family which is expressed in the suicidal behavior. The suicidal adolescent is basically in a double-bind situation with simultaneous fears of total fusion and total abandonment. He is stuck, so to speak, between the devil and the deep blue sea—a running away from symbiosis and running toward symbiosis. A situation of impossible entrapment which Richman (1978) calls "unempathetic symbiosis," where suicide is not just a solution but is perceived as the *only* solution.

These parents, says Pfeffer, are still dependent on their own parents with a consequent loss of family boundaries (Pfeffer, 1981). Symbiosis in her view denies repressed aggression. We may add that it also discharges a lot of aggression directly and indirectly. There is a lot of control and passive aggression in symbiotic families. According to her, symbiosis, like the above-described ambivalence, is a cross-generational problem.

The sado-masochistic family relation leads to the formation of a "sadistic-masochistic nucleus" (Furman, 1984). There is a pattern of fusion of sexual and aggressive drives in such a way that aggression toward the self or others becomes sexually stimulating. In disturbed adolescents, self-cutting may produce pleasure and ecstasy. In object-relation terms there is a fusion (rather than integration) of love and hate. Love may be mixed with rejection, humiliation, or physical pain. A young adult patient reflecting on past physical abuse in the hands of her father said once, "It was the only thing I was sure of. It meant that he still loved me." The same love–hate relationship is found between the parents.

Parental Aggression and Bodily Care

An important consequence of the presence of violence and aggression in the family is the lack of love for one's physical self which is not only the basis for later emotional self-love but is also the basis of the self-preservation. Khantzian and Mack (1983) wrote, "The capacity for self-preservation requires an internalization of parental communication that the child is someone of value who is worth protecting" (p. 220).

According to Shapiro, psychological abandonment is a derivative of ambivalent bodily care (Shapiro & Freedman, 1988). Parental bodily care of these adolescents during infancy and early childhood failed to convey nurturance. Salk found that suicidal adolescent were significantly differentiated at birth on three variables: *Medical negligence during pregnancy, chronic maternal illness,* and *neonatal respiratory difficulties* (Salk et al., 1985). Orbach (1988) commented that it is ironic to note that if these infants had not received medical treatment, few of them would have survived. Shapiro believes that the early care of the child's body is affected by parental ambivalence and narcissistic vulnerabilities. Laufer (1981b) reminds us that the earliest source of the child's own investment in his body is through an identification with the mother's care of that body. When this goes wrong, making the body feel dead and without needs (suicide or anorexia nervosa) is their only defense against experiencing the dangerous wish to be intruded on by the mother.

Alternatively, if bodily care has not been adequately internalized, we may find a demand for parental nurturance metaphorically presented in the form of hunger for material things, addictive behavior, bulimia, psychosomatic illness, and unmanaged sexual and aggressive behavior. Jeammet (1985) coined the term "active passivity" to describe the adolescent who is unable to perform, compete, or tolerate any success—a state of total dependence. An unemployed 22-year-old patient put it in these terms: "If I start making my own money how will I know that my father cares about me?"

In early adolescence, when the child's body changes and his dependency needs increase, there may be a shared family regression to earlier ambivalence leading to lack of responsiveness (Shapiro & Freedman, 1988), or merely functional responsiveness.

If child and adolescent suicide is related to primary care, then at an unconscious level, suicide in the family has to do with killing babies. Abortion (in the adolescent or in significant adults) is a frequent precipitant of suicidal behavior. There is an identification with the unwanted and discarded baby. "I am a deferred abortion," a suicidal young girl once said to me. Bereaved mothers of children and adolescents who committed suicide experience their loss as the loss of a baby. That they feel destroyed is the essence of their motherhood.

Borderline and Narcissistic Adolescents

Shapiro differentiates between the narcissistic suicidal adolescent and the borderline suicidal adolescent in regard to their experience of maternal care of the body. "The narcissistic adolescent uses suicide as a statement that the body, even if dead, belongs to them. Unconsciously the suicidal act both removes the body from the demanding and unresponsive mother and controls the terrifying wish to depend and surrender to her. The borderline adolescent is caught up in passionate attempts to repeat an early satisfying physical relation to the mother which was traumatically interrupted by separation–individuation, accompanied by excessive anger and aggression. He is vulnerable to losing control over anger at those who frustrate this intense longing. Suicide is here an attempt to reunite the body with mother's body" (Shapiro & Freedman, 1988, p. 164).

Violence, Reunion Fantasy, and the Holding Environment

The wish to reunite in death carries, according to Stork (1988), a fantasied realization of an incestuous wish (which, in fact, may conceal a reparatory wish to be born again of a loved and loving mother). He quotes an adolescent suicidal note: "Death is a woman you make love to only once, but for eternity" and "Death is the only woman whom one can trust." Incestuous wishes (just like murdurous wishes) are normally well repressed in adolescents but may emerge within a poor holding environment and in presence of characterological problems.

Another impact of rejection is the absence of an adequate holding environment and emotional containment at a time when the adolescent developmentally needs it most. The preservation of adequate generational boundaries protect against unmastered aggression and constitute an important aspect of the holding environment (Samy, 1992).

For the child to preserve what Galdston (1981) calls "the central dependent fantasy" (a dimension of basic trust, a sense of vital connectedness with the caring one, or what safeguards the good internal object) in the context of his increasing maturation and autonomy, parents must manage their own aggression so that they can provide adequate care. This is also necessary so that they may tolerate the use of aggression in the service of separation without reacting with retaliation or withdrawal.

A trauma during the childhood of the parents (e.g., suicide of their own parent) may limit their capacity to respond to their child and to provide actual or symbolic holding at times of aggressive outbursts. The absence of emotional containment causes a regression to a concrete expression of feelings and desires and leads to their acting out in the form of early and inappropriate erotization of relationships or aggressive and suicidal behavior. With absence of containment the child doesn't experience the limits of his aggression and the boundaries of his body (Shapiro & Freedman, 1988). He loses the securing knowledge that neither he nor his parents will be destroyed by his aggression.

The adolescent with ego deficits and severe characterological problems (where usual defense mechanisms are not in place or are deficient) may experience outbursts of sexual attractiveness and aggression toward his parents (mostly mother) which Furman (1984) associates with suicide as both an expression and a punishment for these wishes.

Adolescents need their family stability as a component of the holding environment at a time when they are undergoing major changes and uncertainties. Freud said, "Every institution is a messenger of the law" (Freud, 1933/1980). Phillippe Gutton (1988) adds: "As such, every institution is a messenger of violence." He equates violence with frustration, that is, potential violence or violence risk. "Violence being the attribute of an affect," Gutton says, "which measures the gap between fantasy and perception, between the cathected internal object and the psychological reality of this other person."

The break-up of families results in their inability to be messengers of the law. In other words, they become unable to maintain the generational boundaries which are essential for oedipal resolution—containment of affect and reality perception (Samy, 1992). Therefore, the break-up of families leads to the breakdown of their holding function. They become "amorphous institutions and the matrix of violence." Aggression which is unmastered cannot effectively be utilized by the child in the service of need gratification nor ultimately for self-preservation.

THE DEVELOPMENTAL CONTEXT

The above dynamics must be understood within the context of adolescent developmental changes. The developmental tasks of adolescents may be grouped under identity formation and the acquisition of autonomy—the two, of course, being closely linked. These achievements translate developmentally into individuation, oedipal resolution, and the establishment of generational and sexual differentiations.

The adolescent uses his aggression to relinquish the primary object. Aggression may also be a defense against his sexual wishes or it may be mixed and confused with sexual impulses like in the sadistic-masochistic nucleus. Aggression toward the same-sex parent may be the result of conflicts over his negative oedipus. On the other hand, the resolution of the negative oedipus is, according to Blos (1979), the very task of adolescence. However, aggression in the adolescent triggers, in vulnerable parents, anxiety over their own unacknowledged aggression.

Puberty necessitates that the adolescent incorporate in his body image the newly acquired and functional genitality and acknowledge the same in his adult objects (Laufer, 1981a). In case of a developmental breakdown, suicide may aim at the killing of the sexual body. Their sexuality becomes either incestuous or emancipatory, and is in either case unacceptable (Samy, 1989). We can assume that parental ambivalence toward the pubertal changes overlap on the earlier experiences of ambivalent bodily care in the suicidal adolescent.

Symbol Formation and the Suicide Option

The above dynamics explain the suicidal conflict but not its actual acting-out. Acting-out involves a regression to a *concrete* mental representation. Conflicts must be handed over to the ego for conflict resolution and acting-out is the short-circuiting of this process.

The intensity of poorly controlled repressed anger prevents symbol formation. Symbol formation was described by Melanie Klein (1975) as a way to control anger and allow its expression while protecting the loved object. Excessive anger, however, forestalls symbol formation. Failure of symbol formation leads to a desperate wish for control of the object and a wish for concrete restitution (vs. true reparation). Concrete restitution is always deceiving, if not destructive, as it denies objective reality. Suicide is an acting-out which expresses the failure of symbolization and verbal representation. Unconsciously it gratifies the wish for total reunion with the object in a concrete restitution fantasy, as described earlier.

In addition, symbol formation in children and adolescents is essential for grasping the meaning of death, its absoluteness, and its irreversibility. Unconsciously they wish "to go away," "to sleep and wake up different," "to not feel pain anymore," "to kill the body but not the soul" (Samy, 1989).

CONCLUSION

I have attempted to describe child and adolescent suicide as a response to overt or covert parental aggression which has not been mastered. It is equally a desperate wish for magical reparation and reunion—a wish to be born of a significant other who wishes them alive and separate, and who acknowledges their self-worth. Unresolved anger doesn't only shape the nuclear suicidal conflict, but also hinders the opportunities for resolution at the level of verbal representation with the resultant final acting-out. If nothing else, the death by suicide of children and adolescents has taught me that these children did not want to die, they only wanted to exist.

The tragic impact of suicide attempts and completed suicide on the parents has also taught me that parents are themselves prey, often in a cross-generational way, to their own unconscious and unresolved central conflicts around parenting that derive from their own childhood experience. Our empathy should extend from the child to the whole family.

If these conflicts are safely unraveled and brought to verbal representation that allows their working through, we may achieve important prevention in the case the suicide attempts as well as crucial reparatory work with bereaved parents.

REFERENCES

Blos, P. (1979). Modifications in the classical psychoanalytic model of adolescence. In P. Blos (Ed.), *The adolescent passage: developmental issues*. New York: International Universities Press.

Feder, L. (1980). Preconceptive ambivalence and external reality. *International Journal of Psycho-Analysis, 61*, 161–178.

Freud, S. (1933). Why War? In J. Strachey (Ed. and Trans.), *The standard edition of the complete psychological works of Sigmund Freud*, Vol. 22 (pp. 197–198). London: Hogarth.

Furman, E. (1984). Some difficulties in assessing depression and suicide in childhood. In H. S. Sudak et al. (Eds)., *Suicide in the young*. Littleton, MA: John Wright.

Galdston, R. (1981). The domestic dimensions of violence: Child abuse. *Psychoanalytic Study of the Child, 36*, 391–414.

Gutton, P. (1988). The external object alone is violent. In A. Asman (Ed.), *International Annals of Adolescent Psychiatry, Vol. I.* (pp.116–121). Chicago: University of Chicago Press.

Jeammet, P. (1985). Actualité de l'agir. *Nouvelle Revue Psychiatrique, 31*, 201–222.

Khantzian, E., & Mack, J. (1983). Self-preservation and the care of the self ego instincts reconsidered. *Psychoanalytic Study of the Child, 38*, 209–232.

Klein, M. (1975). The importance of symbol formation in the development of the ego. In R. E. Money-Kyrle (Ed.), *Love guilt and reparation and other works. 1921–1945. Writings of Melanie Klein, Vol. 3.* (pp. 219–232). New York: Delacorte Press.

Laplanche, J., & Pontalis, J.-B. (1973). *The language of psycho-analysis*. New York: W. W. Norton.

Laufer, M. (1981a). Adolescent breakdown and the transference neurosis. *International Journal of Psychoanalysis, 62*.

Laufer, M. (1981b). The psychoanalyst and the adolescent's sexual development. *Psychoanalytic Study of the Child, 36*, 181–191.

Litman, R. E. (1967). Sigmund Freud on suicide. In E. S. Schneidman (Ed.), *Essays on self-destruction*. New York: Science House.

Menninger, K. (1938). *Man against himself*. San Diego: Harcourt Brace Jovanovich.

Orbach, I. (1988). *Children who don't want to live: Understanding and treating the suicidal child*. San Francisco: Jossey-Bass.

Paulson, M., Stone, D., & Sporto, R. (1978). Suicide potential and behavior in children ages 4 to 12. *Suicide and Life Threatening Behavior, 8*(4), 225–242.

Pfeffer, C. R. (1981). The family system of suicidal children. *American Journal of Psychotherapy, 35,* 330–341.

Richman, J. (1971). Family determinants of suicide potential. In B. D. Anderson & L. J. McLean (Eds.), *Identifying suicide potential* (pp. 33–54). New York: Behavior Publications.

Richman, J. (1978). Symbiosis, empathy, suicidal behavior and the family. *Suicide and Life-Threatening Behavior, 8*(3), 139–149.

Rosenbaum, M., & Richman, J. (1970). Suicide: The role of hostility and death wishes from the family and significant other. *American Journal of Psychiatry, 126,* 1625–1655.

Sabbath, J. C. (1969). The suicidal adolescent—The expendable child. *Journal of the American Academy of Child Psychiatry, 38,* 211–220.

Salk, L., Sturner, W. A., Lipsitt, L. P., Reilly, B. M., & Levat, R. H. (1985). Relationship of maternal and prenatal conditions to eventual adolescent suicide. *Lancet, 16,* 624–627.

Samy, M. (1989). Suicide et adolescence: Perspective sociale et analytique. In H. Caglar (Ed.), *Adolescence et Suicide.* Paris: Editions ESF.

Samy, M. (1992). L'adolescence: Une perspective kleinienne. *P.R.I.S.M.E., 2*(3), 300–321.

Shapiro, E.R., & Freedman, J. (1988). Family dynamics of adolescent suicide. In A. Asman (Ed.), *International Annals of Adolescent Psychiatry, vol. I* (pp. 152–166). Chicago: University of Chicago Press.

Stork, J. (1988). Suicide and adolescence: Reflections on psychodynamics. In A. Asman (Ed.), *International Annals of Adolescent Psychiatry* (pp. 256–266). Chicago: University of Chicago Press.

Toolan, J. M. (1962). Suicide and suicidal attempts in children and adolescents. *American Journal of Psychiatry, 118,* 719–724.

Tustin, F. (1991). Revised understandings of psychogenic autism. *International Journal of Psycho-analysis, 72,* 585–591.

Winnicott, D. (1949). Hate in the countertransference. *International Journal of Psycho-Analysis, 30,* 69–74.

Zilbrog, G. (1937). Consideration of suicide with particular reference to the young. *American Journal of Orthopsychiatry, 7,* 15–31.

Chapter 4

Bereavement after a Suicide: A Model for Support Groups

Carole Renaud

Different group intervention methods exist to temper the impact of a completed suicide upon family members. This chapter presents a perspective on conducting group interventions with the suicide bereaved. [Ed.]

BACKGROUND

Shneidman (1969) estimates that for each death by suicide 6 other persons are intimately affected. A study in Québec (Association Québécoise de Suicidologie, 1990) suggested that an average of 10 individuals are significantly affected by each completed suicide. Colt (1987) found that 33 percent of callers to suicide prevention centers were bereaved by suicide and that 25 percent of their suicidal clients had experienced the death by suicide of a family member. Although bereavement by suicide is an important social issue it is only recently that programs have been developed to help the suicide bereaved. This chapter discusses research on the needs of persons bereaved following a suicide and the implications of these studies for the development of appropriate intervention strategies. We then present a model of a support group for the suicidal bereaved which has been developed at the Suicide Prevention Centre in Québec City. Data from an evaluation of the effectiveness of these support groups are presented and discussed in terms of implication for appropriate interventions for persons bereaved by suicide.

SOCIAL SUPPORT AND PERSONS BEREAVED BY SUICIDE

The support group described later in this chapter is based upon our understanding of the needs of persons bereaved by suicide. Calhoun, Selby, and Selby (1982) reviewed key studies and clinical interviews with persons bereaved by suicide. They concluded that the suicide bereaved see themselves as isolated, have feelings of guilt, and experience avoidance by their friends and relatives. Although this may be their perception, Rudestam (1977) and Solomon (1982) suggest that it is the persons bereaved by suicide who isolate themselves from friends and relatives by refusing to discuss the death or by lying about the cause of death. They feel uneasy with persons they must deal after the death, such as police officers, coroners, and physicians, and feel that they are blamed by other family members for the suicide (Cain & Fast, 1972; Solomon, 1982). Many accept technical or material support from a limited number of friends but avoid discussing the suicide (Dunn & Morrish-Vidners, 1987). A study of students aged 18 to 45 years who lost a friend by suicide shows that they had similar reactions to family members; they avoided discussing the death and sought little emotional support (Sklar & Hartley, 1990). Range and Martin (1990) suggest that the reactions of avoiding discussion of a death by suicide are greater when the suicide was thought to have been caused by emotional or psychological problems. Range and Goggin (1990) found that when the person who died by suicide was younger, the family was more often thought to be to blame for the suicide.

Persons who know someone bereaved by suicide tend to have less negative attitudes than persons who do not know someone bereaved by suicide (Calhoun, Selby, & Abernathy, 1984). Funeral directors have noticed that visitors to families bereaved by suicide react differently from others (Calhoun, Selby, & Steelman, 1988). They tend to express compassion and curiosity but appear to be uncomfortable in expressing their sympathy.

Our review of the research on the nature of bereavement by suicide suggests that one of the primary needs is to express and talk about thoughts and feelings in a "safe" environment where the bereaved will not feel judged. For this reason, many of the programs for the suicide bereaved have involved group meetings with persons who share the common experience of having lost a friend or relative by suicide.

THREE MODELS OF GROUP INTERVENTION
FOR THE SUICIDE BEREAVED

Although it is not always possible accurately to categorize group interventions for persons bereaved by suicide, our review of the literature, experiences with different groups, and reading of descriptions of group programs, indicate that group interventions may be broadly categorized as endorsing a *therapy* model, *self-help* model or *support* model. These three models have several similarities and differences (see Table 4.1). In each model the group functions to help develop adaptational strategies to deal with the loss and related stress. In each model the exchange between group members occurs in a climate of acceptance and respect and is non-judgmental. However, there are important differences in the roles of the group leaders and the participants as well as the nature of group activities. In the following sections, we briefly describe each group model.

Therapy or Treatment Groups

There exists a wide range of therapy or treatment groups from different perspectives and theoretical points of view. These groups are generally led by an expert who determines the group activities, interprets reactions from members, and functions as a therapist with specific group skills (Rosenberg, 1984). One example of a therapy group for persons bereaved by suicide was described by Battle (1984). The intervention objectives were to help the bereaved understand the psychodynamics of the suicide, their own motivations and reactions and to increase their knowledge of themselves by examining of their relationships with those who died by suicide. The group activities consisted of discussions directed by the leader, who took the role of a therapist, interpreting, encouraging participation, and encouraging the participants to help and accept each other.

Rosenfeld (1991) described a therapy group where the objective was to diminish negative feelings and develop a consciousness of how behavior by the bereaved participants may have an effect upon their support systems. The leaders gave information about the process of bereavement and the nature of suicide. Activities included structured exercises for expressing feelings and analyses of the image which the bereaved convey to others.

Self-Help Groups

Self-help groups are based on the ideology that there is a wealth of qualities in different persons who have experienced a traumatic event which

TABLE 4.1 Synthesis of Therapy Groups, Self-Help Groups, and Support Groups

	Therapy	Self-help	Support
Objectives	Personal change Behavioral change, correcting personal and social, dysfunctional behavior	Socialization Decreasing isolation Helping each other change	Adaptation Improving coping and interpersonal abilities
Members are seen as	Persons with adaptation problems or abnormal behavior	Persons having the necessary abilities to give and receive help	Persons whose common stress is increased by negative social reactions
Membership	Sometimes open, but usually closed; determined by the leader	Open No selection process	Closed Determined by the leader
Role of members	Therapy work on individual goals	Act as resources for each other	Act as resources for each other
Role of leaders	Active: expert, therapist	Peripheral, catalyst, resource person, consultant	Shares personal experiences, therapist, model, teacher, facilitator
Program	Time limited. Determined by leader	Time not limited. Determined by members	Time limited. Determined by leader

may be beneficial to developing positive adaptations and behavior change in others who have experienced similar events (Lieberman et al., 1979). In self-help groups each participant is a resource for others (Riessman, 1965), and participants reinforce each other's feelings of competence and self-esteem and provide experiences in problem solving. Self-help groups are directed by the participants, there is no time limit, and new members can usually join at various times. Activities in self-help groups include discussions in small and large groups. Sometime invited speakers may be present, some groups have members paired with other individuals for mutual support, and self-help groups may include other activities such as leisure events, community education, or social militancy (Romeder et al., 1989). Professionals may or may not have an important function in self-help groups (Toseland & Hacker, 1982). A professional may have a role of a catalyst or may provide specific information requested by the group. Usually, professionals are limited in their activities to that which the group members specifically request.

Billow (1987) and Wrobleski (1984) reported on experiences of self-help groups where the group leaders were professional helpers who had themselves been bereaved by suicide. The groups began with the leader identifying himself as both a facilitator and a person bereaved by suicide and encouraging participants to discuss their experiences, the circumstances surrounding the death by suicide, their reactions, reactions by others, and so on. The leader in these groups was relatively active, told of their own experience of bereavement, and encouraged the participation by all members in looking at their own situations and describing it to the group.

Billow (1987) suggests that in this type of group too much heterogeneity in relationship with the deceased person (e.g., mixing parents, brothers, friends, children) was not recommended. Wrobleski (1984) suggested that persons with important psychiatric problems, alcoholics, individuals with drug problems, or those who believe that religion is the major cure for all problems should be excluded from such groups. Silverman (1972) suggested that people who are suicidal should not participate in this form of bereavement group.

Support Groups

Support groups are closed groups that have a fixed number of meetings determined in advance. The objective of support groups is to help members increase their abilities to adapt to a common source of stress by learning new coping skills and increasing their interpersonal abilities (Rosenberg, 1984). The presence of the group worker is needed to help the group members to create the conditions in which mutual aid can take place (Shulman, 1979).

Guillemette (1991), Séguin (1988), and Switzer and colleagues (1988) describe support groups for persons bereaved by suicide. In these groups the leader has the role of a facilitator, whose main responsibility is to develop a climate in which participants feel secure and confident, beginning with the first group meeting. Group activities are discussions focused on sharing feelings, experiences, and strategies for coping with grief. The leaders participate little during the meetings. Guillemette (1991) suggests having discussion in dyads to facilitate the process and encourages group members to maintain contacts between group meetings. Séguin (1988) encourages such contacts as well, and suggests that group members participate in community and social activities together between meetings.

A MODEL SUPPORT GROUP AND ITS EVALUATION

The following section briefly describes a support group as offered by the Suicide Prevention Centre of Québec City. Because of their commom feeling of isolation and frequent inability to share their experiences with others in their entourage it was felt that the support group model would offer the advantage of fostering the development of a mutual aid system in the group to help individuals cope with the stress related to the suicide.

Participants

Participants were recruited from callers to the suicide prevention center who were interviewed in a follow-up contact after a call in which they discussed their suicidal bereavement. The interview concerned their relationship with the deceased person, the nature of their attachment, circumstances concerning the suicide, a personal history, assessment of the bereaved person's ability to express emotions, social situation, and the possibility that the bereaved is suicidal. Persons whose bereavement was complicated by severe personality disorders and those who were suffering from a pathological bereavement reaction were excluded from participation in the group. Each group consisted of 8 bereaved persons and 2 professional group workers.

Nature of the Group: Objectives and Intervention Process

Each group met once a week for 10 weeks with a follow-up meeting 5 weeks after the last meeting. Each meeting lasted approximately two-and-a-half hours, including a short break. The intervention process is summarized in Table 4.2. The main technique was for members to facilitate a mutual aid system between the members in which they can express their feelings and share experiences. The emotional support received from others allowed each group member to better understand and validate their own reactions by comparing them with the reactions of others. Discussions allowed members to identify possible solutions for various problems based upon advice and information provided by the group. Feedback from members concerning their perceptions and attitudes in the group and concerning members

TABLE 4.2   Intervention Process

Emotional Support	Cognitive Support	Normative Support	Adjustment Objectives
Expressing their feelings	Understanding their reactions	Developing mutual aid	Decreased depression
Sharing experiences	Identifying solutions to difficulties		Reduced anxiety
		Improving abilities to use natural support systems	Reduced isolation

of their natural support network encouraged the development of a more positive self-evaluation and increased contact with others. This approach is based in part on the research by Séguin (1989), who conducted a study of persons bereaved by suicide. She found that the lesser negative physical and psychological consequences of bereavement by suicide was related to using coping strategies involving expression of feelings, problem-solving techniques, and positive evaluation of one's personal abilities to master their experience by finding some sense out of what they were going through. A "homework" assignment was given to each group member at the end of each meeting. This assignment provided for a transition in the different meeting topics. This assignment was discussed during part of each group meeting. Specific themes were proposed for each of the group meetings which cover the main reactions to a loss by suicide:

1. Getting to know each other
2. Expressing what is being experienced now; "x" number of days–months after the suicide
3. Guilt
4. Anger
5. Continuing to live without the other
6. Oneself and others
7. New identity, new roles in life circumstances
8. Facing difficulties
9. Help from others
10. Discussion and evaluation of the meetings
11. What has been learned and what must be continued

The first meeting allowed members to get to know one another, to establish a common ground, and to negotiate a contract or agreement concerning how the group would function. Just talking about their experiences and being able to describe to others that the death was by suicide was an important step for many. The first two meetings focused on the expression of feelings. Participants learned that they were not the only ones to experience such pain nor to anticipate life with such anxiety.

The following three meetings allowed members to speak openly about their feelings of guilt, anger, impotence, despair—all the feelings they avoided speaking about with others because of their fear of being judged or rejected. The understanding and empathy from group members allowed for a reevaluation of these feelings and consideration of expressing these feelings more to relatives. The sixth meeting was devoted to summarizing and integrating all that had occurred up until that point.

The seventh and eighth meetings focused upon identifying needs and finding solutions to problems resulting from the loss. Discussions lead to exploring new solutions and alternatives and consideration of the future.

The ninth meeting concerned reflecting upon expectations and attitudes concerning members of their support system. Members were led to see how their own attitudes and prejudices could make their relationships with relatives and friends more difficult. The tenth meeting focused upon integrating and summarizing how each group member and the group as a whole succeeded in attaining their initial objectives. This meeting also prepared members for separation from the group.

The follow-up meeting focused upon how each member was dealing with the bereavement, what has been learned, needs still present, and also emphasized identifying possible means for meeting those needs in the future. This meeting concluded with a meal and party for the members.

An Evaluation

In order better to understand the results of the support groups for persons bereaved by suicide, a detailed evaluation was conducted on several of the groups. A typical group evaluation is presented in what follows.

Characteristics of a Group

This typical group consisted of 8 persons ranging age from 27 to 64 years and including 2 persons who lost a child by suicide, 4 who had a husband or wife die by suicide, 1 who lost a friend, and 1 who lost a sister. The group members were between 2½ and 11 months after the death by suicide. All the participants were considered to have gone beyond the initial reaction of shock and denial which often follows a loss. Three of the bereaved discovered the body of the person who died by suicide, and in six of the eight cases the suicide victim had made at least one attempt prior to the completed suicide.

Evaluation Instruments

Depression was measured by the French-Canadian version of the Beck Depression Inventory (Gauthier et al., 1982). Anxiety was measured with the Situational and Trait Anxiety Inventory of Spielberger et al. (1983). Additional questions concerned the development of mutual support during the sessions and the attainment of individual objectives. Evaluations were conducted on the standard measures before participation in the meetings and six weeks after the end of participation in the support group.

Results

There was a significant decrease in depression as measured by the Beck Inventory ($p<.001$) and there was a significant decrease in situational anxiety ($p<.001$) between the pre- and posttests. As would be expected, there was no significant decrease in the measure of trait anxiety, since trait anxiety is a long-term characteristic of individuals. Overall, participants perceived family members, friends, and colleagues as being more supportive after participation in the support group. There were few changes in perceptions of support given by members of the family.

In addition to these quantitative evaluation, each participant was asked what their objectives were before participating in the support group. They were asked at the end to assess to what extent they attained those objectives. Table 4.3 summarizes the 8 participants' objectives and their self-evaluations and explanations of to what extent these objectives were attained.

Summary of Evaluation

It is evident that support groups may offer significant help to persons bereaved by suicide. Besides significant decreases in depression and anxiety, individuals were generally able to attain their own goal and objectives by participating in the groups. The particular type of group which we chose at the Québec Suicide Prevention Centre, the support group, was based upon our evaluation of the important need to develop better ties with others because of the frequent feeling of isolation among persons bereaved by

TABLE 4.3   Self-Evaluations of Objectives

Objectives (sex, age, relationship to deceased)	Self-Evaluation and Explanation
(F. 27 years, husband) "Find an equilibrium, feel at ease with my feelings."	*Moderately attained* "I know now that my anger is blocking me, I am ready to go on to another stage."
(F. 32 years, boyfriend) "Find my equilibrium, find ways to deal with my feelings and reactions."	*Moderately attained* "My feelings of panic and powerlessness have disappeared, I can face my fears and my contacts with others are easier."
(F. 64 years, husband) "Learn to live alone, find my interest in activities which I had before the suicide."	*Little attained* "I learned to think about myself, to be myself, to stand up for myself but I am afraid of being overwhelmed by my son's needs."
(F. 43 years, son) "Sort things out for myself, my feelings of guilt, unblock my feelings."	*Moderately attained* "I have confronted my feelings, I no longer feel guilty, I take pleasure in my activities."
(F. 53 years, daughter) "Express my inner feelings which I am experiencing in grief."	*Totally attained* "I no longer feel guilty, I am capable of talking about my grief to people close to me."
(F. 20 years, sister) "Be able to express my feelings."	*Totally attained* "I can talk more, I found solutions to many problems and I am confident that I will work through my grief."
(M. 35 years, wife) "Get in touch with myself, learn to think of my needs and meet them."	*Moderately attained* "I feel less mixed-up, I have begun a social life and have gone back to work."
(M. 31 years, brother) "Answer my many questions, regain an interest in activities I had before."	*Moderately attained* "I no longer feel guilty, I have found certain answers and I have learned that other questions do not concern me. I get pleasure from my activities."

suicide. We realize that other forms of groups have been tried elsewhere with success. It would be interesting to conduct comparative research in the future in which different forms of groups are evaluated to see if certain tend to be more effective with persons bereaved by suicide, or certain sub-groups of bereaved individuals who have different characteristics.

There are many other research questions which need to be answered. In our support groups a number of specific themes were developed based upon what the leaders felt was most important to discuss. It would be useful to conduct research to determine to what extent the actual content of the sessions is important and to what extent the content is less important than the development of mutual support in a group for the suicide-bereaved. We hope that these programs will be expanded in the future and that future research will help clarify which group characteristics are related to increased benefits from the group experience.

REFERENCES

Association Québécoise de Suicidologie (1990). *La prévention du suicide au Québec: Vers un modèle intégré de services.* Montréal: AQS.

Battle, A. O. (1984). Group therapy for survivors of suicide. *Crisis, 5*(1), 45–58.

Beck, A. T., Ward, C. H., Mendelson, Moch, J., & Erbaugh, J. (1961). An inventory for measuring depression. *Archives of General Psychiatry, 4,* 53–63.

Billow, C. J. (1987). A multiple family support group fro survivors of suicide. In E. J. Dunne, J. L McIntosh, & K. Dunne-Maxim (Eds.), *Suicide and its aftermath* (pp. 208–214). New York: Norton.

Cain, A. C., & Fast, I. (1972). The legacy of suicide: Observations on the pathogenic impact of suicide upon marital partners. In A.C. Cain (Ed.), *Survivors of suicide* (pp. 145–155). Springfield, IL: Charles C Thomas.

Calhoun, L. G., Selby, J. W., & Abernathy, C. B. (1984). Suicidal death: Social reactions to bereaved survivors. *Journal of Psychology, 116,* 255–261.

Calhoun, L. G., Selby, J. W., & Selby, L. E. (1982). The psychological aftermath of suicide: An analysis of current evidence. *Clinical Psychology Review, 2,* 409–420.

Calhoun, L. M., Selby, J. W., & Steelman, J. K. (1988/1989). A collation of funeral director's impressions of suicidal deaths. *Omega: Journal of Death and Dying, 19*(4), 365–373.

Colt, G. H. (1987). The history of the suicide survivor: The mark of Cain. In E. J. Dunne, J. L. McIntosh, & K. Dunne-Maxim (Eds.), *Suicide and its aftermath* (pp. 3–18). New York: Norton.

Dunn, R. G., & Morrish Vidners, D. (1987/1988). The psychological and social experience of suicide survivors. *Omega: Journal of Death and Dying, 18*(3), 175–215.

Gauthier, J., Thériault, F., Morin, C., & Lawson, J. S. (1982). Adaptation française d'une mesure d'auto-évaluation de l'intensité de la dépression. *Revue Québécoise de Psychologie, 3*(2), 13–27.

Guillemette, D. (1991). *Programme de soutien aux personnes endeuillées*, document non publié. Comité Prévention suicide de Val d'Or.

Lieberman, M. A., Borman, L. D., Bond, G. R., Antze, P. S., & Levy, L. H. (1979). *Self-help groups for coping with crisis*. San Francisco: Jossey-Bass.

Range, L. M., & Martin, S. T. (1990). How knowledge of extenuating circumstances influences community reactions toward suicide victims and their bereaved families. *Omega: Journal of Death and Dying, 21*(3), 191–198.

Range, L. M., & Goggin, W. C. (1990). Reactions to suicide: Does age of the victim make a difference? *Death Studies, 14*(3), 269–275.

Riessman, F. (1965). The helper therapy principle. *Social Work, 10*, 27–32.

Romeder, J. L., Balthazar, H., Farquharson, A., & Lavoie, F. (1989). *Les groupes d'entraide et la santé: nouvelles solidarités*. Ottawa: Conseil Canadien de Développement Social.

Rosenberg, P. P. (1984). Support groups, a special therapeutic entity. *Small Group Behavior, 15*(2), 173–186.

Rosenfeld, L. (1991). *Left to live: Mourning in group*. Paper presented at the 4th meeting of the Canadian Association for Suicide Prevention, Moncton, N.B.

Rudestam, K. E. (1977). Physical and psychological responses to suicide in the family. *Journal of Consulting and Clinical Psychology, 45*(2), 162–170.

Schneidman, E. S. (1969). *On the nature of suicide*. San Francisco: Jossey-Bass.

Seguin, M. (1988). *Programme de soutien aux personnes endeuillées*. Montréal: Suicide-Action Montréal.

Seguin, M. (1989). *Le deuil après un suicide: L'effet des mécanismes d'adaptation*. Montréal: Suicide-Action Montréal.

Shulman, L. (1979). *The skills of helping individuals and groups*. Itaska, IL: Peacock Publishers.

Silverman, P. R. (1972). Widowhood and preventive intervention. *Family Coordinator, 21*, 95–102.

Sklar, F., & Hartley, S. (1990). Close friends as survivors: Bereavement patterns in a "hidden" population. *Omega: Journal of Death and Dying, 21*(2), 103–112.

Solomon, M. I. (1982). The bereaved and the stigma of suicide. *Omega: Journal of Death and Dying, 13*(4), 377–387.

Spielberger, C. D., Gorusch, R. L., Lushene, R. E., Vagg, P. R., & Jacobs, G. A. (1983). *Manual for the State-Trait Anxiety Inventory*. Palo Alto, CA: Consulting Psychologists Press.

Switzer, S. A., Austin, M. A., & Reed, C. E. (1988). Survivor of suicide, *Proceedings of the 21st Annual Meeting of the American Association of Suicidology*, 103–104.

Toseland, R. W., & Hacker, L. (1982). Self-help groups and professional involvemement. *Social Work Review*, July, 341–347.

Wrobleski, A. (1984). The suicide survivors grief group. *Omega: Journal of Death and Dying, 15*(2), 173–183.

Chapter 5

The Development Process of a Community Postvention Protocol[1]

Keltie Paul

Besides helping bereaved individuals on a one-to-one basis, several communities have developped integrated "postvention" plans on how to respond in the event that a death by suicide occurs. This chapter presents a model of postvention strategy which shows how an integrated program was developed to prevent and minimize negative reactions when death by suicide occurs. [Ed.]

POSTVENTION

Edwin S. Shneidman invented the term "postvention" in 1973 to describe follow-up support for all survivors of suicide, including attempters, and family, friends and colleagues of a victim of suicide. Boldt (1985) urged the inclusion of postvention activities within his model for the Province of Alberta, maintaining that a coordinated community postvention outreach was as important as prevention and intervention.

---

1. Earlier versions of this paper were presented at the Tenth Annual Suicide Symposium in Calgary, Alberta, in May of 1992, and at the Canadian Association for Suicide Prevention in Saskatoon, Saskatchewan, in October of 1992.

The primary objective behind any postvention strategy is the development of the means to assist suicide survivors. The strategy used incorporates information access and dissemination. Activities can be diverse, from assisting school boards with Tragic Event Protocol development, to delegating specific postvention activities, to educating community resources, including clergy, natural helpers, and professionals. The goal is improved community-based services to assist survivors. The logic is that a solid postvention plan can identify those affected, and assist survivors by offering a continuum of immediate and follow-up services specifically designed to assist them in adjusting to this tragic loss. This continuum might include: immediate on-site (i.e., school, workplace) critical incident debriefings, interventions with severely distraught survivors, and referrals to appropriate resources. Long-term activities might incorporate support groups, training and education programs, monitoring of survivors, and program evaluation.

Suicide crises invariably produce disequilibrium within social systems (Hill, 1984). This has been most evident in school systems, and the development of protocols, ranging from primarily institutionalized administrative procedures (Butler & Statz, 1986) to comprehensive survivor-based activities (Dunne-Maxim et al., 1992) has been well documented. School system postvention protocols are becoming as familiar as procedures for fire or other school disasters.

However, suicide crises can and do often affect social systems larger than educational systems. The tragedy can deeply affect an entire community (Favelle & Boyd, 1992). This fact, combined with knowledge of the negative effects of a "do-nothing" approach, led to the process of developing the community-wide protocol described below.

CASE EXAMPLE

Fort McMurray is a city of 35,000 with a surrounding hinterland of nearly 96,000 square kilometers. The next urban area, Edmonton, is 534 kilometers southwest of Fort McMurray. The city owes its recent urban status to the influx of workers and administrative infrastructure during the oil boom of the 1970s and 1980s. The average age of the population is 27, with 31 percent below age 20. Only 284 people are over the age of 65 (Statistics Canada, 1991b). Median income is $37,000 per annum. The majority of employed adults (7,327) work in the oil extraction/oil refinement industry. The population is primarily of European descent, with a sizable minority of residents who are of Native Canadian, Chinese, Arabic, Filipino, and East-Indian descent (Statistics Canada, 1991a).

Fort McMurray is typical of many "company," non-renewable resource centers in that it experiences periodic "boom/bust" economic cycles and the accompanying social upheavals. The early 1980s is a prime example. Following a population/economic boom, a multitude of factors contributed to a suicide rate of 18.1 per hundred thousand (1982). The suicide rate fell to 5.9 per hundred thousand in 1989–1991.

In the mid-1980s, Fort McMurray became the host community to a Community Interagency Suicide Prevention Program (CISPP), funded by the Province of Alberta Department of Health, Mental Health Division. Some Other Solutions Society for Crisis Prevention (S.O.S.) became the umbrella agency for both the CISPP and 24-hour distress (intervention) HELPLINE. A Bereavement Program was added in 1989.

The development of interagency protocols mirrors the development of a unique urban area in a unique environment. Geographic isolation, cultural, economic, and historical factors have contributed to the "frontier mentality" of many residents. This worldview of self-sufficiency, local-level problem-solving and decision-making autonomy had produced a unique problem-solving and organizational pattern. The "coordination-of-services" approach is one of the positive components of the interorganizational field, and this particular task environment (Jones, 1975). Along the way, the process also began to reflect the current paradigm shift now being experienced by other communities, with emphasis on interagency collaboration and volunteer staff.

The community has had previous experience in developing a community response to a crisis situation. The Critical Incident Stress Interventions (CISI) protocol for psychological debriefing response to disasters and serious incidents was already in place. The CISI protocol was developed in response to underlying axiomatic principles:

The two oil-producing plants are situated close to the city and the corollaries:

a) When an accident occurs which affects emergency personnel to the extent of possible emotional trauma (i.e., Post-Traumatic Stress Disorder), then:

b) The local personnel must be prepared to deal with psychological debriefing of affected groups and individuals.

Over several months in 1989 and 1990, key agency personnel met to design, develop, and implement the CISI protocol. The result was a document which addressed all aspects of this type of response, including clinical consultation, professional mental health and peer counselor roles, psychological debriefing criteria, training requirements, and reporting procedures.[2]

---

2. Originally entitled the Critical Incident Stress Debriefing Protocols, this first step was a local Employee Assistance Program initiative aimed at providing psy-

In December 1989, the Fort McMurray Separate School District began work on local tragic event protocols which directly addressed suicide postvention. Much of this work was aided by the office of the Provincial Suicidologist, Dr. Ron Dyck. Within the Public School System, most high schools now have a postvention protocol which specifies postvention responses and media releases. The Fort McMurray Separate School System has a division-wide postvention protocol.

Despite the existence of the above protocols, gaps in service delivery and information dissemination were discovered in the community response to two teen suicides in early January of 1992. Some Other Solutions was called upon to arrange a meeting of caregiver stakeholders in mid-January. Twenty-six people, representing 19 agencies, attended.

Two concerns were immediately apparent. First, no systematic reporting system to alert schools or the helping agencies was in place. Both tragedies had occurred at the tail-end of the Christmas break. In one case, the media published the details before most agencies were aware of the tragedy. Caregiver agencies, particularly school personnel, were anxious to have a centralized reporting system where information could be given to affected schools and feeder-schools where survivors attended. A second group concerned with reporting procedures were clergy, who were concerned with contact procedures which might enable them to assist survivors as soon as possible.

Another issue was the lack of a comprehensive plan for postvention services; including agency parameters (responsibilities, action plans, and immediate and follow-up procedures). Stakeholder agencies were interested in seeing a community-wide strategy codified, so that service duplication, agency confusion over reporting procedures, and inappropriate referrals could be eliminated.

The first action of the stakeholder group, which came together in January 1992, was to delegate a subcommittee with the responsibility of examining solutions to the above problems. The Suicide Response Committee, (SRC) as the group came to be called, was made up of representatives from Alberta Mental Health, Some Other Solutions, the Health Unit, the Ministerial Association, the two school systems, the Royal Canadian Mounted

---

chological debriefing for plant-site and city first responders: fire, paramedics, and ambulance personnel. Over the last four years, debriefing requests from other groups (i.e., sports associations, workers, school personnel) prompted a change in mandate to include all community groups requesting this service. To date, psychological interventions (defusing and debriefing) have been accessed by local consumers following suicide, homicide, and accidental death, "near-miss" incidents, deaths of children (i.e., Sudden Infant Death) serious injury, and robberies. All 20 members of the CISI team are volunteers.

Police (RCMP), the Alberta Alcohol and Drug Abuse Commission, and the Venture Program (an outpatient program operating in the local hospital).

This group's first task was to tackle the labyrinth of information access and distribution. A draft "information tree" was adopted as a prototype for longitudinal revision and refinement. The prototype called for extensive contact and information exchange between certain agencies. First, a protocol for information access was established between the RCMP Victim Services Unit (RCMP V.S.U.) and the distress line (HELPLINE), which would then inform the Suicide Response Coordinator.[3] The Suicide Response Coordinator informs designated personnel and coordinates immediate activities, including debriefings.

In order to avoid "re-inventing the wheel," the Suicide Response Committee examined the existing CISI protocol and decided to duplicate its format. This decision seems to have expedited the process. Most committee members were familiar with the CISI document, and familiarity with that process seems to have two outcomes. First, while an initial glance at the project indicated a formidable process, the earlier success showed that such a community-wide protocol was achievable. Second, the CISI protocol is a model that agency personnel are comfortable with, thus reducing the stress of producing an entirely new structure.

In early June of 1992, Suicide Response Subcommittee (SRC) members began working on the "action" and follow-up portions of the four protocols. As with the initial information base and agency contact sections, work was divided among subcommittee members. This process proved to be more challenging than the information debate, as debriefing team training, survivor follow-up, information access, and survivor-rights issues began to be discussed.

The postvention strategies already in place had clearly demonstrated that one or two agencies could not cope with the number of intervention requests received from the community. Also, student reaction to non-school debriefing personnel tended to be mixed. School counselor and teacher attendance at debriefings is essential, yet only a few counselors had training in debriefing techniques. The SRC recommended that the community sponsor a postvention debriefing training and that debriefing teams be recruited from this training. The deployment of these teams would be coordinated through Some Other Solutions.

Last, the SRC decided to have the CISI teams, once expanded and trained, to engage in immediate postvention interventions, thus delegat-

---

3. The Suicide Response Coordinator is the Some Other Solutions Suicide Prevention Coordinator or delegate.

ing work among a broad base of trained community personnel. At present, there are seven team leaders (mental health experts) and thirteen peer counselors. The peers were selected from the sixty-two participants from a three-day postvention intervention seminar held in March of 1993.[4]

Once the structure and processes for postvention information access were in place, the Suicide Response Committee subdivided to produce Youth, Adult, Professional Personnel (death of a helping-service professional), and multiple completed suicide interventions. Each protocol outlines specific survivor identification, intervention actions, and agency follow-up responsibilities.[5] The postvention protocol also contains helping agency and personnel phone numbers, as well as local clergy contact numbers.

ANALYSIS

Communities encountering postvention situations always experience high risks as some survivors may become suicidal themselves. When this situation is complicated by "systems problems" (Hoff, 1983) the results can be increased survivor distress, as well as increased stress and frustration among helping agencies who are scrambling to meet needs that have not been properly identified. A community commitment to immediate identification of, and intervention with survivors, and consistent follow-up collaboration among human service agencies for consumers (survivors) can be the mediation avenue for a communal task which turns postvention reaction into prevention strategies. A secondary, and often overlooked, component of stress in crisis mediation is the "care for the caregiver." This component, now codified in the local CISI protocols, is the defusing and debriefing for "second responders"; helpers involved with survivors who may need stress management following a particular postvention crisis (i.e., colleague, consumer, or multiple deaths) (Mitchell, 1988). Both consumer-oriented postvention and acceptance of self-care may, as in this local protocol process, require paradigm shifts. In short, a paradigm shift is a rapid change in the rules of the playing field of a particular culture. When the rules change, not only can the expected outcomes be enhanced, but the un-

---

4. The CISI training program is currently using local experts for skill-enhancement in suicide prevention, group process, defusing and debriefing skills, and crisis intervention.
5. In addition to regular follow-up, all individuals involved in local suicides meet one week following the suicide to discuss evident service gaps and remedy any service delivery problems discovered during postvention activities.

expected outputs can generate even more changes on the playing field. Continuing on the sports analogy, not only do the rules change, but so do the plays.

Expected outcomes included rapid information access, survivor identification and intervention, and improved follow-up. Success of the protocol has been attested to by agencies, groups, and individuals. For example:

a) The suicide of an educational professional in a community 46 kilometers from Fort McMurray resulted in a three-member intervention team on site in 45 minutes. School staff and school division administrators have applauded their efforts.

b) Consumer complaints about service delivery have greatly decreased.

c) Schools experiencing postvention events have had very positive experiences with response and follow-up.

d) Local psychologists have commented that the survivor identification and referrals have been appropriate and timely.

e) Postvention case conferences have produced opportune and effective service-gap closures.

The unexpected outputs, apart from being surprising, have also been positive:

1. The debate among Suicide Response Committee members regarding survivor rights resulted in work spearheaded by the RCMP Victim Services Unit to produce a Release Form which respects the wishes of the family in regard to notifying agencies which had contact with the victim (i.e., drug and alcohol counselors, therapists) and friends of the victim. If the family is reluctant to accept the death as suicide, then debriefing focuses on bereavement issues in general (i.e., Feelings, Grief Process Information).[6]

2. The postvention training held in March was extended to rural community representatives. The communities of Athabasca, Fort Chipewyan (a northern Alberta Native community), and Lac La Biche now have their own postvention response teams. The recent suicide of a former Fort Chipewyan resident was responded to internally with the suicide prevention program in Fort McMurray acting only as a resource.

3. Community interagencies have formed a Community Interagency Suicide prevention Program Council (CISPPC) which meets biannually to:

a) update protocols

b) discuss future community-based initiates for suicide prevention.

---

6. CISI team members are trained to mention, as information, that "the death is being investigated by the police as a suicide." Legal cause of death is established by the Medical Examiner's office, and is not often immediate.

All members of the original Suicide Response committee are on the CISPPC. The spring meeting of this council initiated a new community goal: a protocol for all treatment agencies following suicide attempts, and inter-agency support for a local study of attempts with the aim of producing a profile on attempters (age, sex, method). The local hospital (Emergency and Medical Records) are collecting these data.

CONCLUSIONS

The Fort McMurray Postvention Protocol is not a static document. Re-search continues on survivors, and the new data must be incorporated into any plan which addresses such a diverse cultural area as an entire community.

A postvention objective also requires a great deal of community co-ordination in order to have stakeholders buy-in to the provision of services and support a wide range of activities. Evaluation is a constant activity, as service gaps are bound to appear even with the most vigorous planning. A continuum of services is not only a goal; it is also a process requiring both knowledge and experiential learning.

Part of this experiential learning process has been the acceptance of Crisis Intervention as a postvention technique. Its aims are to assist survi-vors in resolution of the immediate crisis, restoring the individual to a pre-crisis level of functioning, and follow-up with traumatized individuals. The future of this process is now in further service gap-identification and clo-sure, and in evaluation. Evaluation is currently being conducted of all Suicide Support Groups and within a Goals and Objectives framework through the coordinating agency, Some Other Solutions Society for Crisis Prevention. The CISI committee has raised the issue of thoroughly evalu-ating postvention activities in schools as part of the follow-up activities. This initiative was spearheaded by a local CISI training session during which a recent article by Hazell and Lewin (1993) was discussed. Results of this evaluation will be available in 1996.

Last, there is a powerful paradigm shift toward accountability, broad public participation in planning consumer-based services, and coordinat-ing more services with less financial support. This shift is inevitable, and will effect all future service delivery (i.e., elimination of duplication).

The process of developing a community-based postvention response creates and supports an environment for such a paradigm shift. As demon-strated by this experience, the keys to our first community-wide protocol were stakeholder buy-in, previous experience with a particular approach to crisis management (i.e., The Critical Stress Interventions Program), and stakeholder willingness to tackle sensitive issues in order to produce an objective and vision which was born out of tragedy, thus creating proaction from reaction.

REFERENCES

Boldt, M. (1985). Towards the development of a systematic approach to suicide prevention: The Alberta Model. *Canada's Mental Health, 33*(2).

Butler, R. R., & Statz, M. A. (1986). Preparation for when prevention doesn't work: Responding to a suicide. *NASP Journal, 23*(3).

Dunne-Maxim, K., Godin, S., Lamb, F., Sutton, C., & Underwood, M. (1992). The aftermath of youth suicide, providing postvention services for the school and community. *CRISIS, 13*(1).

Favelle, G., & Boyd, L. (1992, October). *When bad things happen to good communities, the community trauma postvention process. A case example.* Unpublished Paper Presented at the 2nd Annual Canadian Association for Suicide Prevention Meeting, Saskatoon, Saskatchewan.

Hazell, P., & Terry, L. (1993). An evaluation of postvention following adolescent suicide. *Suicide and Life-Threatening Behavior, 23*(2), 101–109.

Hill, William H. (1984). Intervention and postvention in schools. In H. S. Sudak, A. B. Ford, & N. B. Rushforth (Eds.), *Suicide in the young.* Boston: John Wright/PGS.

Hoff, L. (1983). Interagency coordination for people in crisis. *Journal of the Alliance of Information and Referral System, 5*(1), 79–89.

Jones, T. (1975). Some thoughts on coordination of services. *Social Work, 5,* 375–378.

Mitchell, J. (1988). Stress development and functions of a critical incident. *Journal of Emergency Medical Services, December,* 43–45.

Shneidman, E. S. (1973). *Deaths of man.* New York: Quadrangle Books.

Statistics Canada (1991a). *Census area profiles.* Ottawa: Queens Printer.

Statistics Canada (1991b). *Vital Statistics and Health Statistics Section.* Ottawa: Statistics Canada.

Chapter 6

How Family Members and Friends React to Suicide Threats

Brian L. Mishara

Most people think about suicide at some time in their life and many express their suicidal thoughts to others. This chapter discusses the impact of learning that a friend or family member is thinking of suicide, how people react in these situations, and how they may be supported as a potential helper. [Ed.]

BACKGROUND

It is a commonly accepted fact that most people who attempt suicide express their desire to kill themselves to friends and/or family members before initiating the attempt (e.g., Suicide in Canada, 1994). Suicide prevention and crisis intervention centers often receive a substantial number of calls from persons who are not themselves suicidal but who are concerned about a friend or family member who has threatened or talked about suicide. For example, approximately one out of five callers to Suicide-Action Montréal, the Montréal area suicide prevention center, are so-called "third-party callers," persons who are calling because of their concern for someone else who they feel may be suicidal. Government and non-profit organizations in many different countries have publicized the importance of appropriate reactions to suicide threats by friends and family members as a mean of primary prevention. For example, brochures published by the American Association of Suicidology, the Canadian Association for Mental Health, the Government of Québec, tell how to recognize danger signs (including suicidal threats) and what to say and do in those situations.

Research conducted years ago (e.g., Mishara, Baker, & Mishara, 1976) showed that two-thirds of college students in their sample had the experience of a friend telling them that they were thinking of committing suicide. Approximately half of persons who were told by someone else of their desire to commit suicide gave appropriate "open" responses of discussing the person's problems and asking questions about the situation. However, the other half of the sample reacted with a clear message that it was not appropriate to continue serious discussion on the topic: they either ignored the statements concerning suicide, made a joke about the situation, or took the suicidal threat seriously but said that they were not qualified to discuss the matter, and suggested that their friend seek professional help rather than continue discussion with them.

Although there is much recent research on how to deal with bereavement following a death by suicide, there are few studies of how people handle the expression of suicidal ideation by friends and relatives. This chapter presents some models for understanding how so-called "third parties," those who are concerned about suicidal ideation expressed by friends and relatives, may react to suicidal ideation. The chapter then presents suggestions for helping persons better react and help when they are concerned about the possibility of the suicide attempt by friends and relatives. The information presented in this chapter is based upon clinical experiences with "third-party" callers to the Montréal suicide prevention center, Suicide-Action Montréal, as well as face-to-face interventions with persons concerned about the suicidal risk of people they know and how they can be of help.

MODELS OF REACTION TO SUICIDAL THREATS AND VERBALIZATION

This section describes several ways in which people may react to suicidal threats and verbalization. Each section describes a "model" of how the "third party" may react. These models are not mutually exclusive and individuals may have a combination of reactions or change in their reactions over time. Nevertheless, these models may help explain the nature of the reactions of friends and relatives to suicidal threats and verbalizations.

The Helper

The helper, in her/his most idealized form, does exactly what the textbooks would describe as appropriate behavior when a friend or relative talks about suicide. The helper listens without being judgmental, asks direct, clear and appropriate questions about how and when the person is thinking about committing suicide, asks questions about what is going on that is resulting in the person contemplating suicide, expresses empathy and concern as well as a desire to help the person find alternative ways of resolving their problems, and makes appropriate referrals and suggestions. In this "perfect" idealized version, the helper behaves like the most skilled volunteers in telephone interventions but has the added advantage of being available to stay with the suicidal person and offer concrete instrumental help.

However, there are inherent difficulties in reacting as a helper to a friend who is contemplating suicide. First, few individuals have received the training and information necessary to know what one "should" and "should not" do when faced with a suicide threat. For example, many people may feel that to say, "look on the bright side, you have so many reasons to continue to live and not consider suicide, for example, a good job, a loving wife, etc." is a useful and appropriate response. However, those who work in suicide prevention suggest that such a response of trying to convince a suicidal person *not to be suicidal* because their suicide is not "justified" may increase feelings of guilt. *Despite* those reasons not to kill oneself, the person is still suicidal; trying to tell the person that they have no right to be suicidal may not be helpful.

Helpers often feel incompetent to deal with a suicidal situation. For this reason, they may call a suicide prevention center or crisis intervention center to seek support or look for alternative means of helping their possibly suicidal friend or relative. Such organizations can support helpers in their dealing with the suicidal person and may often encourage persons who feel uneasy about assuming a helper role to do so, at least to some extent.

The Future Victim

The future victim anticipates a possible suicidal death by a friend or relative and focuses upon the devastating nature upon her/him of the future loss. The future victim may experience an anticipatory grief reaction and begin mourning for the suicidal person before the person has actually attempted suicide. The future victim shifts the focus from the anguish or problems which the suicidal individual is experiencing to an egotistical concern for "what you are going to do to me should you kill yourself." Future victims may suffer and anguish, but may be immobilized and unable to offer much help to the suicidal acquaintance because they become too focused upon their own anticipated suffering.

The Devil or Bad Person

The devil or "bad person" feels guilty and may be convinced that their friend or relative is suicidal because of what they have done or failed to do. They may say to themselves, "I am a horrible mother if my son is thinking about suicide." "She is killing herself because I have stopped dating her." Or, "If I had just done . . . or if I were just able to . . . , this person would not be suicidal—but I am no good." The devil or "bad person" feels personally responsible for anything which may occur to the person expressing suicide and feels that if they had been "better" in some way, the other person would not be suicidal.

The Martyr or Saint

The saint feels that she/he has done everything possible to help and support the suicidal individual and feels that there is nothing more they could possibly do to be of help. The martyr goes a step further and feels an injustice in the fact that the friend or relative is suicidal: "I have done everything possible for her, I have tolerated so much and put myself out so much, and despite all I have done she is considering suicide."

The Blind Person

The blind person simply does not believe that the friend or relative is "really" suicidal. In fact, the more extreme version of the blind person would ignore even the most blatant warning signs and suggestions by others that the friend or relative may be dangerously suicidal. The defense of denial can be extremely strong and the blind person may continue that denial even after a tragic death by suicide in believing that it was just an "accident."

The Lamb of God

In the Bible, the Lamb of God is the scapegoat, which carries the sins of the people into the wilderness and relieves them of their sins. People who are contemplating suicide often feel greatly relieved when they talk with someone else about these thoughts. The suicidal person may feel much less at risk and the danger of an imminent attempt may be minimized. However, some friends and relatives who help such a person may feel that they have taken on the other person's troubles and anguish. They may be extremely troubled since they now carry the emotional and psychological burden of their friend or relative, regardless of whether or not the relative is feeling better and working toward resolving their problems.

The Traitor

Sometimes suicidal intentions or a suicide plan is revealed to a friend or relative "in secret." The suicidal person says, "I am going to tell you something but I don't want you to tell anyone else." The suicidal person then reveals a plan to end his/her life in a specific way at a specific time or reveals that he/she possess the means and intent to complete the act. In some situations, the suicide may be highly probable but the suicidal person tells a confidant not to reveal his/her troubles or anguish to anyone else. If, despite this, the confidant calls a suicide prevention center or speaks to a family member or calls an ambulance to save the person's life during an attempt, the confidant may feel that they have betrayed their friend or relative. This feeling of betrayal may be tempered by receiving information about the ambivalence which frequently accompanies suicidal ideation and explanations about how suicidal persons may cry out for help while at the same time saying that they do not want anyone to help them.

The Extortion Victim

The extortion victim feels that the suicidal threats are being used as a means to manipulate others or extort some form of reaction. The extortion victim focuses upon the possible manipulative aspects of the suicide threat and ignores the person's anguish. In some instances, the extortion is quite explicit. For example, a boyfriend who says to his former girlfriend, "If you don't start dating me again, I will kill myself."

The Strong Soldier

The strong soldier sticks to the facts and does not allow the suicidal threats to have much conscious emotional impact. The strong soldier may be helpful to a person who is suicidal by focusing on concrete ways to solve the person's problems. However, in other situations the strong soldier may be of less help because the emotional impact of the events are ignored.

The Person in Crisis

The experience of having a friend or relative who is suicidal is a crisis situation for many individuals. As such, the friend or relative may need help to deal with the crisis. In some cases, the crisis may evoke suicidal ideation and a potential suicidal risk in the confidant. Aggressive crisis intervention may be warranted depending upon the extent of the stress and anxiety the third party experiences.

COMMON MYTHS

Although suicide is a phenomenon which is present in all cultures, it is a problem for which there is little formal education or training. Most people have not learned much about the nature of suicide and the role of friends and relatives in helping people who express suicidal ideation. Because of this, it is common for friends and relatives to have erroneous thoughts and beliefs concerning their potentially suicidal acquaintance, which influence their ability to be of help. Here are some of the common myths which friends and relatives may believe:

1. *I am the only person who is able to help this suicidal individual.* This false belief may be reinforced by overt statements by the suicidal individual, such as "you are the only one who understands me," or "no one else can help me." In reality, this is rarely the case.

2. *The suicidal person made a poor choice in confiding in me.* It is common to feel inadequate when confronted by a suicide threat or discussion about someone's thinking of killing themselves. Friends and relatives may not recognize that it is relatively difficult to be harmful to someone who is suicidal by discussing the topic. Most discussions with a concerned friend or relative are helpful regardless of the confidant's feelings of inadequacy or lack of training.

3. *Suicidal people can't wash the dishes.* Some people believe that someone who is potentially suicidal or contemplating suicide should be "treated with kid gloves" and relieved of normal daily responsibilities. "Taking care of" someone who is suicidal may be a useful means of expressing that one cares for the person and is concerned. However, being relieved of everyday responsibilities, such as washing the dishes, may lead to a feeling of infirmity and more free time to focus upon one's problems. In general, being suicidal or having thoughts about suicide does not limit one's capacities to engage in everyday activities; in fact, the continuation of such activities may even be helpful.

4. *If the suicidal person wants to be left alone, this wish should be respected.* People who are considering suicide may not use good judgment and often are not aware of what is best for them. If the danger of committing suicide seems high, it is generally best to not leave a suicidal individual alone.

5. *Other "normal" people don't experience situations like this.* When a friend or relative is suicidal, one may feel that this is an abnormal, unusual circumstance, which other "normal" people like myself do not undergo. In reality, suicide affects people in all walks of life and in all situations and it is common to have a friend or relative talk about suicide.

6. *The suicidal person has so many problems that my own problems do not matter.* When suicide is evoked some friends and relatives are so impressed by the extent of the other person's problems that they ignore their own difficulties and the importance of dealing with their own troubles.

7. *Suicidal thoughts are the result of some family genetic psychiatric problems.* Most families have one or several members who have had psychiatric problems. When another person in the family talks about suicide, some friends and relatives jump to the conclusion that this family pathology has been inherited by this individual. Conceptualizing the problem as genetic pathology may lead to an attitude that "there is nothing we can do about it."

8. *If I talk about why the person is suicidal, I might learn things that I don't want to know.* It is easy to feel guilty about things we have done or failed to do in our intimate relationships. For this reason some people are reluctant to discuss the situation of an intimate friend or family member who is thinking of suicide. We are afraid that we will learn something about ourselves and our personal failures and inadequacies which we may be afraid to face. Although this type of revelation rarely occurs, the fear of discovering something we did not want to know is more frequently present.

9. *The situation is so serious that I must refrain from having fun in my life.* All the manuals on suicide prevention insist on the fact that suicidal threats and suicidal ideation should be always taken seriously. However, taking discussion of suicide seriously does not imply that the suicidal person or the confidant cannot laugh at something funny or find amusement in life events.

10. *I should not burden others with her/his problems.* We live in a society where the heroes in film and fiction are often superconfident individuals who win the battles and solve the problems by themselves. In everyday life, there are few situations which do not benefit from the importance of help by many members of a person's support system. Friends and relatives of suicidal individuals should benefit from discussing the situation with members of their entourage as well as specialized support resources such as counselors or crisis centers.

HELPING POTENTIAL HELPERS

What should be done to help friends and family members be better helpers in situations where someone they know talks about suicide? Experience with friends and relatives of suicidal individuals suggests that there is often ambivalence: there is a desire to help and, at the same time, the person experiences a feeling of lack of competence or a fear of becoming too involved. The first step in helping potential helpers is to support the individual and particularly their interest and desire to be of help. It may be useful to tell family and friends that they are capable of helping, regardless of their feelings of inadequacy—that those feelings of inadequacy are common and that it is all right to feel inadequate. It is even acceptable to tell the person they want to help that they are feeling a bit inadequate or that they think they may not have all the necessary competence.

The desire to be of help may also be complicated by other feelings such as anticipatory grief at the potential future loss or feelings of anger because someone close is considering doing something so hurtful to others. Therefore, it is important in helping potential helpers discuss these different feelings. The objective is to allow the friend or family member to recognize their different feelings and at the same time realize that, despite feelings of anger, being manipulated, and so on, one can still express concern and help work toward solving problems.

In some instances one of the immediate needs is to help the helper remain calm—to help diminish the crisis situation which the family member or friend is experiencing. Crisis intervention with the confidant may be as important as helping with the crisis the suicidal person is experiencing. However, efforts to diminish the crisis experienced by the potential helper should not include minimizing the potential dangers when suicide is threatened (don't say, "I am sure it is not that serious").

Some people tend to dwell on past history and ignore much of what is going on at the present time. Some family and friends focus upon events which occurred months or years ago for which they feel guilty, past psychiatric problems in the family, or other events which may have questionable relevance to the crisis the suicidal person is undergoing now. It is often useful to help focus the potential helper by emphasizing the importance of what the suicidal person is feeling, experiencing, and doing *now* and ways to deal with the problems in the present and in the future.

Suicide prevention centers find it important to give information to family and friends on the nature of suicide and how to be of help. This information includes an explanation of different "myths and realities" concerning suicide, as well as specific information on how to evaluate the urgency and suicidal risk, what questions to ask (e.g., asking directly about methods and when a possible suicide is anticipated). This information includes telling the helper that talking about suicide does not increase the risk, and knowing that a friend or relative cares and is available in a crisis may be quite useful.

Some friends and relatives feel that they should lie or not tell the truth in order to be of help. There may be a tendency to "say what they think the suicidal person wants to hear" in order to calm the crisis, even if it is not true. These tactics sometimes backfire and some potential helpers need to be encouraged to recognize that it possible to be honest and still be helpful.

In some situations the friend or relative has certain beliefs which complicate the situation. For example, "If I don't lend him the car, he might kill himself," or "Telling his parents of his suicidal intents would be a betrayal." The friend or family member's beliefs should be explored and their implications examined in detail.

Any helper should be encouraged to involve as many other individuals as possible. Besides referring someone who is suicidal to appropriate agencies, giving the person the telephone number of a crisis or suicide prevention center and suggesting alternative ways to deal with their problems, it is important to involve as many different members of the suicidal person's support system as possible.

Although thinking about suicide is quite common, suicide attempts are relatively rare in comparison to suicidal ideation. Family and friends are generally encouraged to evaluate the suicidal risk by asking many appropriate questions and looking for common danger signs. Sometimes a careful evaluation indicates that the expression of thoughts concerning suicide was of minimal risk and further preoccupation with the problem may not be appropriate. However, in other situations, appropriate reactions, interventions, and referrals by friends and relatives may avert a suicide attempt. It is important in helping potential helpers to communicate to them that they are not alone with the situation and may have support. Even if the situations turn out to be of low suicidal risk, their interest and concern are appreciated and their seeking advice in dealing with the situation is appropriate.

REFERENCES

Mishara, B. L., Baker, A. H., & Mishara, T. T. (1976). The frequency of suicide attempts: A retrospective approach applied to college students. *American Journal of Psychiatry, 133*(7), 841–844.
Suicide in Canada (1994). *Update from the National Task Force on Suicide Prevention.* Ottawa: Health Canada.

Part II

The Impact of
Suicide on Helpers

Chapter 7

"To Engrave Herself on All Our Memories; To Force Her Body into Our Lives": The Impact of Suicide on Psychotherapists

Alan L. Berman

Therapists and other helpers are profoundly affected when one of their clients dies by suicide. This chapter presents poignant case histories and discusses how therapists may cope with the suicide of a client. [Ed.]

We begin with the broadest of themes: The *impact* of suicide.

> **Impact**, *n.* **1.** The striking of one body against another; collision. **2.** The force or impetus transmitted by a collision. **3.** The effect or impression of one thing upon another.
>
> (*The American Heritage Dictionary*, 1982)

Collision, force, and effect; *impact* is a Newtonian word. I'm reminded: Newton's Three Laws of Motion—The first law (the law of inertia): A body

85

moving in a straight line or in a state of rest will remain so unless acted upon by some outside force. The second law: The change which any force makes in the motion of an object depends upon the size of the force and the mass of the object. The third law: For every action there is an equal and opposite reaction. But Newton spoke only of the ideal case; to fully analyze the *impact* of force, I must also remind myself of frictions; in the real world there exist frictions or resistances to motion. Resistances are also psychological processes of opposition to motion, to change; defenses designed to protect the ego.

Thus I am asked to speak of the mechanics of suicide, to analyze the action of force, the effect of a collision between two objects: the outside force, the suicide, its effect defined as a transfer of energy determined by its size; and the object upon which that force has effect. I speak of "the helper" as the object upon which the suicide has effect, the helper defined by his or her mass and those resistances presented to any impact he or she experiences. My Newtonian association is not overly loose. In real life, the suicide, truly now an inert body, does transfer energy to and actively change the helper. Moreover, there are indeed significant resistances to that energy transfer.

But this association remains much too much in a vacuum. In developing four separate topics on the theme topic of "The Impact of Suicide" this book has necessarily divorced the helper from the individual, from family and friends, and from the larger society. In our real world, as in Newton's abstractions, these divisions have scientific merit for our understanding complex phenomena, but lose value in observing that complexity in action.

Were we to illustrate Newtonian law in the classroom we might simply set up a billiard table, place two balls on its surface, force one ball to strike another, and observe the proposed energy transfer from the first to the second ball, with the second ball then caroming off the table's side walls until friction eventually slowed this ball's motion to a stop. But our billiard table has many balls on its surface (family members, friends, helpers), each in its own way to be impacted by the first ball (the suicide), each potentially to carom off others creating a series of rebounding impacts on each other. In the real world, the suicide of a patient invariably means that family, society, and the helper may, and often do, collide, impacting each other in successive transfers of energy having the potential to persist for years.

With my premise so established, let me further propose to you that the impact of suicide on helpers is both universal and idiosyncratic. There are general principles, already well defined for you by previous speakers; principles of bereavement specific to a suicidal death and commonly experienced by those in the community of the suicide's object relations. An insufficient list of these includes: compromised mourning rituals, inadequate coping responses, feelings of isolation, and crises of identity and control; modern-day variants on the forfeitures to the crown demanded as punishment for the suicide being defined as a *felo de se*. Today those of us in the community of survivors, including helpers, are asked to surrender parts of ourselves in payment for the act of a patient's suicide.

I will have more to say of these effects, but wish mostly to speak of idiosyncratic impacts, of effects tempered by the character and resistances of the helper, by rebounding impacts between helpers and surviving family members, and by successive interactions among the survivor family, society, and the helper, interactions having the potential to leave indelible marks of collision.

I wish to present but two illustrations, two case studies. I have chosen to focus on the *psychotherapist as helper*, simply because I have the greatest familiarity with this role. I trust that those helpers among you defined by other titles, such as volunteers or crisis line workers, will come to understand that my selectivity neither is meant to nor should exclude you. There are more than enough similarities in our experiences to justify our community of roles.

I chose these illustrations with the cooperation of both psychotherapists. Each was willing to share his or her story with you. Their stories are rich in detail and as profoundly different as they are similar. Their experiences speak eloquently to the universal and idiosyncratic effects of suicide on the helper.

Among their commonalities: both therapeutic dyads consisted of a patient and therapist from different countries. Both therapists were understandably surprised by their patients' suicides; neither patient gave any direct warning of their intention to suicide. Both therapists sought counsel from others in the immediacy of their coping. Both met with and exchanged correspondence with surviving parents. Both immediately were concerned about issues of confidentiality and about the potential for a malpractice complaint. Both therapists struggled with their anger, questions of omnipotence, and feelings of vulnerability; both grew from their experiences. Yet, their stories describe two quite different experiences. I expect you will empathize with much in their experiences and, with the distance of hindsight, perhaps find much to criticize. My intent is to let them tell their stories with a minimum of adulteration. First their schemata:

The psychotherapists: Peter, about 50, is a married American psychiatrist; board certified and in solo private practice some 16 years. He is known to me as a brilliant and gifted thinker. Trained in psychoanalysis, his therapeutic style has moved some distance over his years of practice. He is a therapeutic force, passionate, combative where he believes necessary, rarely doctrinaire. He is actively involved with his patients; at times, the traditional among you might think too much so, shifting roles, blurring distinctions between the personal and the professional. His style is often highly personal and self-revealing. I have no doubt he is an effective psychotherapist. I have no doubt that his patients number many of Washington's powerful and monied.

Marissa, in her early 40s, is a divorced Latin-American social worker; on a student visa while working as one of six fellows in training at a postgraduate mental health training center in Washington. Her supervised clinical practice (she is yet to be licensed) is at the center's sliding-scale private clinic. The clinic (and Marissa) is psychoanalytic in orientation; its patients are young, intelligent, and typically without funding to support more expensive psychotherapists. Marissa is introspective and gentle; a caring, sensitive therapist in touch with her vulnerabilities. She is deeply immersed in learning and employing object relations theory in her practice and through her own ongoing psychoanalysis. She remains the novice learning her craft, comfortable enough with its language but still insecure in its application. I have no doubt Marissa is becoming an effective psychotherapist. I have no doubt her patients are *not* the monied and powerful of Washington.

I trust you have heard clearly the marked differences between Peter and Marissa. A married male psychiatrist; a divorced female social worker. He in solo private practice for many years; she in postgraduate training in a clinic setting. He licensed, she not. He atraditional in style; she decidedly traditional. He passionate and intense, injecting himself into other's lives; she maintaining boundaries, interpreting transferences and attending to countertransferences. And so on . . .

The patients: Peter's patient, *Juan*, was Latin-American, in his 20s, the unemployed divorced son of a diplomat. Juan was being seen by Peter in weekly group psychotherapy sessions. Juan bled to death after cutting himself on both arms with a razor blade.

Marissa's patient, *Matthew*, was American, single, in his 20s, studying to be an architect. Matthew had been in once-weekly individual sessions with Marissa, but had not been seen for a month because he had requested some time to catch up on financial obligations, before he scheduled, then missed, his last appointment.

Matthew, Marissa's patient, went to a neighborhood park and sat down behind a large oak tree; he then put a gun to his head and a bullet in his brain. Juan, Peter's patient, wandered through his house after making his initial cuts, leaving a trail of blood until he finally sat down to die leaning against a living room couch. Both patients were symptomatically depressed; both also were characterologically disturbed.

Let me tell Marissa and Peter's stories, in parallel sequence, in their own words, both articulate and wanting in their expression.

The collision: Marissa: I arrived at the clinic somewhere between 6:00 and 7:00 p.m. for my training class. There was a telephone message for me from a detective. My first thought was that my adolescent patient had run away from home again; but then my heart lurched to my throat: Matthew had not come to his appointment yesterday after being away a month in order to catch up with his payments. I called the detective. I don't remember his exact words, but he told me Matthew had been found shot to death in the park and they had reason to believe that he had been seeing me in therapy. I explained who I was, that he had missed his appointment last evening, and that I had called and left a message on his telephone answering machine. He said, 'I know; that's how we realized you must be his therapist.' I felt a surge of anxiety and my body began to tremble . . . 'When did this happen?' I asked. 'Somewhere between 6:00 p.m. last night and early this morning,' he answered. I felt the chills intensify.

Thus began the most traumatic experience of my life, both professional and personal. I hung up the phone and went to join my classmates. I must have looked pale, because they immediately asked me what was wrong. As I related the phone call, I began to cry. I had been through a tough time in my own life, having moved to the U.S. only a year and a half ago. These people knew about some of the hardships I had been through the last few months. They asked me about Matthew, and, as I related what I could about him and his treatment, terrifying thoughts flashed through my mind. What if he had come to his session with the gun and shot himself in front of me? or shot me in a transference reaction? Was he killing himself instead of me? How had I failed him? Would his family sue? Would I have to leave the country? Would they throw me out? My anxiety grew. Images of his deep blue eyes looking up at me with a yearning to feel better flashed before my eyes. I had cared a lot about Matthew and had had faith in him when he had none. What did I miss? Had I not heard him?

The Collision: Peter: On September 26th, Juan killed himself, sometime between noon and 6:00 p.m. It was a Saturday, the day before my youngest daughter's birthday party, the day after his last therapy session. At about the time he was drinking the vodka to give him strength (or release his inhibitions) to do it, I was trying to save my rhododendrons. Three of them were about to die. They had to be dug up and replanted on higher ground to improve the drainage.

I found out about it the following evening. Vanessa and I had just come back from a delightful evening with a friend and his new girlfriend, whom we saw perform in concert, a stride-Jazz pianist *a la* Fats Waller. I later found out that her father had also committed suicide.

The baby sitter wrote me the message, "Juan committed suicide" and followed with instructions to call his ex-wife. My initial reaction was an angry denial. "No," I slammed my fist down. I punched out the phone number. It was midnight, I woke her up. My disbelief continued, "Are you sure?" I asked, desperately trying to find some escape from this preposterous news. I don't recall much of that phone conversation. I'm not sure whether I tried to soothe her or vice-versa. She asked something about the propriety of her coming in to see me. What I do recall was the fear already creeping into my voice. "He never told me, he never talked about suicide." As the pain penetrated, I was already defending myself against criticism, the inevitable lawsuit, and my own guilt. I cried some but did not weep. My wife tried to console me. Was the restraint with my tears professional distance? Was it the therapist maintaining an observing posture? Was it simply my own inability to let the sorrow unfold? or was it that alienation that Juan fostered so poignantly, never fully connecting in some enduring way? Anger, contempt, "How stupid . . . what a waste . . . why didn't he call me?" I fell asleep, fitful, feeling sick and dread.

Coping and supports: Marissa: My colleagues began suggesting people to talk to: the clinic director, my team leader, my analyst—for an extra appointment. I talked briefly with the clinic director and he advised me to call a lawyer in the morning and to talk to our clinic consultant on suicidal patients. He then did the kindest thing. He told me of his own experience with patients who had committed suicide and what he had felt. I was so relieved to hear that someone I saw as my superior had not been able to avoid such a trauma. Somehow it helped relieve me somewhat of my self-reproach. Actually, in the ensuing days I was surprised to hear from a number of others who had had similar experiences. It was so generous of them and so healing for me.

The Lawyer: Marissa: The lawyer confirmed my suspicion that I couldn't really say anything to anyone.

The Lawyer: Peter: I called my lawyer the next morning. 'Was I free to tell Juan's parents what I wished? What were the restraints of confidentiality? I don't remember his advice. I just needed to talk to someone who liked and respected me, someone who was a professional. For I was fully in a *professional* crisis—coming on the heels of the ethics committee debacle, I now had very serious doubts about my professional abilities. These doubts, I now believe, were the beginning of my emerging understanding of my *therapeutic grandiosity.*

The Parents: Marissa: Matthew's parents contacted me a few days after the funeral. They wanted to talk about what had happened. They wanted to try to understand. I was anxious about the meeting, but also hopeful that this would give the family and myself an opportunity to mourn our loss.

We scheduled a meeting for later that week and I asked the clinic director to join us. They had not known Matthew was seeing me, only one of his brothers. They knew he had been obsessed over his lost girlfriend. They also felt him to be an enigma, different from the rest of the family. They told me Matthew had decided to apply to graduate school and had been working on a resume with a friend several nights before his death. How could he be doing this at the same time he was planning his death . . . was he dissociating? We were careful during this meeting to attend to *their* guilt feelings. *They* were concerned about me. I was as honest as I could be about my feelings and as open as I could be about Matthew without divulging information I could not give. It was a good meeting and ended by our suggesting some books, and groups to attend, as well as offering our continued service.

The family: Peter: On Monday, two days after Juan's death, I met with his divorced parents. His mother said nothing; father did most of the talking. Only in retrospect did I realize I was numb, a capacity I have to protect myself from pain and sorrow. I tell them I am sorry, what a tragedy, that I liked Juan. They ask me . . . I ask them: why did he do it? I decide to tell them about the embezzling Juan told me about in our last session. A light bulb. "Oh, yes, that's Juan . . . he always wanted more money." I feel glad I told them; I'm off the hook, but not really satisfied. We had talked a year earlier of his stealing when he was a child from both his mother and father. He was never disciplined for it.

Tuesday: 4:30 a.m.: I found my session (essentially) with Juan's father clarified little. He thinks of Juan as having a "weak character." How can I disagree, although his final act was vicious, angry, strong, and the ultimate pathos. . . . The same whining pathos that all who knew him had grown callous to. I am left with a sense of failure, a failure of empathy. Did he lie to me? Was the die cast already somewhere in his soul? Would he get the ultimate revenge? . . . I spoke of dignity; he wanted power and revenge and a capitulation of all love.

A friend of Juan's from childhood called me. To her credit she is furious with him. She said, "I wish he could come back to life so I could choke him." I cannot yet feel the rage. I am suppressing it, still in the therapeutic harness, bridled by the ethics and mores that plague this fucking profession. I don't even know if I will send the final bill to his father, who asked me to. I probably will send it. The son of a bitch has perpetrated enough pain on me.

Tuesday: I both dreaded and eagerly anticipated telling the group on Tuesday. I am reminded of the Great Imposter, hired to teach Latin, not knowing a word of Latin himself. So he would simply study the chapter to be taught the night before teaching the chapter. I had had 48 hours to begin the working through process before having to face the group. More important, I sought solace from the group, a group that had begun to be a vehicle of nurturance after many months of difficulty, disjointedness, and dissatisfaction.

I read the letter (I wrote this morning to Juan's parents) to the group. As I re-read the letter, I can hear the wisdom, feel the sorrow, and see the self-serving qualities of it, both the desire to help them and to protect/defend myself and my group. Whatever else the letter was, though it reflected what I and the group were attuned to, the group endorsed the letter unanimously. "Send it, Peter," they said. I did. I wished I hadn't.

Peter's letter: Dear Mr. H . . .

As you requested, I've enclosed Juan's final bill. I've had a few more thoughts since our discussion that I'd like to share with you. In retrospect, I have a different understanding of what Juan and I discussed about "dignity" in our final therapy session. It was not dignity Juan was after. Rather, it was control, and the power associated with some sort of revenge. Suicide, whatever else it is, and it is many things, is a hostile act, a lashing out at those who have loved you in their imperfect way. But it was not our love that failed, it was Juan's . . .

Juan was expert at getting love, advice, help, sympathy, and support. He left in his wake a whole collection of people who attended to him. He came into his last session with a subtle smile on his face. He told me: "I play so many games, and now everyone knows me, knows what I am really like." What I think he meant by "games" was personal interactions geared to increasing his control over others. He left with that same smile. Did he already know what he was to do? Was the plan already in place? Did he not tell me because he knew I could somehow prevent him from going through with it? You said that Juan had a "weak character." I must agree even though his character was strengthening. His final act, however, was meant to neutralize once and for all that very weakness. He would take charge, he would have the power, he would repudiate all those who would help him. We then are feeling weak and inadequate. The lovers are left feeling unloving and angry . . . impotent and guilty. Grieving normally is not easy. Grieving a suicide is a torment.

I was glad to have the opportunity to meet and talk with you and Ms. H. My impression of you both was a quite positive one, that you *would* grieve this loss and get on with your lives. As it should be. In the final analysis, the revenge of the suicide is empty and painfully foolish . . . His reasons for killing himself could very well have been a reason for living . . . My regards and condolences. If I can be of further assistance, please contact me . . . Sincerely, . . .

Juan's mother's letter written in response to Peter's letter (2 weeks later): This letter began writing itself almost as soon as I had read yours; it seemed to me, however, that I needed other people's reactions to it before I could put my thoughts on paper. Your letter was read by Dr. M . . . , who was so incensed by the contents that he telegraphed his disagreement to Juan's father; by my own therapist who is appalled at the smugness and lack of sensitivity which speaks from every line; and by a number of people who knew Juan well and loved him, and we are all shocked at the shallowness of your thinking, . . . and—in my case, most of all—the fact that you seem to feel no responsibility for the tragedy but push it all on to Juan. No one expects a psychiatrist to be clairvoyant, but shouldn't an experienced psychiatrist have some perception of the fact that a patient he has been seeing for two years is in a frame of mind in which he might turn to suicide?

Before anything else, I wish to disassociate myself from the remark made by Juan's father that Juan had a "weak character." I kept quiet at the time because it did not seem a good moment for an argument between him and me. I do not agree with this description. Juan was not weak; he was gentle but he had strong convictions to which he clung. Gentleness is often mistaken for weakness by those who do not truly understand it.

To take your letter paragraph by paragraph, the word "dignity" is an odd word to use in therapy but, what is much worse is that you go on to say ". . . it was not dignity, it seems, that Juan was after. Rather, it was control, and the power associated with some sort of revenge." The word control implies over something or someone; if Juan was striving for control, could it not have been self-control, or rather, control over his own life, and if that were the case, it could mean he felt he had lost it, something it seems to me you should have noticed . . . The word "revenge" jars. Revenge against whom? Why revenge? Juan was never vindictive, and he had nothing about which to be vindictive, so that is nonsense.

In the same paragraph you say "Suicide . . . is a hostile act, a lashing out at those who have loved you in their imperfect way." Have you never heard of the suicide of the terminlly ill person who wants to spare him/herself and family further pain? There is nothing hostile about that kind of suicide; it is beneficient to those who commit it as well as to their family who have had to watch them suffer . . . I am sure there are other non-hostile suicides.

The next paragraph of your letter makes Juan out to be a manipulator, which he certainly was not. None of us have been able to figure out what you mean by a "subtle smile," and we question very seriously your interpretation of what he may have said. That whole story about playing games to increase his sense of control over others rings untrue to every one of us.

You were so kind to say . . . that your impression of Juan's father and me was "positive" (I wish we could return the compliment). And that we "would grieve the loss and get on with our lives." This is one more example of your shallowness of perception; you were confronting two people who were deeply shocked and under sedation. How dare you even make a judgment under the circumstances? Of course, we have to go on for the sake of our other two children, but I have become a zombie for whom the light has gone out of life and who has the greatest trouble facing the beginning of each day. Juan's father has great responsibilities and therefore goes on, but he tells me that, whatever he does, . . . the image he saw of his bleeding son when the door to Juan's house was opened stands between him and whatever he is trying to accomplish. How can a psychiatrist be so unbelievably imperceptive?

Apart from your letter and your whole attitude in this dreadful tragedy, I need to mention something else to you . . . I had always had a particularly strong bond with Juan . . . As soon as he entered therapy the whole relationship changed. He began to reject me . . . even to hurt me. I can only blame this change in him on his therapy, on you. Perhaps in the U.S. young people need to annihilate their parents to become adults; this does not happen in other countries.

Lastly, I want to add two requests. One is that you get some more training before you take on vulnerable young people. You badly need more insight, more sensitivity, although I don't know whether these are qualities that can be taught. The other request is that you do not attempt to reply to this letter. Any communication from you to me would be returned unopened.

Matthew's father's letter to Marissa: Several weeks after Matthew's suicide, Marissa received a brief note from Matthew's father and the homily from his funeral. Matthew's father had written a poem, as follows:

> Architect
> Matthew,
> Isn't there a flaw
> in this design?
> Look how these lines
> Clash and wander.
> The image is not whole:
> The start of one vision
> Cut off by the end of another,
> And all the in between . . . lost.

Son,
Can't you
Erase the ending
And tease again from the start
Lines that make sense,
Not ending in the dark?

Some story, some ending
Would surely please your eye—
And give us, too
A truer view of you.

Marissa remarks, "This letter was a gift from them to me and felt very healing. They provided me with some new information which helped tie things together for me and ease my pain. I was grateful for their kindness and wrote the following letter in response."

Dear Mr. and Ms. T,
Thank you for your moving letter. I was especially touched by the poem you wrote for Matthew. It captured for me, in so few words, the most intense feeling I have experienced since his death: my sadness and help-lessness at not knowing.
Learning that Matthew had already taken steps toward his unhappy ending makes me feel even sadder that he did not feel able to share this with me or anyone, and allow us the opportunity to help him find another way to deal with his pain. It is so very difficult to really know why Matthew, and others like him, choose this alternative. Like you, I have searched my soul for possible explanations. I have consulted with numerous people who have been so generous as to share with me their experience with a patient who has . . . decided not to live. All have experienced similar feelings to those we all now share; and finally were able to reach the conclusion that one can never really know and understand all the elements that lead to such an unfortunate outcome. Yet, I still find myself caught up in that search and can only hope that one day I will be able to feel at peace with this . . .
I want to also thank you for sending me a copy of the homily from Matthew's burial. As Father Lozano wisely wrote, "gratitude, sharing, and caring are the three tasks of healing." In writing to me and sharing your process and pain, you have generously contributed to my healing process as well. I am deeply indebted. I can only hope that in sharing my feelings with you, I, too, may contribute to yours as well . . . Sincerely yours, . . .

Epilogues

Marissa (one year later): I still feel sad about Matthew from time to time. In the summer I attended a conference in London. As the lecturer explained his views about how a patient actually gets to the point of suicide, I felt as if, for the first time, I was understanding what Matthew had gone through. Oh, how I wished I had understood that then! Once again all the painful feelings I had felt returned: the sadness, the impotence, the anger; but, it was a healing experience and together with those feelings came a deepening awareness of the important lesson I had learned from it: the knowledge that we are all quite vulnerable and can only hope that we are not exposed to such pain in our work. I realized then that I will never stop reworking the loss. It is not something that is on my mind all the time, as it had been for many weeks and months after it occurred, but I know it will come up again when something happens to trigger it. I also know that what Matthew did by leaving treatment was, at some level, to spare me both from his own rage and from the blame. I wish that he could have trusted me to protect him from his own rage. I will never really know what went on in his mind during those last hours. I can only imagine different scenarios . . . perhaps thinking that he wanted to protect me is my way of trying to preserve Matthew in a positive light and put my anger to rest.

Peter (soon after): The literature emphasizes the "working through" process in using family, friends, colleagues, and supervisors. I would add to this list our other patients! I realize that this is, unfortunately, a controversial position to take given the ethical injunction that therapists should not *use* their patients for anything other than paying the bills, that psychological help should flow only from the therapist to the patient. Empirically, however, I observed that for several weeks after his suicide I felt most comfortable, most helped in that group with the other suicide survivors. I've observed substantial growth on my part as a therapist and substantial therapeutic movement in every patient in that group . . .

These patients helped me come to grips with what I see now as the biggest barrier to working through the suicide, what I call *therapeutic grandiosity, therapeutic attachment,* or *narcissism.* One patient, an attorney, shares with me, professional to professional, an insight about his past litigation work; he loses the case and blames himself, completely forgetting the complexity of factors which might go into a conviction or acquittal. Even more profound, another patient takes the side, sympathetically and without rancor, of Juan's mother. As she supports the wounded mother, she inadvertently supports the wounded therapist and the wounded group . . .

Did therapy *contribute* to Juan's suicide? The proposition that therapy killed him is indeed grandiose. A mix of factors so complicated came together to set the stage for the suicide, it is foolish to say one thing did it. One could hypothesize that Juan had great hopes for therapy and that one insight he gleaned was that it, like all other "props," was "inadequate." He certainly reminded me and the group that we were not enough.

The "group memory" of Juan's anguish, in many ways, is clearer than my own. When I listen to each of them talk . . . , they seem to understand his suicide better than I. I sense in myself a fear of understanding this too clearly. When I nick myself shaving, I must quickly stop the bleeding. The idea of letting it bleed, watching the dripping blood of my own life appalls me. Was Juan's blood, its flow, hypnotic? Enjoying the dripping, the bright red, the mess, streaking his arms, soiling his clothes. Calming instead of frightening. Peaceful. It was the blood that soothed him, not any alcohol. I could watch another's blood, not my own; a big leap between experience and empathy.

My philosophy has changed about suicide. I now consider *all* of my patients suicidal as well as myself.

It is now over a year since Matthew's suicide, better than five years since Juan's. Both Marissa and Peter have moved on, wounded but well healed. In the end, neither was sued; the potential to be held liable for the suicide of a patient being a risk, perhaps more in the United States than in the few other countries, mostly European, where civil law holds the caregiver responsible for negligent care.

Neither they, nor we, will ever be free of our vulnerabilities to the suicide of a patient; nor of the unanswered and unanswerable questions that come in the aftermath, of feelings of guilt, or of incompetence.

I think their stories, reflecting the idiosyncratic collisions (dynamics) between and among these patients, the characters and therapeutic styles of the therapists, and the characters of their survivors should give us pause. In each of our intimate autobiographies we harbor narcissistic wounds. At some level of our shared consciousness, we might agree that in seeking to "save" others we secretly wish to be likewise nurtured. Suicide wounds. It rips off our scabs. It reveals our ultimate nakedness and our ultimate powerlessness. It teaches us, perhaps more profoundly than any other example I can think of, about humility and our humanity.

I have given you little here to help you better know Marissa and Peter's patients. The reasons for their suicides were secondary to my purposes. In truth, we are left to wonder with their therapists, *why*? Did they truly want to die? Did they know no other way to end their pain? Were these acts of rage? or simply despair? Unanswered questions. In the end, what we can truly know is only our own experience; we can share our own stories, we can empathize, we can cry together.

What I have tried to convey, in Marissa and Peter's voices, is something of *impact*, of collisions, effects, and resistances; of therapists being caught unaware, facing crises of novelty and threat, colliding with their own fears and anxieties, with their own narcissism, with impotence and naked vulnerability. Through them I have tried to convey how the same experience can take unique paths as the character and defenses of each therapist further carom off those of other survivors, in these cases the parents of their patients. As with the everyday application of Newtonian law, suicide does not take place in a social vacuum.

For the suicide the act of killing oneself (*selbstmord*) ends pain; for those impacted by the suicide, the pain can be enduring. It is for this reason I chose the quote which titles and now ends this paper. Taken from Milan Kundera's (1991) novel, *Immortality*, the following dialogue takes place between Agnes and Paul, discussing Agnes' suicidal sister:

> Agnes says, "I can imagine a person longing to take his life. Not being able to bear pain any longer. And the meanness of people. Wanting to get out of their sight and vanish . . . I have nothing against suicide as a way of vanishing."
>
> She felt like stopping, but violent disapproval of her sister's behavior made her go on: "but that's not the case with her. She doesn't want to *vanish*. She is thinking of suicide as a way *to stay* . . . To stay with us. To engrave herself forever on all our memories. To force her body into our lives. To crush us."
>
> "You're being unjust," said Paul. "She's suffering."
>
> "I know," said Agnes, and she broke into tears . . .

EPILOGUE

What can we conclude from Marissa and Peter's experiences? What lessons should be derived?

First, that s____ happens. I trust you read that as "suicide." Perhaps, especially to therapists, suicide happens. Perhaps, most especially to experienced therapists. These are the clinicians most likely to be referred seriously or acutely pathological patients and there is a clear and robust relationship between pathology and suicidal behavior.

Second, that disturbed patients are likely to have disturbed families. Peter undoubtedly would wish us to remember this the next time we miscalculate, either telling too much and/or misreading the silent member of a grieving family system.

Third, that there is a clear legal proscription regarding the privelege which succeeds the death of a patient as continuing to reside with that patient.

Marissa got and heard the correct legal advice. Peter may not have gotten the correct advice; if he did, he either did not hear or choose to heed it.

Fourth, that one dynamic inherent in therapist bereavement, equaled perhaps only by that experienced by parents, is conveyed by the theme of impotence–omnipotence. Like parents, we are charged with responsibilities for our patients. As long as we are not visited by traumata such as suicide, our omnipotence is reinforced. However, once a patient suicides, we are forever reminded of how little control we truly have over the lives and choices of our patients; and that felt responsibility does have the potential to be reinforced by the courts, should a legal action ensue.

In this vein, it might be helpful to remind ourselves of a fifth lesson. Patients and therapists view the dimension of time quite differently. To the therapist, time is an ally, allowing better understanding, opportunity for change, and so on. To the suicidal (hopeless, despairing, ideationally constricted) patient, the idea that time is forever is an oppression. Time is the enemy, promising only more torment.

Sixth, that the key to helping the suicidal patient is embedded in the quality of the therapeutic alliance. Each has to come to see the world, the future (time), and the patient's dynamics and experience from a shared perspective. It is from this empathic pairing that weaning occurs, weaning from the patient's constricted perspective to that of the therapist's more rational and reasonable perspective. It is easy to conclude from Marissa and Peter's words that neither Matthew nor Juan allowed that alliance to develop; it is more probable that their pathologies and their histories interfered.

Seventh, because of this, that it is essential we take complete histories from our patients, that we meet their families where possible (before rather than after any unforeseen suicide), that we establish thorough diagnostic workups and treatment plans based on these workups. These actions allow us to best understand what we might expect in the way of alliances, to form alliances with family members, to match treatments to pathologies and dynamics, and to maximize the management of malpractice risk, should the worst-case outcome of suicide ever visit our offices. This is the ultimate lesson Peter and Marissa must teach us: There . . . but for the grace of our actions, go I. S____ happens.

REFERENCE

Kundera, M. (1991). *Immortality*. New York: Grove Press.

Chapter 8

After A Suicide: A Helper's Handbook

Bryan Tanney

"I do not believe that it is possible to do meaningful psychotherapy when issues concerning suicide may arise."
   A. Explanation offered by an experienced outpatient psychotherapist for declining the referral of a person at risk of suicide.
   B. Example of the avoidant, fearful, helpless response of a therapist-survivor.

—B. Tanney

This chapter presents a detailed analysis of how caregivers can assess their reactions to a suicide and develop strategies to better cope in the event that they experience a completed suicide in their work. [Ed.]

INTRODUCTION

This work is presented as a handbook for caregivers who are concerned about the impact of completed suicide either on themselves or on other caregivers. It intends to be of practical value to caregivers who have experienced the impact of suicide in their personal and working lives. This commitment to helping the helpers grows from a firmly held belief that caregivers are an absolutely critical factor in suicide prevention. After more than a decade of designing and developing learning experiences to improve caregivers' intervention competencies, we have learned to value the importance of the helper's attitudes in ensuring the best prospects for success for this process. We observed that a helper's values and beliefs about suicide and about persons at risk of suicide often interfered with their ability to master new knowledge and skills needed for suicide intervention. Some of these feelings and ideas appeared to be in place long before they had any professional or occupational exposure to suicidal people. Others clearly derived from experience with suicidal behaviors, especially the impact of being the helper when the person you were helping ended their life—and the intervention—by suicide. In a caregiver's responses to this event, we identify three important issues. All are minimally addressed in the available literature.

1. Caregivers are people, real individuals, who must survive a suicide. Just as for family members and friends, issues of care for these bereaved caregivers are important. The adage that helpers are better able to tell patients how to deal with emotional issues than to deal with them personally, can be applied.

2. In often complex ways, caregivers also respond to a completed suicide in their work or professional role. There are unique issues to be considered, and specific tools, techniques, and strategies for dealing with them.

3. Sooner or later, 'professional caregivers' impacted by suicide will encounter another person at risk. Painful lessons, learned from experience, will shape and modify their attitudes and their helping behaviors in these future encounters. Appreciating this impact allows for adjustments to be made to their caregiving practices that will ensure the effectiveness of future helping interventions.

This handbook proposes no new formulations and offers no original research. It is, instead, a synthesis and organization of available knowledge beginning with Havens & Litman. (Havens, 1965; Litman, 1965). A surprising coherence in the observations and suggestions available in the literature made this a straightforward undertaking. As a draft, it is not "failsafe" nor is it represented as a "gold standard." It is intended as a distillation of good, healthy clinical practices. As expected, there are areas of controversy based on divergent opinions or incomplete data. Within the text, these are appropriately flagged (***) for further study and examination.

There are several conventions proposed in this text:

1. *A helper or caregiver* is anyone whom another person turns to in times of trouble. Using many different approaches, some occupations specifically prepare their practitioners to respond to such invitations to help. Most of the literature about the impact of suicide on caregivers describes the responses of trained practitioners, usually either psychiatrists or psychologists. Although these professionals have some special issues to consider, the largest part of their experiences can be generalized to helpers of all kinds.
2. A helper or caregiver intervenes with a *Person at Risk* (PAR, *plural* PARs) for suicidal behavior.
2a. A helper or caregiver specifically engaged in a longer-term encounter with a PAR is undertaking either management and/or therapy.
3. A helper or caregiver who experiences the loss through suicide of a PAR with whom they are intervening is a *survivor-caregiver*, or *survivor-therapist* (*also caregiver-survivor, or therapist-survivor*).

IS THIS NECESSARY? IS THERE A PROBLEM HERE?

Suicidal behavior is an unfortunately common occurrence. Between 1% and 3% of all deaths annually are attributable to self-destruction. In response to direct inquiry, 4% of North American adults report an episode of self-destructive behavior during their lifetime. All ages and socioeconomic groups are at risk. With a behavior of this magnitude, virtually all caregivers are likely to be in contact with a person at risk of suicidal behaviors (PAR) during their working lifetime. Such contact is clearly not limited to mental health practitioners, as PARs indicate they would approach a friend, a family physician, or clergyman before sharing thoughts of suicide with a mental health specialist/professional. In numerous studies, almost half of those who undertook suicidal behaviors that required treatment reported approaching a primary care or other physician resource in the month before the occurrence of the self-harm behavior. For those in the emergency room environments of a general hospital, 3% to 7% of patients present with complaints related to self-destructive behaviors. In our survey of 1,500 community-based caregivers, 61.5% reported a "professional" contact with persons who had undertaken suicidal behaviors. Of more interest was the finding that 17% reported personal contact.

The frequency of professional caregivers' experiences with completed suicide has been surveyed. Chemtob et al. (1988a, 1988b) reported that 51%

of psychiatrists and 22% of psychologists responding to their study had experienced a completed suicide during their years of clinical practice. Other estimates range from 20% to 43%. In our sample, 43% reported either professional or personal experience with completed suicide. Particularly during the formative years of training, experiences with suicide may have long-term developmental consequences for professional practice. Summarizing nine studies, about 15% of trainees experienced a completed suicide during their training, with one of these reporting that 37% of psychiatrists had survived such a loss during their residency training programs.

Although such numerical estimates give credibility to the issue, the qualitative impact on the individual caregiver may be more important. Completed suicide is "the most significant event in the training of a psychiatrist" (Sacks et al., 1987). Others have characterized it as having a "strong," "severe," or "major" impact. Suicidal behavior is ranked second only to physical assault as a stressor for therapists (Rodolfo et al., 1988). In a recent national survey, 97% of clinicians were afraid of losing a patient to suicide (Pope et al., 1993). For both completed suicide (4.25 on a 1–5 scale) and for nonfatal suicidal behavior (3.7), the emotional impact is significant. Of much interest, the perceived stress level within a caregiver is reported at the same level for both fatal and nonfatal behaviors.

To summarize, suicidal behavior is common. PARs come to caregivers of all kinds when they are concerned about self-harm issues. Because it involves far-reaching issues, suicide may be a particularly stressful challenge to a caregivers' intervention competencies. The stakes are high. Death may be involved. For many mental health caregivers, including psychiatrists, death is not a familiar, expected, or usual outcome of their interventions. Caregivers of a PAR are further stressed because the majority question their own confidence in being able to handle the issues of suicide. In fact, suicidal behaviors are often conceptualized as a crisis for the helper because the competencies to cope effectively with these behaviors are simply not within their repertoire. For this reason, an experience with suicidal behavior, like any other crisis, may have an outcome in growth (opportunity) or in disability (danger) for the involved helper.

WHY SHOULD I READ THIS? IS IT USEFUL FOR ME?

If you are a survivor, whether recent or longstanding, this text has likely reawakened sometimes disturbing and always strong emotional memories. This is an ongoing reminder that the professional and personal impact of being left behind after a suicide is large. Although short-lived, one-half of professional mental health caregivers experience intrusive stress that reaches clinically significant levels after a completed suicide. As a survivor-caregiver, another suicide is more likely to occur in your work than in that of a helper who has never (yet) experienced work-related suicide. Caregiver-survivors should definitely read on.

It is possible that you are a survivor, but are unaware of your nomination to this role; for example, the impact of nonfatal suicidal behavior emotionally rivals that of completed suicide for some helpers. Clues to unrecognized survivor status include: having a strong emotional reaction to all PARs, labeling them "manipulative," distancing oneself from them as a therapist, or making demeaning comments directed toward persons presenting with self-harm behaviors. These clues have been especially noted in emergency room and crisis personnel. Status as a survivor may also not be recognized because the experience of loss to suicide is unavailable to conscious memory, or it has simply not been considered because it occurred in a personal and not in a caregiving relationship. In fact, issues of personal survivorship are seldom explored in caregivers unless they occur in the context of their being a patient or client, or as part of a training process.

Age of the caregiver and their years of clinical practice do not correlate with the likelihood of a suicide loss experience. The observation that professionals with more postgraduate training appear to experience less suicide in their work may simply be related to the duties or to the types of patients/clients that are encountered in their subspecialty practice and not to any particular effect of better preparation with prolonged training. It has been said that "There are two kinds of therapists: those who have experienced the suicide of a patient, and those who will" (Marshall Swartzburg, personal communication, 1981; in Jones, 1987).

THE BASIC FACTS OF GRIEVING

Humans experience grief in response to loss. Two components are recognized: *subjective, individual* (bereavement) and *societal-familial* (mourning).

Grief = Bereavement + Mourning

Grief is a time-limited, naturally occurring process. The process is continuous, but (usually) three phases or stages are recognized: impact or avoidance, confrontation, and resolution/renewal/ integration.*** It can be complicated by delay or by extreme bereavement response. Although the process is a natural one, there is value in receiving the support offered by the rituals and customs of mourning. A specific helper may guide or accompany one through the process. For the helper, designated tasks during each stage include resuscitate, rehabilitate, and renew.

Bereavement is the state of having suffered loss, including physical, psychosocial, spiritual, and behavioral responses.

Mourning is the social and familial rituals that help the bereaved to grieve and to express thoughts, feelings, and memories related to the loss.

Is Suicide Grief Different?

Mourning. Mourning after suicide is different. Normal rituals are compromised by a notable lack of social support that is related to and perpetuates the denial, stigma, and shame surrounding death by suicide. (Landers, 1993). There is often a failure to mourn. Most societies have a decidedly ambivalent response to suicidal behaviors and to all those who are involved with them.

Bereavement. The impact phase is characterized by shock and disbelief, reminiscent of a crisis experience when adaptive coping mechanisms and defenses are briefly overwhelmed by the intensity of a stressful event. Active denial and avoidance, including expressions of disbelief in the reality of the loss, are not uncommon. When the loss is confronted, there may be intense, strong, and sometimes extreme expression of affects: guilt, shame, anger, hurt and sadness, and anxiety (see Table 8.1).

The final phase is a decline of grief-related emotional responsiveness and the beginning of emotional and social re-entry. It includes saying good-bye, connecting with ongoing supports, accessing personal strengths, and realistically testing the future. There is controversy about the end-point of

TABLE 8.1 Confronting a Suicide Loss: How Affects Can Be Expressed

Guilt	Searching for the fatal mistake, repeated review of events preceding the loss: the theme of responsibility
Anger	Directed both in and out, often accompanied by blaming
Hurt/sadness	Experienced as despair, defeat, a syndromal depression; sometimes a late response deriving from anger internalized
Anxiety	Thoughts of failure and loss of self-confidence are accompanied by anxiety: defensive efforts to preserve mastery include regression, denial, projection, displacement (blaming), distancing, identification with the deceased with surges of suicidal ideation or continuing reminders in both reality and dreams is not uncommon.

the grief process.*** For some, there is an experience of resolution or clo-sure, suggesting some "successful" working-through of a conflict to a state of recovery. For other helpers, the final product is a diminishing but ongo-ing process in which the experience of loss and the feelings attached to it are integrated into the personal and professional self, thus serving to re-define that 'self' adaptively through experience.

Whether invoked by suicide or some other cause of death, there are more similarities than differences in the bereavement process. Due to un-expectedness, suddenness, and often violence, the impact/avoidance phase in accidental and suicide deaths may involve an anxiety response very simi-lar to, and often perpetuated as, post-traumatic stress disorder. Although the guilt and anger experienced when confronting suicide are strong and intense, there do not appear to be any significant differences in severity when bereavements due to suicide or accident losses are compared.

Although controversial, a recent study suggests that the time course of bereavement following suicide may be different, especially around one year (Farberow et al., 1992). Compared with other bereavements, suicidal grief was felt more intensely at one year, suggesting that the process might be somewhat prolonged. (The bereavement response at 2 months and at 30 months was of similar intensity.) This study suggests that applying a common clinical guideline of one year's duration for the grief process may lead to an artifactual designation of suicidal grief as being "complicated".

Although suicide bereavement resembles the general bereavement process in most aspects, it is still vital to recognize that maladaptive griev-ing responses are common (see Table 8.2).

Are Caregivers Allowed to Grieve, or Even to Mourn?

Caregivers should feel very uneasy if they do not experience grief follow-ing a loss through suicide. It cannot be emphasized too strongly that caregivers are expected, and must be allowed, to be survivors of suicide. In their bereavement, caregivers react in much the same ways as do other survivors. Although the choice is a personal one, it is entirely appropriate to attend the funeral and to make appropriate contact with the family and loved ones as a fellow human being learning to survive with the loss. Un-fortunately, Litman found that the most common bereavement response, in the 200 caregiver survivors that he surveyed was denial—with no sub-sequent movement through the bereavement process or with no support in mourning.

In addition to personal grief, caregivers can expect specific role or occupational responses to suicide loss. Their work may require a response

TABLE 8.2   Recognizing Maladaptive Grief

1. Failure to grieve
     Compromised mourning
     Bereavement prohibited
2. Anger expressed inappropriately
3. Preoccupation with the deceased—searching for meaning and responsibility
4. Feeling shame, thinking stigma, and becoming isolated
5. Disrupted coping devices leading to a crisis with emergence of suicidal behavior as an escape phenomenon.

as a team member, institutional representative, teacher or supervisor, or trainee. This handbook focuses on the most common role: being the helper or caregiver who was intervening with a PAR when that person ended their life by suicide. This is a unique experience because both personal and professional responses are present, intermingled and blended in highly individual combinations/patterns.

What Can I Expect as a Survivor-Caregiver?

Expect all of the phases of bereavement experienced personally by other survivors. Add to this specific professional or occupational responses that may be different or may simply add on to the impact of the personal bereavement responses. As a survivor-therapist, add a further response labeled (for now) as an interaction between roles: person in therapist or, alternatively, therapist as person.

In the helper or therapist roles, guilt and self-blame is a major issue. Concerns, sometimes realistic, about responsibility in the clinical, ethical, and legal spheres amplify these affects. A generalized experience of impaired competence in all helping activities is very common. There are worries about a loss of standing with patients, peers, and consultees. Anxiety around damage to one's "professional" reputation, ongoing employment prospects, and the possibility of censure or recrimination by peer associations is not unusual. Legal issues around incompetence and medicolegal litigation are also a threat.

A second disturbing affect is anger, and it has two components. Anger felt in response to completed suicide may be directed in straightforward fashion at the deceased patient, with feelings of betrayal for "not letting me do my job of helping him"; "how could he/she do this to me." A more complex elaboration of anger involves a resonant, empathic response with the patient's anger, an anger that was so intense as to lead them to self-destruction. Further identification with the patient around this issue may lead to considerations of one's own mortality, to the possibility of suicide, and to a generalized anxiety over broad issues surrounding one's own death.

Caregivers recognize that these strong and unpleasant emotional experiences mobilize intrapsychic mechanisms and overt behaviors to defend against or cope with them. In response to guilt, often-used mechanisms including blaming, intellectualizing, and overanalyzing. Compensation and/or reaction formation may lead to increased caution in ongoing involvements with other persons at risk: a physician helper-survivor may limit passes, or increase levels of care and observation (variously labeled as suicide observation or suicide watch) for other inpatients. Of greater concern, and variously observed in up to 20% of survivor caregivers, may be responses of fatalism, denial, or a "Polyanna—the suicide was all for the best"—response. These responses are used to establish emotional distance from survivor-caregiver feelings. Krieger (1968) also described four other reactions by staff following a suicide in a hospital: professional (50%), projectors (19%), ultra-rightists (5%), and tangentialists or intellectualizers (5%).

A final coping behavior (or lack of same) involves a withdrawal from any further professional interaction where there might be a possibility of suicide. Referrals of PARs are refused, and those presently in care may be prematurely discharged, often with a clear indication that they are being punished for being at risk of suicide.

How Strong Can This Experience Become?
How Long Does It Last?

Experiencing impaired competence and intrusive stress is to be expected. These disturbances are relatively short-lived, resolving within six months.

Using the Impacts of Events Scale, psychiatrists and psychologists experienced a level of stress similar to those grieving the recent death of a parent (Kleespies, Smith, & Becker, 1990). In both professional groups, one-half of the survivors had a clinical stress level (IES intrusiveness score) comparable with that of a group of bereaved persons seeking therapy for the intensity of their distress. It is noteworthy that these survivor-therapists did not have increased avoidance scores on the IES. This stands in some contradiction to Litman's finding that the most common survivor response of caregivers was denial.***

Loss of a PAR to suicide appeared to have less impact in those who were older, had more years of clinical practice, and presumably were more experienced in helping. Psychiatry trainees experienced a more intense impact than psychiatric clinicians, but psychologists did not appear to have similar protective effect with increased helping experience.

As measured by duration and intensity of therapy, investment in the treatment alliance influences the impact of the suicide loss. This follows the general rule that "investment changes attitudes." More specifically, impact was larger when there was considerable expression of anger or hostility within the treatment alliance. (Of course, such affective expression is critical to the helping process with most persons who are at serious risk of suicide.) Discussions by survivor-therapists of the role of the treatment alliance as a proximal factor in the suicide of a PAR further validate this investment-impact correlation. In longer therapies there was more focus on the interpersonal aspects while discussion of techniques and methods were the main issues mentioned when the helping encounter was of shorter duration.

WHAT IS GOING ON IN ME? HOW DO I MAKE SENSE OF ALL THIS?

For the survivor-caregiver, the post-suicide experience is a difficult one. There is a sense (and sometimes a reality) that their technical, professional, and even general helping competence is being scrutinized from without. For most therapists, there is also a clear experience of injury to both their personal and professional beliefs about self. The damage to self-image is two-fold: a) Feelings of defeat, impotence, and failure to acknowledge a blow to the helper's narcissism; and to their belief in an omnipotent ability to "heal all, know all, love all" (Maltsberger & Buie, 1974); b) When responsibilities accepted as a helper (to prevent death by suicide) are not fulfilled, painful emotion is also experienced in the punishment demanded and meted out by everyone's internal arbiter of expectations, the superego. It may be useful to distinguish whether depressive guilt or failure of omnipotence dominates in the helper's experiencing of defeat, depression, and failure after a suicide. Depressive guilt responses include preoccupation with the hopelessness of helping, and specific concerns about self-worth and competency. Issues of narcissism/omnipotence are pre-eminent when the caregiver denies guilt or failure, engages in blaming, represses guilt, and emphasizes issues of responsibility. This focus on failure, defeat, and responsibility is emphasized in a literature which enumerates the errors made by therapists in working with PAR, but seldom addresses potential solutions.

There are interactions between personal and professional responses that contribute to understanding the survivor-caregiver's experience. Each is independent, but there is much overlap between them. Particularly for guilt and anger, the contributions are additive. For other parts of the experience, professional attitudes and demeanors serve a defensive and reparative function for the helper. This is a general, nonspecific function to protect the helpers whose role it is to absorb so much of the personal pain and suffering that cannot be shared and expressed within general society. There are also complex interactions between these role-bound responses. Professional skills influence the form that personal reactions may take, and personal reactions in their turn may influence the way that professional skills can be utilized (Marshall, 1980). These two interactions may be stated as "caregiver in person" and "person as caregiver," respectively, where "in" infers melding of one response into the other, and "as" suggests the direct application of skills and responses derived from experience in one role into actions carried out in the other role. Interactions of "caregiver as person" and "person in caregiver" are also possible. This model is useful in understanding all aspects of a caregiver in their encounter with a PAR, including the responses of being a survivor-caregiver.

The caregiver who struggles with and thoughtfully considers issues of professional role competency following a suicide faces a true conundrum. If the suicide is accepted as inevitable, there is a very real question about the purpose or value of any helping intervention. Either intervention efforts were not helpful with this PAR (ineffective) or perhaps they are not helpful at all (nihilism). If therapy is regarded as effective, and a suicide results anyway, the caregiver must recognize and (hopefully) address shortcomings and limitations in the process and technique of their intervention. This critique is not without an emotional price. In whichever direction, the professional self is in a lose–lose situation.

What Can I Do about Feeling So Awful?

Review all aspects of the experience with colleagues and others. Goals of receiving support and obtaining consultative expertise are appropriate.

Support. The objectives are to air issues and attitudes and to permit a thorough expression of the feelings and thoughts attached to the experience ("ventilate and validate"). An informal forum for such support appears the most common venue. The environment must feel safe. This includes a respect for process, whether administrative or personal, and a commitment to protect those who are open in their discussions of the feelings and events surrounding the suicide. In addition to a supportive, nonblaming atmosphere, two other basic conditions are suggested: 1) a nonjudgmental consultant should be available on an ongoing basis for a period of up to 12 months; 2) staff and others who offer support in this safe forum should have established their own comfort level based on training and experience in working with persons at risk.

Ongoing support groups for therapists who have experienced a completed suicide are another resource (Jones, 1987; Richman, Caffrey, & Gold, 1994). Most helpers experience contact with the family and significant others of the PAR who suicides as a positive and supportive experience. It may be useful to have such meetings facilitated by another caregiver so that the bereaved caregiver can be present in both survivor and helper roles.

Be aware that some supports can be unhelpful. Peers and colleagues who do nothing, ignoring the event, offer not only an unhelpful but also a potentially destructive lack of response. Intrusive and unwanted support is not helpful. This is most often an issue of timing when others interrupt bereavement by encouraging talk about the death too early in the stages of this process. When support is received from professional peers and colleagues, some supporters may experience a survivor syndrome: relief that the suicide was not one of their persons at risk; some sense of triumph as in a competition; even a feeling of envy that the survivor-caregiver has experienced an important rite of passage in their experience of survivorship. Finally, therapists feel little consolation from "permissive" philosophical statements that the suicide was acceptable because a person has the ultimate right to choose their own fate.

Consultation. It is entirely appropriate to meet with a professional colleague to reflect upon the therapeutic relationship. Issues of the treatment alliance, handling of transference and countertransference, responses to ambivalence, and fully appreciating the meaning of suicide to both the deceased PAR and to the caregiver are all deserving of consideration. There is a more formal process, which may or may not arise from the needs of some institution or organization. It usually takes one of two forms (Little, 1992). The first is a *psychological autopsy*. This attempts to reconstruct the problems and processes within the person at risk, their interpersonal environment, and their therapeutic encounters. It is most interested in understanding how and why the suicide occurred. The second formal process involves a *procedural review*, using audit or quality control protocols. Both of these are primarily for the institution and have been regarded as not especially helpful by individual caregivers. In fact, 60% of psychiatrists participating in a psychological autopsy procedure felt that it compounded their doubts rather than aiding in the process of understanding or recovery (Goldstein & Buongiorno, 1984).

Timing

Resuscitation involves the immediate provision of a supportive emotional response. After this, personal and/or professional support must be available on an ongoing basis. Early on in the task of rehabilitation, it is important to relieve immediate issues of clinical and legal responsibility by ensuring that appropriate "paperwork" involving protocols or reports is in order and complete. Fuller clarification and understanding through psychological autopsy, or some administrative review process is appropriate at any time more than six weeks after the suicide. These reviews have different purposes and may be ongoing for extended periods of time. As the experience of the suicide is integrated into work and personal practices, formal reviews of progress are appropriate with a chosen support or consultative resource. Six months, 12 months, and 18 months (optional) are suggested intervals. Appropriate issues for consideration are preparations for reinvolvement with persons at risk and relative resolution vs. ongoing doubt about the personal and professional issues surfaced by the experience of being a survivor-caregiver.

What Are the Long-Term Impacts for Me as a Caregiver?

"I would qualify this (indicating that the experience of suicide did not have a major effect on career) by saying that I do not choose to carry chronically suicidal patients in my caseload. I am not sure whether this is due to this one experience or to my overall practice/personal experience" (Brown, 1987). As with this Psychiatry Resident, a small number of caregivers will discontinue all further work with PARs. (Some may even entirely abandon their career as a caregiver.) If this is not completely possible, they will avoid assuming responsibilities for suicidal patients. The intensity of these avoidant responses depends upon how well the survivor experience has been integrated into their work role. Responses range from feeling helpless with persons at risk, through being fearful of future work with high-risk suicidal persons, to simply acknowledging a feeling that they are less comfortable as caregivers working with persons whose motivation for seeking help might involve the consideration of suicide.

"For the better." Most survivor-caregivers indicate that they have learned valuable lessons. They no longer minimize complaints of suicidal ideation or suicidal behavior, and are willing to initiate explicit questions and explorations surrounding the potential for self-harm. Many therapists have made some resolution of the conundrum referred to above (p. 110).

They are willing to assume greater responsibility and to be more active in their encounters with PARs. At the same time they appreciate that their therapeutic efforts have limitations and these are accepted without becoming discouraged.

Other caregivers redefine personal and professional expectations concerning their work as caregivers: acknowledging fallibility, accepting limitations, giving up magical expectations and fantasies of therapeutic omnipotence, and practicing benign self-forgiveness. Many caregivers ultimately acknowledge the difficult and painful experience of losing a patient to suicide as an important "rite of passage" in their growth as an effective and caregiving helper.

What Are the Long-Term Impacts for PARs I Encounter in the Future?

Life-saving. In the first weeks up to a few months after becoming a survivor-caregiver, restrictive and conservative responses toward other PARs may be an important compensating mechanism. Caution includes increasing requests for consultation, more restrictive levels of observation, and fewer passes or early discharges for at-risk inpatients. In the inpatient environment, this may be a truly life-saving response because there is a reality in the possibility of suicide clusters in these care settings.

With realistic integration of the bereavement into personal and work roles, the "for the better" lessons noted above may be applied. Suicidal behavior is anticipated as a real possibility, and helping activities directed specifically toward suicide and suicide intervention may be incorporated into caregiving practices. Finally, the awareness of a need for increased competency in the skills of suicide intervention may motivate the caregiver to learn more about these competencies and to assiduously practice them in their everyday work as helpers.

Life-Taking? In reviewing completed suicides, two studies recognized "some aspect of the treatment process" (Holden, 1987), perhaps an "unrecognized failure in the relationship" (Modestin, 1987), as a precipitating factor in the suicide event. This is reminiscent of the old *nostrum* concerning psychotherapies: if the treatment process is effective, the possibility of negative outcomes must be considered equally with that of positive or therapeutic ones.

In working with PARs, there is consistent technical advice that more direct activity of the caregiver is required. This involvement in the life (and death) of the PAR requires the helper to move away from the "benevolent neutral" stance adopted in many therapeutic approaches. There is a strong possibility that feelings in the therapist may spill over and impact the intervention process. For a survivor-caregiver, their feelings in some future encounter with a PAR may be even more volatile. Many of the same feelings that would be evoked in any caregiver intervening with a PAR (anger, helplessness, sadness) may already be present within the helper-survivor as they are moving through the various phases of bereavement. Even before the encounter begins, any person at risk will serve as a reminder of anxieties, concerns, and misgivings over professional competency. In fact, the PAR not only reminds, but presents a challenge not to do whatever it was (if anything) that led to the earlier suicide.

The impact on here-and-now work with a PAR of thoughts and feelings attached to a similar situation, whether personal or professional, in the past experience of a therapist is recognizable by those readers with a psychodynamic orientation as countertransference. There are complex explanations of the mechanisms by which these past experiences and memories intrude on our actions in present realities. Whatever the process, each of the major feelings of the survivor-therapist experience may motivate specific behaviors. When either the feelings or the resulting thoughts and behaviors are unacceptable, defensive behaviors against them may also motivate helping behaviors. In most instances of suicide intervention, this aspect of the therapist's activities is described in negative terms: never positive, not helpful, the source of malignant therapy or of counterproductive interventions.

As caregivers experience and deal with their own anger, they may:

1. become impatient or feel restless with the progress of therapy, and maneuver toward premature termination;
2. respond to anger in the PAR with aggression. This can include identifying with the object of the PAR's feelings, then becoming angry back at the PAR, with this anger being partly from the role, and partly owned by the helper;
3. find the angry affect unacceptable either personally or professionally and invoke defense/coping mechanisms to diminish it;
4. make themselves the object of the hostility with resultant self-devaluation personally and professionally.

When a survivor-therapist responds to feelings of blame or blaming, they may direct this at themselves with self-devaluing, at others including former therapists or significant others, or toward the PAR with whom they are now intervening:

1. When there is self-devaluing by the helper, less activity or less confident intervenings are likely. In the encounter, the PAR may experience the lack of action as fear or hopelessness on the part of the helper. This may validate the similar feelings they already hold about themselves and their situation. When the survivor-therapist experiences blame directed at him/herself by the person at risk, a compensating response toward rescue maneuvers or trying too hard on the life side of ambivalence is not uncommon.

2. If blaming others is unacceptable, perhaps because of issues of therapist omnipotence that no one else could be as important as the therapist to the PAR with whom they are intervening, the survivor-caregiver may protect and defend significant others of the PAR even when such supports are neither warranted nor justified.

3. Blaming the PAR whom they are now helping may take the form of being too permissive with unclarified statements such as, "suicide is always your choice," or, alternatively, too restrictive with a suggestion that the patient must either cooperate with the offered treatment—or else. This has been described as "the highwayman's formula: your cooperation or your life."

When the survivor-therapist experiences feelings of defeat and depression, they may:

1. be overwhelmed by hopelessness or pessimism and neglect certain active and direct activities that are useful in suicide interventions;

2. feel pity for the person at risk in the hopelessness of their position;

3. respond to the PAR's expressions of sadness, dependency, and a need for support with aggressive rejection: in their sadness more is being asked of the helper than they can provide. Rather than deal with their feelings, they push away the PAR who stimulates them.

When the surviror-therapist experiences feelings of anxiety directly they may:

1. become more aggressive in their helping activities, hoping to bring speedy resolution for the issue and the person at the source of their discomfort;

2. convert these into anger, blaming, and defeat/depression: with these feelings then handled as above;

3. mobilize inner psychological mechanisms to defend or cope with this painful emotion.

Defenses mobilized against any or all of these disturbing feelings will lead to some of their helping activities being based on countertransference reactions. As the choice of such defenses is multidetermined, each therapist may employ some or all of these protecting mechanisms:

1. *Indifference, boredom, or inattentiveness.* In lesser degree, this defense presents as a decreased capacity to empathize. It is most commonly a defensive response to guilt feelings that may arise from any of anger, blaming, or sadness. One response to this "psychic numbing" has therapists offering rigid, theoretical intellectualizations as helping interventions.

2. *Projection.* Either preoccupation with or neglect of suicide because of a pessimistic nihilism about the effectiveness of therapy.

3. *Reaction formation.* Oversolicitousness and conservativism as a protection against anger; elaborating rescue fantasies as a response to feelings of hopelessness; forcing an acceptance of professional competence as a "savior" with demands for regression and dependency— evidenced by premature struggles over control and too-hasty decisions for hospitalization.

4. *Suppression or denial.* Negating suicide potential in the PAR, failing to make appropriate inquiries, refusing to permit the surfacing or ventilation of sad or painful material. In therapy, this may take the form of colluding with the patient in prolonging an idealized positive transference situation.

The nature and variety of responses of a survivor therapist in working with another person at risk is clearly complex, and only incompletely reported here. In brief summary, two counterproductive patterns of caregiver activity in such future interventions are recognizable. The first are various maneuvers to deny and diminish the reality of painful emotions being experienced by the therapist. These strategies lead to failures to recognize and to errors of omission, sometimes called "blind spots" (Zee, 1972) in the process of intervention. The second pattern is a more active and direct rejection of the person at risk, protecting the therapist against further injury to their already impaired senses of professional and personal competence. If there are no persons at risk to remind, then painful affective memories related to the therapist's experience with completed suicide will not be activated. Both the rejection and the denial responses have been associated as contributing proximal factors in the suicides of persons who are in therapy.

What Can I Do? Strategies for Competent Caregivers Offering Effective Suicide Interventions

This is not a simple issue. To handle feelings or impulses toward rejection of a PAR, only general guidelines are available.

1. Endure their anger and hostility without retaliating through either hostility or withdrawal. Understand their feelings as erotic or aggressive transference: "hungry for warmth, they enflame the therapist."
2. Contain your own anger and hostility toward the PAR and make every effort to remain loyal to them. Be especially alert that never feeling angry with a PAR may be just as dangerous.
3. Tolerate their dependency needs, balancing these with realistic limit-setting. In practice, this may involve your being available and accessible beyond a fixed appointment time, and may at times require direct, supportive, real-world interventions on your part.
4. Strategies to aid you in tolerating your own responses while working with a PAR include: 1) obtaining regular supervision with a special focus and frank discussion of your own personal protective (defense or coping) responses to painful or unacceptable feelings; 2) limiting the number of seriously suicidal patients that you have in therapy at any one time—maximum of three or four; 3) fully experiencing your survivor role and obtaining support to integrate this experience into your helping practices; 4) accepting and defining the limits of your therapeutic skills with a recognition that you can be neither savior nor executioner.

The other counterproductive intervention has been summarized as a response of denial, viewed by some as *passive rejection*. It includes either an inability or an unwillingness to mobilize appropriate competencies in working with PARs. Denial may be a more common response in helpers who were never prepared for the turbulence and pain that arise following a completed suicide. In their general abilities to intervene with PARs, most caregivers feel inadequately prepared. Only one-half of psychologists in professional or clinical programs in the United States have had access to learning experiences about suicide (Bongar & Harmatz, 1989). Virtually all education and training efforts emphasize intellectual mastery, and this focus has been assessed as minimal or only moderately helpful by helper-survivors. National and international strategies for suicide prevention all recommend the improved preparation of caregivers who will be undertaking suicide interventions. Specific caregiver competencies for working with PARs have been identified. Involving attitudes, knowledge, and skills, they are appropriate for all caregivers, whatever their professional discipline or helping orientation.

Although there are no clear data that such educative efforts might be beneficial, a realistic anticipatory approach in a training program seems warranted. In addition to this handbook, specific topics in a curriculum addressing patient suicide might include: the development and discussion of personal philosophies, the clarification of personal responsibilities, the awareness of realistic limits on therapy and on helpers, and a discussion of specific agency policies. Issues of personal survivorship which predate involvement in professional training should be surfaced and integrated. All training programs should ensure that general suicide-intervention competencies are promoted, that supervisors are fully comfortable in working with PARs, and that direct opportunities to analyze and to practice helping situations with PARs are available. This might include simulations, roundtable discussions of PARs, and even "impossible patient" conferences. If preparedness is important in training to be an effective suicide interventionist, similar preparedness on the part of institutions and agencies must be expected. Protocols for dealing with a completed suicide should be in place, with every effort made to ensure that these incorporate ongoing strategies of support for staff members impacted by a completed suicide.

CONCLUSIONS

Be actively prepared for the possibility of completed suicide in a PAR whom you are helping. Be aware of the intense though probably short-term impact of the suicide loss on your personal and professional life. Expect the experience of being a helper/survivor to hurt. When ready, seek consultation and support from colleagues. Though it will not resolve all issues, actively cooperate in psychological autopsy or quality assurance investigations that may enlighten your understanding of the many reasons why the suicide occurred. Appreciate your bereavement as a process moving through various phases toward the goal of integration and renewal. Use this painful experience as an opportunity "for the better" to improve your future interventions with persons at risk.

Wide distribution of this handbook offers one approach to preparing caregivers for the experience of completed suicide in their work. In Rothman's schema for development research (Rothman, 1980), this literature synthesis represents the completion of Stage 2B. Prior to pilot and field testing, this core content draft will undergo further revisions by the Calgary group whose goal is the preparation of caregivers who are both competent and confident in their suicide intervention activities. As a work in progress, feedback, changes in emphasis, corrections, and additions are welcomed.

REFERENCES

Bongar, B., & Harmatz, M. (1991). Clinical psychology graduate education in the study of suicide: Availability, resources and importance. *Suicide and Life-Threatening Behavior, 21*(3), 231–244.

Brown, H. N. (1987). Patient suicide during residency training (1): Incidence, implications and program response. *Journal of Psychiatric Education, 11*(4), 201–216.

Chemtob, C. M., Hamada, R. S., Bauer, G., Kinney, B., & Torigoe, R. Y. (1988a). Patients' suicides: Frequency and impact on psychiatrists. *American Journal of Psychiatry, 145*(2), 224–228.

Chemtob, C. M., Hamada, R. S., Bauer, G., Kinney, B., & Torigoe, R. Y. (1988b). Patient suicide: Frequency and impact on psychologists. *Professional Psychology: Research and Practice, 19*(4), 416–420.

Farberow, N. L., Gallagher-Thompson, D., Gilewski, M., & Thompson, L. (1992). Changes in grief and mental health of bereaved spouses of older suicides. *Journal of Gerontology: Psychological Sciences, 47*, 357–366.

Goldstein, L. S., & Buongiorno, P. A. (1984). Psychotherapists as suicide survivors. *American Journal of Psychotherapy, 38*(3), 392–398.

Havens, L. (1965). The anatomy of a suicide. *New England Journal of Medicine, 272*, 401–406.

Holden, L. D. (1987). Therapist response to patient suicide: Professional and personal. *Journal of Continuing Education in Psychiatry, 39*(5), 23–32.

Jones, F. A. (1987). Therapists as survivors of client suicide. In E. J. Dunne, J. C. McIntosh, & K. Dunne-Maxim (Eds.), *Suicide & its aftermath: Understanding and counselling the survivors* (pp. 126–141). New York: Norton.

Kleespies, P. M., Smith, M. R., & Becker, B. R. (1990). Psychology interns as patient suicide survivors: Incidence, impact, and recovery. *Professional Psychology: Research and Practice, 21*(4), 257–263.

Krieger, G. (1968). Psychological autopsies of hospital suicides. *Hospital and Community Psychiatry, 19*, 218–220.

Landers, A. (1993, February 15). Don't ignore tragedy. *Calgary Sun.*

Litman, R. E. (1965). When patients commit suicide. *American Journal of Psychotherapy, 19*, 570–576.

Little, J. D. (1992). Staff response to inpatient and outpatient suicide: What happened and what do we do? *Australian and New Zealand Journal of Psychiatry, 26*, 162–167.

Maltsberger, J. T., & Buie, D. H. (1974). Countertransference hatred in the treatment of suicidal patients. *Archives of General Psychiatry, 30*, 625–633.

Marshall, K. A. (1980). When a patient commits suicide. *Suicide and Life-Threatening Behavior, 10*(1), 29–40.

Modestin, J. (1987). Countertransference reactions contributing to completed suicide. *British Journal of Medical Psychology, 60*, 379–385.

Pope, K. S., & Tabachnick, B. G. (1993). Therapists' anger, hate, fear, and sexual feelings: National survey of therapist responses, client characteristics, critical events, formal complaints, and training. *Professional Psychology: Research and Practice, 24*, 142–152.

Richman, J., Caffrey, T., & Gold, R. (1994). *A self-help group for therapists with the suicidal.* Panel presentation, 27th Annual Conference, American Association of Suicidology, New York, 1994.

Rodolfo, E., Kraft, W., & Reilley, R. (1988). Stressors of professionals and trainees at APA-approved counselling and VA medical center internship sites. *Professional Psychology: Research and Practice, 19*, 43–49.

Rothman, J. (1980). Research and development in the human services. In *Social Research & Development.* Englewood Cliffs, NJ: Prentice-Hall.

Sacks, M. H., Kibel, H. D., Cohen, A. M., Keats, M., & Turnquist, K. N. (1987). Resident response to patient suicide. *Journal of Psychiatric Education, 11*(4), 217–226.

Zee, H. J. (1972). Blindspots in recognizing serious suicidal intentions. *Bulletin of the Menninger Clinic, 36*, 551–555.

Part III

The Impact of Suicide on Individuals

Chapter 9

Persistent Suicidal Ideation and Its Enduring Morbidity

Robert D. Goldney, A. H. Winefield,
M. Tiggemann, and H. R. Winefield

The subject of suicide is not limited to completed suicides in which the person dies, but includes suicide attempts and ideation. This chapter looks at the impact of suicidal thoughts and mental health problems upon future suicidal ideation and behaviors. The authors present a longitudinal study of the complex issue of the relationship between suicidal thoughts and feelings and measures of psychopathology over time. [Ed.]

The deceptively simple words "suicidal ideation" convey a broad range of emotion, varying from fleeting thoughts that life is not worth living to intense delusional preoccupations with self-destruction. Not unexpectedly, there is a great diversity of opinion as to how prevalent suicidal ideation is in the community. Indeed, a recent review demonstrated that reports have varied from 6 percent to 74 percent in different populations, with most studies demonstrating that about 20 to 30 percent of persons have, at some time in their lives, had suicidal thoughts to some degree (Goldney et al., 1989).

It is difficult to know what to make of these widely varying reports of suicidal ideation. Some philosophers, such as Camus, have argued that the contemplation of suicide is the one truly significant philosophical question and, by implication, it is worthy of consideration by all persons. However, although such an argument might have some appeal to those with an existential view of the world, the reality of the situation is that most research demonstrates that the majority of persons do not have suicidal thoughts. Indeed, those surveys which have examined thoughts about suicide in subjects who most approximate community samples are those which have generally reported the lower range of suicidal ideation (Paykel et al., 1974; Vandivort & Locke, 1979), whereas the reports of high incidence of suicidal ideation have come from more specialized groups such as those of psychology pool subjects in universities (Bonner & Rich, 1988). The latter subjects could hardly be seen as representative of the community at large, as it is well recognized that, on occasion, students participating in such surveys do so under the misapprehension that certain responses may enhance their chances of academic success. While that may be a somewhat skeptical view of some research in this area, it is important to keep an open mind as to the meaning of what any delineation of suicidal ideation may be in any given group of subjects. Notwithstanding these caveats, it is fair to state that, in general terms, most persons would regard suicidal ideation, at least that of a persisting nature, as being of some concern and worthy of study in the overall context of suicide and attempted suicide.

The majority of studies investigating suicidal ideation have been cross-sectional examinations of subjects without follow-up. Indeed, to the best of our knowledge, there have been no studies that have used a random population sample with subsequent follow-up over an extended period of time with recurrent assessment of suicidal ideation and its relationship to various measures of psychological morbidity.

We have undertaken a longitudinal study of a group of young school leavers over a period of eight years and this has allowed us the opportunity of examining suicidal ideation over a period of time (Goldney et al., 1991). Initially we were constrained by school authorities from asking about suicidal thoughts, but questions related to such thoughts were included in four-year and eight-year follow-up samples.

This chapter examines suicidal ideation over a four-year period in young adults, and also reports on the correlates of suicidal ideation with a number of measures of morbidity taken both at the time of the most recent assessment of suicidal ideation and also four and eight years previously.

METHOD

The original subjects were 3,130 students who were attending 12 randomly chosen metropolitan secondary schools in Adelaide, Australia, in 1980. They have participated in yearly postal follow-up surveys and the return rate has been about 80 percent each year. In 1984 there were data from 1,014 subjects and in 1988 the number had reduced to 472 young adults. A full description of this study has been published elsewhere (Winefield et al., 1993).

In 1984 suicidal ideation was assessed on the basis of responses to the four questions which address suicidal ideation in the 28-item General Health Questionnaire. The individual G.H.Q. responses have four anchor points and can be measured in a Likert-type manner from 0 to 3, which gives a range of scores from 0 to 12, or they can be scored in a binary manner, with scores of 0 and 1 allocated for lesser and greater degrees of acknowledgment of suicidal thoughts, respectively, giving a range of scores from 0 to 4.

In 1988 subjects were asked directly whether or not they had ever had thoughts of killing themselves.

Subjects were given a number of psychological instruments in 1980, 1984, and 1988. These included measures of depressive affect, locus of control, self esteem, hopelessness, the G.H.Q., and an anomie scale, and a description of these instruments has been provided in our more detailed report (Winefield et al., 1993).

RESULTS

In 1984, with the Likert-type scoring method, as few as 3.3% of males and 3.0% of females, or as many as 20.2% of males and 17.5% of females could be considered to have had some degree of suicidal ideation, depending on the austerity of the cut-off point of definition of suicidal ideation. Using the more conservative, binary G.H.Q.-derived score, 11.7% of males and 9.7% of females reported suicidal ideation.

In 1988, 112 (24 percent) of 472 subjects reported a history of suicidal ideation on the basis of direct questioning. Of those 472 respondents, data were available from 1984 for 432, of whom 40 acknowledged suicidal ideation, using the more conservative, binary G.H.Q.-derived score, at that time. Significantly more of the subjects who recorded suicidal ideation in 1984 still reported suicidal ideation in 1988 (chi square = 34.6, $df = 2$, $p < 0.001$). It is also of interest that 16 of those 40 subjects who had acknowledged suicidal ideation in 1984 denied ever having had suicidal ideation when assessed in 1988.

For those subjects who acknowledged suicidal ideation in 1988 there was a highly significant relationship, at the 0.001 level of statistical significance, with measures of self-esteem, depressive affect, locus of control, anomie, hopelessness, and the general health questionnaire measurements also taken in 1988.

When those subjects with suicidal ideation in 1988 were examined in regard to their responses to the instruments administered in 1984, it was of note that there was still a highly significant, at the 0.001 level, relationship with measures of self-esteem, depressive affect, and hopelessness, and a lesser degree of association, at the 0.05 level, with measures of anomie and the general health questionnaire (see Table 9.1). When subjects who had acknowledged suicidal ideation in 1988 were examined in regard to their responses to instruments which had been administered in 1980, there were still significant associations. Only three instruments pertinent to mental health were administered in 1980, and depressive affect at that time was significantly associated with suicidal ideation in 1988, at the 0.01 level, and measures of self-esteem and locus of control in 1980 were also significantly associated with suicidal ideation in 1988, although at the 0.05 level.

DISCUSSION

We have discussed problems in the assessment of suicidal ideation in some detail in our earlier reports (Goldney et al., 1989, 1991; Winefield et al., 1993), but they are worthy of reiteration. Suicidal ideation in 1988 was measured by direct questioning, whereas in 1984 it was derived from responses to individual questions on the G.H.Q. It is possible that that may have led to error, but it is reassuring to note that our results were similar to those of previous studies which examined suicidal ideation in general community subjects (Schwab et al., 1972; Sorensen & Golding, 1988).

It is also of some concern, and it highlights the fact that one must have reservations about any data pertaining to suicidal ideation, that no less than 16 (40%) of 40 subjects who acknowledged suicidal ideation in 1984 denied ever having had such thoughts when assessed in 1988. This is a problem

TABLE 9.1   The Statistical Significance of Suicidal Ideation in 1988 in Relation to Psychometric Measures in 1988, 1984, and 1980

	1988	1984	1980
Self-esteem	.001	.001	.05
Depressive affect	.001	.001	.01
Locus of control	.001	N.S.	.05
Anomie	.001	.05	not tested
Hopelessness	.001	.001	not tested
G.H.Q.	.001	.05	not tested

common to all studies examining this issue, and there is no reason to believe that our results should be biased in any direction.

The fundamental criticism of longitudinal studies is the fact that it is impossible to provide data for all subjects. Indeed, we only had access to 1,014 subjects in 1984 and 472 subjects in 1988 from the original sample of 3,130 subjects. Although we acknowledge that this is a significant attrition rate, taken over an 8-year period during which subjects have had some form of assessment each year, this represents an 80% annual return rate and is comparable to what can be anticipated from similar survey methods (Dillman, 1978). Furthermore, retrospective analyses of those who did not continue participating demonstrated that they did not differ systematically on any of the social or clinical variables measured (Winefield et al., 1990).

It could also be argued that a number of the psychological variables measured lacked specificity in terms of mental illness, and this certainly must be acknowledged. Nevertheless, each of the instruments used has been devised with the intention of assessing specific parameters of psychological distress.

Notwithstanding these caveats, we believe our results are robust, and not incongruent with clinical reality. Thus the fact that those who reported suicidal ideation in 1984 were significantly more likely to have suicidal ideation in 1988 demonstrates that suicidal ideation is an enduring phenomenon for some subjects. This is consistent with the recent clinical study of Kovacs et al. (1993), who reported that suicidal ideation was stable over a period of up to 12 years (mean 6.6 years) in a follow-up study of children.

The strength of association between suicidal ideation in 1988 and scores on instruments measuring differing aspects of psychopathology at that time was not unexpected. Indeed, each of the instruments used was significantly associated with suicidal ideation at the 0.001 level. This high degree of statistical association between suicidal ideation and measures of emotional distress does not allow us to dismiss suicidal thoughts as simply a manifestation of an abstract search for a meaning about life and death.

What was not anticipated in the present study was that there should have been such strong associations between the report of suicidal ideation in 1988 and psychometric variables measured 4 and 8 years previously.

These results indicate that suicidal ideation and its associated morbidity, at the very least that morbidity measured by the tests in this study, are more enduring than has been believed previously. While these findings may be surprising to some who have regarded suicidal ideation as a relatively nonspecific and fleeting phenomenon, they are probably not unexpected to clinicians who have to grapple with suicidal subjects over a period of time.

The expression of suicidal ideation should always be considered seriously, as suicide is the most extreme outcome of any of the emotional conditions with which clinicians have to deal. We have found that patients usually express a considerable degree of relief after having divulged suicidal thoughts and feelings, and more often than not they are able to speak about their mixed feelings of living and dying, rather than feeling that any suicidal ideation will inevitably and inexorably lead to death by suicide. We have also found in the clinical situation that subjects almost invariably respond better to an open-ended question such as, "What are your thoughts about living and dying," rather than a more direct question such as, "Have you felt suicidal?," or the even more direct and threatening question, "Did you want to kill yourself?" By asking about mixed thoughts of living and dying in an open-ended manner people will often speak about their feelings of hopelessness or feelings that they really don't care whether they live or die. Not infrequently it is patients in this category, those who do not care whether they live or die, who take risks with their lives, risks that may lead to death by suicide.

Most clinicians in the field of suicidal behavior have had the sobering experience of the unexpected death of a patient by suicide. The present results indicate that we must maintain our vigilance in the longer term. Indeed, when one considers the present findings of the persistence of suicidal ideation and its association with measures of emotional morbidity over an 8-year period it is not surprising that short-term measures to reduce overall suicide rates have yet to be proven effective.

These findings have implications in terms of our understanding of both the natural history of suicidal ideation and its associated morbidity, and also the duration of treatment which may be required for some suicidal patients. Thus they are consistent with hypotheses such as those of Clark (1993), who suggested that there may be "a lifelong character fault" in persons who ultimately commit suicide, and of O'Carroll (1993), who has delineated the differing components of lifelong vulnerability to suicidal behavior. Furthermore, they are consistent with emerging views about the chronic nature and need for long-term treatment of some psychiatric conditions, particularly depression (Kupfer, 1992), the condition most commonly associated with suicidal ideation.

REFERENCES

Bonner, R. L., & Rich, A. R. (1988). A prospective investigation of suicidal ideation in college students: A test of a model. *Suicide and Life Threatening Behavior, 18,* 245–258.

Clark, D. C. (1993). Narcissistic crises of aging and suicidal despair. *Suicide and Life Threatening Behavior, 23*, 21–26.

Dillman, D. A. (1978). *Mail and telephone surveys.* New York: John Wiley.

Goldney, R. D., Smith, S., Winefield, A. H., Tiggemann, M., & Winefield, H. R. (1991). Suicidal ideation: its enduring nature and associated morbidity. *Acta Psychiatrica Scandinavica, 83*, 115–120.

Goldney, R. D., Winefield, A. H., Tiggemann, M., & Winefield, H. R. (1989). Suicidal ideation in a young adult population. *Acta Psychiatrica Scandinavica, 79*, 481–489.

Kovacs, M., Goldston, D., & Gatsoni, C. (1993). Suicidal behaviours and childhood onset depressive disorders: A longitudinal investigation. *Journal of the American Academy of Child and Adolescent Psychiatry, 32*, 8–20.

Kupfer, D. J. (1992). Maintenance treatment in recurrent depression: Current and future directions. *British Journal of Psychiatry, 161*, 309–316.

O'Carroll, P. (1993). Suicide causation: Pies, paths and pointless polemics. *Suicide and Life Threatening Behavior, 23*, 27–36.

Paykel, E. S., Myers, J. K., Lindenthal, J. J., & Tanner, J. (1974). Suicidal feelings in the general population: A prevalence study. *British Journal of Psychiatry, 124*, 460–469.

Schwab, J. J., Warheit, G. J., & Holzer, C. E. (1972). Suicidal ideation and behaviour in a general population. *Diseases of the Nervous System, 33*, 745–749.

Sorensen, S. B., & Golding, J. M. (1988). Suicide ideation and attempts in Hispanics and non-Hispanic whites: Demographic and psychiatric disorder issues. *Suicide and Life Threatening Behavior, 18*, 205–218.

Vandivort, D. S., & Locke, B. Z. (1979). Suicide ideation: Its relation to depression, suicide and suicide attempts. *Suicide and Life Threatening Behavior, 9*, 205–218.

Winefield, A. H., Tiggemann, M., Winefield, A. H., & Goldney, R. D. (1993). *Growing up with unemployment.* London: Routledge.

Winefield, A. H., Winefield, H. R., & Tiggemann, M. (1990). Sample attrition bias in a longitudinal study of young people. *Australian Journal of Psychiatry, 41*, 75–85.

Chapter 10

Attempted Suicide and Depression: Initial Assessment and Short-Term Follow-Up

Anthony T. Davis

What happens after a suicide attempt and what is the impact of the suicide attempt upon the individual? This chapter provides insight into the issue of what happens after a suicide attempt by presenting a longitudinal study of persons hospitalized for an attempted suicide. [Ed.]

INTRODUCTION

Depression is the most common psychiatric disorder in patients who have attempted suicide. Reports of the association of depression with attempted suicide vary between 35% and 80% of cases. This variation reflects the diverse terminology and multiplicity of study methods used to explore this issue. Researchers have used, variously, case record reviews (Burke, 1974; Holding et al., 1977), clinical diagnoses (Lukianowicz, 1972; Pablo & Lamarre, 1986), diagnoses based on specific diagnostic criteria and/or structured clinical interviews (Newson-Smith & Hirsch, 1979; Reeves et al.,

1985), self-report questionnaires (Beck et al., 1975; Goldney & Pilowsky, 1980), observer rating scales (El-Gaaly, 1974; Weissman et al., 1973) and comparisons with other psychiatric patient groups (Bridges & Koller, 1966; Bruhn, 1963). It is not possible to reach any definitive conclusion from these diverse studies other than that depressive symptoms are common at the time of attempted suicide. Clinical experience has shown that in some patients these are relatively short-lived phenomena, yet in others they are manifestations of a more profound depressive disorder which renders the patient at risk of further suicidal behavior.

It is important to continue to systematically explore the issue of depression in attempted suicide, to clarify its nature and significance, and to provide optimal guidelines for the management of suicidal patients. Depression can usually be treated and clinicians can vigorously pursue this with every hope of reducing mortality rates in this vulnerable group.

A number of studies have examined the change in mood state immediately following attempted suicide, in an attempt to understand the impact of a suicide attempt on mental state, which will have a bearing on the nature of psychiatric intervention.

Platman et al. (1971) reported a single-case study of a 49-year-old woman admitted to a research unit with severe depression. She was studied systematically in terms of physiological state, daily behavior, self-reports of mood, and regular psychiatric evaluations before and after a suicide attempt that occurred in the ward approximately six weeks after admission. Observer ratings and self-ratings showed an increase in depression and other emotions up to the time of the suicide attempt, and a rapid recovery afterward. Within two weeks she was almost free of depression and ready for discharge.

In a detailed study, Newson-Smith and Hirsch (1979) assessed 131 inpatients immediately following "self-poisoning." Seventy-nine completed an initial assessment, which included a Present State Examination (PSE) diagnostic interview and a General Health Questionnaire (GHQ). Sixty-one patients were reviewed one week later and 51 were followed up at three months. They constituted the central study group.

The initial PSE and GHQ scores were high. According to the PSE for the 51 patients, 60% were identified as having a "definite" or "at threshold" psychiatric disorder at initial assessment and all but one of these subjects had a diagnosis of depressive disorder. At 1 week this figure had reduced to 40%, and at three months 22% of the sample. The authors concluded that the reduction in "caseness" over 1 week was in keeping with an impression that "the act of self-poisoning can have a cathartic therapeutic effect." Patients reported a high level of "neurotic" symptoms over 4 weeks prior to the suicide attempt. There was a significant reduction in symptoms over one week but this was less likely in patients with a high initial GHQ score and a PSE diagnosis of "definite" mental disorder.

Van Praag and Plutchik (1985) studied the relationship between presuicidal and postsuicidal mood conditions in a group of 25 hospitalized suicide attempters and 50 control patients who were hospitalized with depression but with no previous suicide attempt. Using the Hamilton Rating Scale for Depression, the Zung Self-rating Depression Scale, and a Global score for depression, they demonstrated a significant decrease in depression in the suicidal patients within a few days of hospitalization. This was not found in depressed patients without prior suicide attempts. The authors considered that the drop in depression ratings could be attributed to the suicide attempt and offered several possible interpretations of this phenomenon: 1) the suicide attempt served to palliate feelings of guilt or remorse, or gratified hostile feelings toward others; 2) an expectation effect or bias exists connected with the recall of feelings and experiences before the suicide attempt; and 3) depressive feelings may be denied or repressed in order to promote speedy discharge and escape from a situation seen by others as shameful; and 4) the physical consequences of a serious suicide attempt could play a role in the observed mood changes.

The findings of these studies are in accord with clinical experience that patients may have a significant reduction in level of depression soon after attempted suicide, irrespective of the clinical diagnosis. Early writers used such terms as "catathymic crisis" (Farberow, 1950) and "catharsis" (Stengel, 1960) to describe such changes.

Against this background, I would like to report a study that was recently completed in Adelaide, South Australia. It was anticipated that a detailed study of suicidal patients, that included an examination of the short-term changes in mood state, could provide useful information for the clinician involved in making diagnostic and treatment decisions and contribute toward a greater understanding of depression in attempted suicide and the optimal management of such patients.

The specific aims of this study were threefold:

1. to identify the extent of depression in a large cohort of patients hospitalized after attempted suicide;
2. to examine in detail various aspects of depression in a sample of these patients; and
3. to examine the short-term course of depression over one week following the suicide attempt and define predictors of persistent depression at one week. It was anticipated that this would help define the impact of a suicide attempt upon the individual and identify patients

at risk of persistent depression and possible repeated attempted suicide or suicide.

MATERIALS AND METHOD

Subjects

Subjects for the study were drawn from patients, aged between 18 and 65 years, admitted following a suicide attempt to the Royal Adelaide Hospital (RAH) over a 3-year period.

A suicide attempt was defined as a non-fatal act in which an individual deliberately caused self-injury or ingested a substance in excess of any prescribed or generally recognized therapeutic dosage. Patients with primary drug and alcohol intoxication were excluded. The RAH admission policy is that all suicidal patients are evaluated in the Accident and Emergency Department by a Psychiatric Trainee and are then admitted as inpatients if there are concerns about the physical sequelae of the suicide attempt, signs of significant mental disorder, or the persistence of suicidal ideation. During the study period, 70% of all suicidal patients were hospitalized. For each of these patients, basic demographic data, details of method of suicide attempt, and day of admission were obtained from hospital files.

Procedure

The study proceeded in three phases.

1. *Screening.* Once medically stable patients who consented were screened for the presence of depression with the Zung Self-rating Depression Scale (SDS) and the Levine Pilowsky Depression (LPD) Questionnaire, and where indicated, cognitive function was assessed with the Mini-Mental State Examination (MMSE).

2. *Initial clinical assessment.* Patients were eligible for further assessment if they had 1) SDS Index of 50 or above, and 2) MMSE score of 24 and above. Of the eligible patients, one subject per day was randomly allocated to participate in the initial clinical assessment. Each patient was assigned a formal diagnosis according to DSM-III criteria and the Hamilton Rating Scale for Depression (RSD) and the Suicide Intent Scale were completed. Patients completed the Hopelessness Scale and again were asked to report their mental state as it was over the few days prior to the suicide attempt. Subsequently, a specific depressive symptom profile of each subject was

recorded, using all items of the DSM-III Major Depression criteria and the Hamilton RSD.

3. *Follow-up assessment*. Those patients who completed the initial clinical assessment were invited to participate in a follow-up assessment one week later.

Results

Screening. During the study period, 1,091 suicidal patients aged between 18 and 65 were assessed in the Accident and Emergency Department and 784 were admitted to the hospital. Four-hundred-thirty-two patients were screened with the Zung SDS and the LPD questionnaire. The mean age of this group was 31.5 (SD = 11.2) years. There were 194 males and 243 females. Three-hundred-eighty-two (88%) had a drug overdose and 50 (12%) had used other self-damaging means.

Zung SDS. The mean SDS Index was 64.9 (SD = 12.7) and 379 (87%) had a SDS Index of 50 or greater (the "morbidity cut-off score"). Seventy-one (16%) had a SDS Index of 50–59 (minimal to mild depression), 152 (35%) had an Index of 60–69 (moderate to marked depression), and 156 (36%) had an Index of 70+ (severe to most extremely depressed).

LPD Questionnaire. The mean LPD score was 11.3 (SD = 5.9). Three-hundred-thirty-three (77%) were categorized as depressed, with 151 (35%) "non-endogenous," and 182 (42%) "endogenous." Ninety-nine (23%) were "not depressed."

Initial clinical assessment. Of the 432 screened patients, 359 (83%) satisfied all inclusion criteria for the initial clinical assessment, and 201 patients were allocated to the assessment interview and completed this.

Depression scores. The three measures of depression severity were positively correlated. Each measure indicated moderate severity of depression. The self-report measures showed significant differences between sexes but not the Hamilton RSD. The older age-group (above the median of 29 years) had a higher Hamilton RSD than the younger group.

LPD Categories. One-hundred-seventy-eight (89%) were depressed, with 108 (54%) in the endogenous category and 70 (35%) in the non-endogenous category. There were no significant differences between the sexes but there was a significant difference between age-groups, with the older group having more endogenous and less non-endogenous depression than the younger group.

DSM-III Diagnoses. The DSM-III diagnoses were divided into three groups: a) (90 [45%]) Major Affective Disorder–Major Depression, Dysthymic Disorder, Bipolar disorder–depressed and Atypical Depression; b) (56[28%]) Adjustment Disorder; and c) (55 [27%]) Other Disorders/No Diagnosis/Major Depression in Remission.

Depressive Symptom Profile. The 10 symptoms most commonly reported to have been present over the two weeks prior to the suicide attempt are listed in rank-order frequency in Table 10.1.

Follow-up. One-hundred-twenty-eight subjects were reassessed one week after the initial assessment. At the time of follow-up, 52 (41%) were inpatients of psychiatric units and 76 (59%) were outpatients. The mean length of hospital stay following the initial assessment of the latter group was 1.2 days.

The mean age of the study group was 33 years (SD = 11.8) and the median age was 30 years, with a female:male ratio of 1.5:1. Twenty-nine (23%) subjects were married or living in a de facto relationship and 99 (77%) were either single, divorced, separated, or widowed. Eighty (63%) were occupied with full time work, studies, or home duties and 48 (37%) were unemployed or on a pension. One-hundred-six (83%) patients had taken an overdose of medication and 22 (17%) patients had used other self-damaging means (self-laceration 10, gunshot 2, carbon monoxide poison-

Table 10.1   Rank-Order Frequency (%) of the 10 Most Commonly Reported Pre-Attempt Symptoms

Symptom	Frequency (%)
Anxiety—psychic	175 (87)
Dysphoric mood	148 (74)
Anxiety—somatic	144 (72)
Initial insomnia	113 (56)
Loss of energy/fatigue	112 (56)
Recurrent thoughts of suicide	104 (52)
Middle insomnia	104 (52)
Feelings of worthlessness	97 (48)
Loss of interest/pleasure	93 (46)
Diminished ability to think/concentrate	93 (46)

ing 5, hanging 1, poison 1, and multiple methods 3. Twenty-seven (21%) subjects had a high-lethality suicide attempt (i.e., required intensive care management or surgery) and 101 (79%) had a low- to moderate-lethality attempt. The mean Suicide Intent Scale score of the group was 12.9 (SD = 8.0), indicating a moderately high level of suicide intent.

The 128 study subjects were compared with the 231 patients who were eligible but not selected for the clinical assessment or did not complete the follow-up. There were no statistically significant group differences in terms of age, sex, marital status, employment status, day of admission, method of suicide attempt, or mean SDS Index.

In addition, the 432 screened patients were compared with the 352 age-related patients not screened but admitted to the hospital during the study period. There were no statistically significant group differences in mean age, sex, marital status, employment status, or method of attempt. There was a significant difference in day of admission, with screened patients admitted less on Fridays and Saturdays than the non-screened group ($p < 0.001$). Of the 352 non-screened patients, 185 were discharged by the medical and surgical units out of study hours, 36 discharged themselves against medical advice, 64 had cognitive impairment, 57 refused to participate in the study, 6 died following admission, 1 had language problems which precluded inclusion in the study, and 3 failed to complete the questionnaire.

Depression Scores. The total group mean depression scores reduced at a significant level over 1 week, as did male and female subgroups.

LPD Categories. The overall change in the distribution of the three LPD categories between T_1 and T_2 was found to be highly significant ($p < 0.001$) with the "non-endogenous depression" and "non-depressive" categories showing the most significant changes. The "endogenous" group showed a relatively small change in frequency.

DSM-III Diagnoses. The same analyses as applied to the LPD category data were carried out on the grouped diagnostic data and a significant change in diagnostic groups was found ($p < 0.001$). The Major Affective Disorder group showed a significant reduction in frequency across time, while the "Other Disorders/No Diagnosis/Major Depression in Remission" group showed a significant increase. The Adjustment Disorder group had a lesser reduction from T_1 to T_2.

It is of interest that a diagnosis of personality disorder was made in 45 (35%) subjects.

Depressive Symptom Profile. It is noteworthy that there was a significant reduction in frequency of depressive symptoms at the $p < 0.01$ level in 8 of the 10 symptoms.

Further Analyses—Prediction of Persistent Depression

It was apparent that, while there were significant changes in all measures of depression, a substantial number of patients remained depressed, as defined by the LPD category "endogenous" or a Hamilton RSD score greater than 17. The next phase of the study aimed to define T_1 predictors of persistent depression at T_2 in this subgroup. The predictor variables of interest were a number of demographic, clinical and state characteristics that have been shown to be associated with depression and suicidal behavior.

In order to define T_1 predictors of depression at T_2, a stepwise logistic regression model was utilized. The dependent variable was the presence of depression, as defined successively by a Hamilton RSD score greater than 17 and the LPD category "endogenous." Three steps were taken to identify variables that may have some predictive value in this model. First, each demographic, clinical, and state variable was defined in a dichotomous form to give subgroups of each variable. Second, significant differences in subgroup mean depression scores at T_2 were identified by paired *t*-test. Third, depression frequencies of variable subgroups at T_2 were examined by χ^2 analysis to locate variables that were associated with a significant difference ($p < 0.05$) in categorization.

These univariate analyses revealed a subset of variables that could have some predictive value. These variables were entered into the logistic regression model in a stepwise fashion.

With the Hamilton score greater than 17, the variables listed as significant indicated that the following T_1 subgroups had a higher probability of being depressed at T_2: a history of previous depression, non-overdose method of suicide attempt, female sex, high level of hopelessness, and absence of acute psychosocial stressors within 48 hours.

With the LPD category "endogenous," a history of previous depression, a history of attempted suicide, absence of acute psychosocial stressors, the use of prescribed medication, and being single/widowed/divorced were identified as the subgroups with higher probability of depression at T_2.

Table 10.2 lists a combination of the variables that emerged from the analyses. These variables suggest a clinical profile of patients presenting with attempted suicide who have a high probability of persistent depression one week following a suicide attempt.

Table 10.2   Predictors of Persistent Depression

History of previous depression
History of previous attempted suicide
Non-overdose suicide attempt
Female sex
High level hopelessness
Absence of acute stressors
Use of prescribed medication
Single/widowed/divorced

DISCUSSION

While a number of methodological issues need to be considered, including the effects of statistical regression or repeated measurement, the lack
of control subjects and the possibility of spontaneous remission, several
important findings have emerged from the study. In summary, in this cohort of patients hospitalized following attempted suicide:

1. The vast majority had a significant level of depression, as defined by
   self-report measures. Seventy-one percent were defined by Zung SDS
   as moderate, marked or extreme severity, and 77% were categorized
   as depressed by the LPD questionnaire, with 42% "endogenous"
   depression.
2. Observer ratings of 201 subjects demonstrated a moderate level of
   depression and a diagnosis of a major affective disorder in 44%.
3. In a subgroup of 128 patients, there was a significant reduction in
   severity of depression, depression categories, and diagnoses and
   depressive symptoms over 1 week following admission.
4. In this subgroup a number of variables were predictive of persistent
   depression over the week, namely a past history of depression and
   attempted suicide, a non-overdose method, a high hopelessness score,
   female sex, absence of acute stressors, use of prescribed medication,
   and being single, widowed, or divorced.

The finding of an initial high level of depression in the study group
is in keeping with the reports of several research groups (Dyer & Kreitman,
1984, Morgan et al., 1975, Weissman et al., 1973), although this finding is
by no means universal. Comparisons with other studies requires a careful
appraisal of methodological differences between studies. A striking finding of this study was the large proportion of hospitalized patients with a

significant depressive disorder and a high frequency of symptoms usually associated with endogenous-type depression.

With regard to the impact of the suicide attempt upon the individual, the observed reduction in depression over one week added considerable support to the notion of attempted suicide having "a cathartic therapeutic effect." This issue has been raised by several authors, including Farberow (1950), Newson-Smith and Hirsch (1979), Stengel (1960), and Van Praag and Plutchik (1985). It is conceivable that, at a psychodynamic level, the punitive act of self-destruction, laden as it is with aggressive affect, may bring symptomatic relief through the surrender to impulse and discharge of powerful emotions, albeit against the self. Other factors are no doubt important in this reduction in depression. At the interpersonal level, there are a number of important sequelae to the suicidal act. Not uncommonly, the behavior follows a critical interpersonal event, such as loss of or rejection by a loved one. Whatever the duration of hospitalization, there is a significant infusion of care and support from nursing, medical, and paramedical staff. Family members and significant others are often mobilized such that care and support are offered and interpersonal crises are resolved. Psychiatric assessment provides the opportunity to define more clearly the nature of problems, and arrange for further specialist treatment. Other community agencies can be mobilized as the need is identified. The impact of these multiple factors over a short period can be such as to engender a degree of hopefulness and optimism in patients who have experienced despair and hopelessness at the time of attempting suicide. In general, a corresponding shift in affective state can be expected. When this change is not observed, it is important to question the role of endogenous-type depressive illness and the need for physical treatments as well as the possible negative effects of psychosocial influences.

It could be argued that the predictor variables identified in this study are of critical importance in the detection of patients at high risk of further morbidity and mortality following a suicide attempt, through persistence of depression. Thus clinicians should be alert to presence of these high-risk characteristics when assessing all suicidal patients and make every effort to ensure that such patients receive adequate psychiatric follow-up. In many instances this will require use of hospital outreach teams and other community-based services.

This study has focused on changes in mental state over one week. What happens beyond one week is not clear. A recent paper by Bronisch (1992) reported the course of depression over two weeks in a group of 32 females hospitalized with a major depressive disorder. Twenty-one had attempted suicide and 11 were matched as a control group. All patients were treated with short-term dynamic psychotherapy. Measures used were the Munich Personality Test, the Diagnostic Interview Schedule, Inpatient Multi-dimensional Psychiatric Scale, and three self-rating depression scales.

Bronisch found a similar course of depressive symptoms and somatic complaints in both groups over the two-week period, and could not support the notion of attempted suicide having a cathartic effect. However, there were several important differences between this study and the other controlled study of Van Praag and Plutchik (1985). Bronisch's subjects were all female, had less severe depression (non-melancholic), used less violent means of attempted suicide, and had a specified psychotherapeutic intervention. He does question if the cathartic effect of attempted suicide is restricted to severe major depression, to violent attempts, or other variables such as older age and male sex.

Newson-Smith and Hirsch (1979) reported further changes in depression in their study group between one week and three months but they were reluctant to comment on the significance of this, given the large numbers of intervening variables that have to be considered over that time.

This highlights the need for further controlled studies of this subject, using methods that can be replicated across centers and across time. This is one area of inquiry that deserves much closer attention, as it could yield important insights for clinicians who often confront the problem of managing patients who have attempted suicide.

Having clarified the phenomenology of depression and the short-term course of depression following attempted suicide, and identified clinical predictors of persistent depression, future research could be directed at elucidating the important intervening variables that influence outcome. Areas of interest would include measures of the response of significant others to the suicidal behavior, alterations in life circumstances, and the specific psychological interventions immediately after the suicidal crisis. Further follow-up studies of changes in mental state from one week to three months and beyond would provide important information on the outcome of suicidal behavior and the efficacy of various interventions.

REFERENCES

Beck, A. T., Kovacs, M., & Weissman, A. (1975). Hoplessness and suicidal behavior: An overview. *Journal of the American Medical Association, 234*, 1146–1149.

Bridges, P. K., & Koller, K. M. (1966). Attempted suicide. A comparative study. *Comprehensive Psychiatry, 7*(4), 240–247.

Bronisch, T. (1992). Does an attempted suicide actually have a cathartic effect? *Acta Psychiatrica Scandinavica, 86*, 228–232.

Bruhn, J. G. (1963). Comparative study of attempted suicides and psychiatric out-patients. *British Journal of Preventive Social Medicine, 17,* 197–201.

Burke, A. W. (1974). Clinical aspects of attempted suicide among women in Trinidad and Tobago. *British Journal of Psychiatry, 125,* 175–176.

Dyer, J. A. T., & Kreitman, N. (1984). Hopelessness, depression and suicidal intent in parasuicide. *British Journal of Psychiatry, 144,* 127–33.

El-Gaaly, A. A. (1974). Social dysfunction in depressives and attempted suicides. *Acta Psychiatrica Scandinavica, 50,* 341–345.

Farberow, N. L. (1950). Personality pattern of suicidal mental hospital patients. *Genetic Psychology Monographs, 42,* 3.

Goldney, R. D., & Pilowsky, I. (1980). Depression in young women who have attempted suicide. *Australia and New Zealand Journal of Psychiatry, 14,* 203–211.

Holding, T. A., Buglass, D., Duffy, J. C., & Kreitman, N. (1977). Parasuicide in Edinburgh—A seven year review. *British Journal of Psychiatry, 130,* 534–543.

Lukianowicz, N. (1972). Suicidal behaviour: An attempt to modify the environment. *British Journal of Psychiatry, 121,* 387–390.

Morgan, M. G., Burns-Cox, C. J., Pocock, M., & Pottle, S. (1975). Deliberate self-harm: Clinical and socio-economic characteristics of 368 patients. *British Journal of Psychiatry, 127,* 564–574.

Newson-Smith, J. G. B., & Hirsch, S. R. (1979). Psychiatric symptoms in self-poisoning patients. *Psychology and Medicine, 9,* 493–500.

Pablo, R. Y., & Lamarre, C. J. (1986). Parasuicides in a general hospital unit: Their demographic and clinical characteristics. *General Hospital Psychiatry, 8,* 279–286.

Platman, S. R., Plutchik, R., & Weinstein, B. (1971). Psychiatric, physiological, behavioural and self-report measures in relation to a suicide attempt. *Journal of Psychiatric Research, 8,* 127–137.

Reeves, J. C., Large, R. G., & Honeymoon, M. (1985). Parasuicide and depression: A comparison of clinical and questionnaire diagnosis. *Australia and New Zealand Journal of Psychiatry, 19,* 30–33.

Stengel, E. (1960). The complexity of motivations to suicidal attempts. *Journal of Mental Sciences, 106,* 1388–1393.

Van Praag, H., & Plutchik, R. (1985). An empirical study on the cathartic effect of attempted suicide. *Psychological Research, 16,* 123–130.

Weissman, M., Fox, K., & Klerman, G. L. (1973). Hostility and depression associated with suicide attempts. *American Journal of Psychiatry, 130,* 450–455.

Chapter 11

The Impact of Mass Media Reports on Suicide and Attitudes Toward Self-Destruction: Previous Studies and Some New Data from Hungary and Germany

Sándor Fekete and A. Schmidtke

This chapter discusses how the impact of a mass-media report on suicide may affect attitudes and behaviors in the general population. [Ed.]

There is worldwide interest in the effects and influence of the mass media. It is no accident that this influential means of matters economical and political, the mass media, can influence the opinions, thinking, attitudes, and emotions of huge numbers of individuals. This interest has recently appeared in Eastern Europe, and there are "media wars" where political powers fight for the control of the mass media. The effects on human behavior that are achieved by the mass media in informing, forming values and attitudes, or influencing forcefully may seem evident, but their direct analysis is quite difficult. At the same time, the reflection of general social attitudes can be seen and analyzed in the way that the media present different human or social phenomena—such as suicide. This chapter analyzes two questions concerning the relationship between mass media and suicide: First, how the mass media present suicide and what social attitudes are reflected in mass media reports; second, how the changing presentations of self-destruction in the media effects suicides in a society as well as attitudes toward suicide.

Empirical studies regarding suicide and the mass media have been conducted in only a few countries and even fewer studies are available involving content analysis of the suicidal reports. The majority of these studies have reported a correlation between media reports of suicide and increasing suicide rates; heavily publicized reports (presenting the suicidal event in spectacular, accepting, even heroic way) have often been found to be followed by a significant increase of imitative suicides. The suicidal models presented in the mass media can play a role in the sociocultural transmission of suicide; they are a part of the suicidal culture of a country. This culture gives meaning, influences attitudes concerning suicide, and, by different attributive processes, influences the understanding of this phenomenon. This chapter, after reviewing some studies on the relationship of mass media reports to suicide, presents an investigation of mass media reports in Hungary and Germany.

Hungary has been consistently very high when comparing suicide rates. The high rate of suicide in seen in emigration and among Hungarian minorities living in the neighbouring countries points to the role of sociocultural factors and the common culture as an important influence upon suicide. In our study we used Germany as a comparison country. There is a remarkable difference between Hungarian and German populations regarding suicide rates. Furthermore, analyses comparing German and Hungarian newspaper reports seem to reveal some typical cultural differences in attitudes concerning suicide as expressed in the media, which may have an affect upon the maintenance of the suicide rate differences between the two countries. The study presented in this chapter was conducted to better understand the process of possible cultural transmission of suicide, transcultural differences in attitudes toward suicide, and the impact of mass media reports on suicide. It was hoped that this study might help in our understanding of suicide and contribute to a decrease in the possible negative effects of portraying suicide stories effectively as "advertisements" in the media.

This approach takes the point of view that the media may influence an ambivalent, vulnerable person by its presentation of a suicidal act which may be viewed as "the natural advertisement" of self-destruction (Phillips,1990), and which can lead a person to suicide rather than to some alternative solution to his distress. It is possible that "copy cat" suicides may occur or even have a protective effect. Our aim is to understand these interactions by content analysis of reports on suicide in Hungarian newspapers from different periods (before and after the political changes in Eastern Europe), and by comparing and analyzing suicidal news (headlines) of the German and the Hungarian press from a transcultural point of view.

PRECEDENTS AND THEORETICAL BASES

It is not new to analyze the effects of the media on suicide. Phelps (1911) published a book on this subject at the beginning of the century; later, in the 1960s, mostly in the U.S.A., several systematic research projects on the topic were conducted. Motto (1970) analyzed suicide statistics in large American cities at a time when journalists were on strike and there was no news from the written press. He found that the number of suicides among women under 35 years of age decreased during this period. Phillips (1974, 1990) analyzed American suicide statistics in relation to news about real and fictitious suicidal acts in newspapers and on television, and found a significant increase in the number of imitation suicides (and of car and plane accidents with one passenger on board—a suicidal equivalent) in accordance with the so-called "Werther effect." The increase could be seen mostly among young people, in the geographical region affected by the given media, and its rate depended on how much publicity was diffused. After publication of some contradicting reports by several researchers which did not show such an increase in suicide following media reports, Phillips analyzed various alternative explanations. He refined his methodology and took into account seasonal changes and economical cycles. He argued that it is improbable that the main effect of media reports is to advancing suicides which would already have occurred in the future since, if this were true, the suicidal peak following the media reports should be followed by a decrease in suicide, which was not the case. A "common preceding evoking condition" (e.g., economical crisis) for both the increase in suicidal rates and in suicidal news is not probable either, since if this were the case, the rate increase after the suicide story would not be correlating with the rate of publicity. If the effect of media news would only be that more deaths would be labeled as suicides, this would have resulted in a parallel decrease in the other causes of death, but this phenomenon was not observed.

Some European analyses have shown less of a connection between media news and the suicidal rate (Riaunet, 1991), but this may be due to methodological differences in the studies. Dutch researchers, in contrast to their American colleagues, found only half as many evident wordings of suicide in the titles of new stories. It is also characteristic of Dutch suicide stories that there is a high (50 percent) rate of news about suicide and murder together, which, of course, decreases the phenomenon of identification–imitation. A Hungarian study (Fekete, 1990) indicated a media effect in an analysis of the imitation consequences of a Hungarian beauty queen's suicide. Several researchers explored the effect of stories from the electronic media (television and radio) about fictitious and real suicides, and their effects on the suicidal rate (Schmidtke & Hafner, 1989; Welz, 1992). The appearance of imitation effects was supported and justified in several works—in spite of the difficulties of empirical analysis. The effect, as with newspaper stories, was limited to the given broadcasting area, and was proportionate to the rate of publicity. Our present study concentrates on the written press, the nature of the reports, and their effects. Unlike the surveys mentioned so far,we tried to analyze more or less theoretically the news and articles about suicides in the written press, and through it reconstruct the culture-dependent circumstances and nature of suicidal acts. An earler study by Bourgeois (1969) investigating the content of reports on suicide, found a statistical connection between political crises and self-burning suicides. Gappmair (1980), analyzing six daily papers in Salzburg found 631 suicide news reports in a year, and he found that the presentation was generally condemning, criminalizing, and it neglected the social background and the possibilities of prevention. In opposition to Tantalo's and Marchiori's (1981) similar results in Italy, Niedermaier (1985) analyzed 144 articles in five supraregional German newspapers with very large circulation and recorded a less prejudicial, sensational presentation which took into consideration motivational and preventive aspects. Pell's (1982) Canadian, and Kuess and Hatzinger's (1986) Austrian analyses show the sensational highlighting of public suicides, suicides in which unusual methods were used, or suicides committed by prominent personalities, without mentioning either psychic or social causes nor possibilities for prevention. An interesting counterexample may be Etzensdorfer and Sonneck's (1990) empirical analysis of the suicide epidemic in Vienna, that was apparently spread as a consequence of highlighted sensational articles in newspapers. Publication of these articles stopped after the consultations with Austrian media experts and suicide experts.

Sometimes these researchers have been accused of not having a theoretical perspective to explain their findings. It is obvious that content analysis of cultural values and attitudes, and studies of imitation behavior can be interpreted from several different theoretical perspectives. Beside classical imitation theory, the modeling approach of social cognitive theory (Bandura,1986) may offer some help in understanding these findings. It may be useful to take into consideration the selective function of "recipients" of information, the role of reinforcement; as well as the approach of symbolic interaction (Blumer, 1969); and if we complement this frame of reference with the dynamic point of view of identification–projective identification at the level of the individual (Taiminen,1992).

What are the implications of such a frame of reference for the planning and conducting of practical research work? According to the rules of social-cognitive learning theory, suicide as a problem-solving method can be built into a person's behavioral patterns resulting from social transmission. The magnitude of the model-effect is related to the fame or prominence of the suicidal model and to the amount of publicity given to the event in a geographic area. This influence would appear to be dependent partly on the correspondence between the publicized models' attributes and those of the "imitators," for example, their age, sex, social status and geographic location. In media presentation, positive consequences, effects and values can evoke imitation effects, as well. The nature of the effects and attitudes suggested by the media may be shown in the language used. For example, in German there are several expressions for suicide ranging from the two extremes of *Freitod* (free death) and *Selbstmord* (self-killing).

To understand the intrapsychic mechanisms of suicidal contagion, the analytic concepts of identification and projective identification may be of help, at least in the group of model followers with a weak identity, where the suicidal model is not particularly attractive or important. In such instances, the model follower may project his best qualities on his internalized representation and then identify with the model. The weakness of distinguishing the internal self and the object, in cases of borderline, narcissistic, or psychotic persons, makes such identification with a real or fictitious model easier.

According to symbolic interaction, the population is in interaction with the symbols shown by the media. The sensitivity of those who react to the pattern is essential, for example, if some sociological suicidal conditions are given (high unemployment, high divorce rates, anomie in the society, great political transitions), there is real "receptivity" for the suicidal news in the media. The degree of media influence on the public is contingent on audience receptivity to suicide stories (Berman,1988; Stack, 1992). In our research this is particularly relevant considering the consequences of the recent important political and social changes in Hungary.

Before actually getting down to describing the methodology of our research, we will allude to Phillips'(1990) conclusions. According to

Phillips, the most important and essential elements in suicide presentations in the media are the following: presentation of idealized romantic, prominent personalities' suicides, highlighting positive or negative consequences, showing alternative solutions other than suicide, connecting with other suicides, explicit, concrete, or indirect titles, highlighted first-page article or a short piece of news on another page, avoiding sensation.

METHODS AND MATERIALS

In the first transcultural, comparative part of our research, German and Hungarian newspaper headlines concerning suicide were collected. Reports, articles about suicide from daily newspapers from the period of January 1, 1991 to May 31, 1992 (altogether 249 articles from German newspapers of high circulation), and 184 articles from Hungarian central and regional papers, were gathered. Concerning Hungarian papers, the data collection was complete, while we could only randomly select material from West German papers of conservative, socialist, or liberal views. Since the German sample was not complete, we could not compare the frequency of suicidal news reports in the two countries. A similar study is now being conducted in the territory of the former GDR in order to compare the two German states and Hungary from the point of view of differences in their cultural and political systems. We would just like to comment on the fact that we did not find a single article of suicidal news during the year 1981 in the daily papers of the GDR. We separated the headlines, subtitles, and parts printed in italics. The effect of the headlines seem to be the most essential; readers mostly scan the titles instead of reading the whole story. The title's basic role is to attract attention, to summarize the basic message of the text. The content analysis was performed on basis of the variables demonstrated in Table 11.1. By comparison of the German and Hungarian data, similarities and differences in the presentation of suicidal stories were investigated and interpreted.

In the second part of our research we analyzed the entire articles about suicide in Hungary. Our aim was to investigate changes in public attitudes reflected in the evaluation of suicidal events in complete newspaper reports. We compared the material from periods before and after the change of political system (1990). Our analysis in Hungary included as well a number of electronic media reports on suicide (TV, radio), however, the comparisons mainly concerned printed media reports. We analyzed the entire material of one national and another regional daily paper with a wide circulation from the years 1981, 1991, and 1993 (5 months). We gathered all the articles and reports on suicides. We then carried out content analysis

TABLE 11.1   Demonstrated Variables in
             Suicide Stories
_____

- Suicide or attempted suicide
- Prominence of the person
- Mentioning of a name, profession, positive or
  negative characteristics of the prominent
  person
- Suicide method
- Age, sex, motives of the suicidal person
- Mentioning of a certain geographic location
- Positive or negative consequences of the suicide
- Labeling, qualification, interpretation
- Prevention, possible alternatives to the suicide
- Expression used to refer to the suicidal act
- Murder-suicide, extended-suicide stories
- Statistics, scientific report
- Explicit (versus ambiguous) headline stories
_____

comparing the texts dated before and after the great political transitions in Eastern Europe. Reports about suicide were analyzed on the basis of the variables presented in Table 11.1.

Another comparison concerned two suicides which also date from the given periods and which received a lot of publicity. In 1986, the suicide of the first Hungarian beauty queen (articles, reports, and books were published on this topic) started an imitative suicide wave in young people using the same method. We also studied the suicide in 1992 of a new "protesting hero," a taxi-driver, who set himself on fire in front of Parliament. We analyzed the media reports that were published at the time the events occurred and those that were released within a month after they had taken place.

Content analyses were carried out on the basis of the occurrence of the following variables in the headlines and in complete newspaper articles shown in Table 11.1.

RESULTS

In 1991–1992 we collected 249 headlines of suicide stories in Germany and 184 headlines of suicide stories in Hungary. Chi-square analysis was conducted to determine whether any significant differences existed in the characteristics in the two countries (see Table 11.2).

TABLE 11.2 Characteristics of Media-Reported Suicide Stories

Variables	Germany		Hungary		SD
	N	%	N	%	
Suicide	198	79.5%	164	89.1%	0.01*
Attempted suicide	51	20.5%	20	10.9%	0.01*
Prominent's name	37	14.9%	30	16.3%	0.78
Prominent's profession	16	6.4%	11	6.0%	0.85
Prominent's positive	4	1.6%	3	1.6%	0.49
Prominent's negative	22	8.8%	6	3.3%	0.03*
Positive consequence	23	9.2%	35	19.0%	0.005*
Negative consequence	51	20.5%	26	14.1%	0.04*
Labeling					0.008*
psychiatrization	14	5.6%	4	2.2%	
criminalization	52	20.9%	15	8.2%	
moralization	16	6.4%	13	7.1%	
belittlement	5	2.0%	6	3.3%	
self-punishment	3	1.2%	4	2.2%	
Bilanz-suicide	9	3.6%	6	3.3%	
political protest	3	1.2%	9	4.9%	
tragedy	3	1.2%	20	10.9%	
denial	1	0.4%	6	3.3%	
Method of suicide	119	48.0%	96	52.0%	0.94
Concrete geographic site	42	16.9%	57	31.0%	0.03*
Mention of a motive	117	47.0%	49	27.0%	
Prevention, alternatives	6	2.4%	7	3.8%	0.57
Murder-suicide	37	14.8%	12	6.5%	0.02*
Extended suicide	16	6.4%	3	1.6%	0.03*
Used expression of suicide-only by method	79	31.7%	73	39.7%	0.087
Ambiguous headline	33	13.3%	52	28.3%	0.002*
Explicit headline	216	86.7%	132	71.7%	0.002*
	249		184		

*p<.05

The rate of prominent persons' suicides is equal (about 15%) in both countries, but suicides of "negative" celebrities were found more frequently in German texts. There were not any significant differences regarding the age, sex of the person, and the concrete method of the suicide. The only exception was self-burning, which occurred more frequently in Hungary. In both countries the proportion of spectacular methods described in headlines was higher than in real life. There were significant differences between the two countries in worthlessness, divorce and drug problems, which were described more frequently in Germany, but we did not find any other significant differences among the other motives. Preventive possibilities and alternatives to the act is infrequent in both countries. As the figures show, the mentioned negative consequences of suicide are described as significantly more frequent, and the positive consequences as less frequently in German headlines. The labeling process in the media seems to be very interesting as well. The negative qualification such as criminalization, psychiatrization the news about murder-suicide, and about extended suicide can be found much more frequently in German headlines. The "positive," accepting labeling—suicide as a tragedy, as a political protest—occur more frequently in the Hungarian headlines. Also, the rate of ambiguous headline stories was significantly higher in the Hungarian material.

Significant Changes of Attitudes Toward Suicide in the Mass Media in Hungary Comparing the Years of 1981 and 1991–1993

- Occurrence of prominent persons' suicides has decreased
- Spectacular way of description has decreased
- Rate of spectacular methods among the others has decreased
- Psychiatric labeling occurs more frequently
- Labeling as a political protest has become less frequent
- Statistics and scientific reports are more frequent
- Direct verbal formulation and openness in the expressions referring to the act have become more frequent

Changes as Tendencies

- Mentioning prevention, alternatives, and therapy is more frequent
- Criminalization, the mentioned psychiatric illness and depression are more frequent
- Moralization and the verbal formulation reflecting the suicidal person's passiveness have decreased
- Mentioning the relation to other suicides, to age, to concrete location of suicide has become less frequent
- Extreme formulations and the rate of the mentioned negative and positive consequences have simultaneously decreased
- Several more frequently demonstrated motives

DISCUSSION

On the basis of knowledge of the differences in German and Hungarian suicidal statistics and the fact that suicide is much more frequent in Hungary, we had hypothesized that this difference might be reflected in the mass media reports as differences in cultural values and attitudes toward suicide. This sociocultural difference may be interpreted as contributing toward the maintenance of the differences of suicidal rates. Additional data from the GDR in 1981 support this contention, with our finding of the media's "deadly silence" about suicide. In spite of a suicidal rate nearly as high as in Hungary, the suicide was not mentioned once in a central and two regional papers in a year. The frequency of suicide is traditionally, historically higher than in West Germany and there is still the presence of West German electronic media (radio and TV channels), despite the denying silence of local mass media.

Intercultural differences did not appear in our survey data concerning the imitation of suicides of attractive, prominent personalities, as both countries had the same rate of 15 percent. But it important that the rate of "negative" prominent persons as models was significantly lower in the Hungarian reports, so the identification possibility may be considered to be higher. It is also significant that in the Hungarian material there are more positive consequences shown. By these we refer to reports on the "effectiveness"of suicide, the effects influencing human relationships, showing the suicide may have a "communicative force." We recall Teleki, the Hungarian prime minister, whose suicide in the second World War, highlighting honor, honesty; the extensive effects of the act in opposition to other actual possible action alternatives. This parallels discussion of the political results of a taxi driver's self-burning in May 1992 (for example, one may consider the supporting letter by the president of the state in the mass media). Also there are certain wordings in the texts of collected newspapers which support the "positive" outcome of suicide (e.g., "A fatal jump into life").

The German material showed the negative consequences of suicide at a significantly higher rate and this may be interpreted as possibly decreasing the possibility of imitation–identification. The German media had more emphatic presentations of the pain and awful circumstances of suicide, highlighting extended suicide, the joining of murder and suicide, and the consequent sufferings and deaths of other people. The values as reflected in the labeling seen in media presentations reflected the different attitudes of the two cultures toward suicide. Negative, one-sided depictions of suicide, its criminalization and psychiatrization are much more frequent in the German material, while positive, sometimes heroic presentations—suicide as a tragedy, as a heroic mode of political protest or its denial—are found more often in the Hungarian media. In contrast to Phillips' notion that obscure, vague titles or highlighted parts of text can have a protective effect from the point of view of suicide imitation, we suggest another possibility. It is interesting that in the Hungarian material the rate of texts which allude only indirectly, implicitly, not evidently to suicide, or even deny it, is much higher than in the German one, and their effect is not at all protective. On basis of certain learning theories (*Zeigarnik* effect), we propose that vague wording may be risky from the viewpoint of potential imitation. Uncertainty can be seen in the expressions denoting suicide in Hungarian mass media. Interesting examples are two euphemisms in our material (in the context they are evidently suicides): "The under-ground killed again" and "It's the end of the murderous Gramoxon." Summarizing, it seems that on the basis of presented consequences, qualifications, and wordings in the Hungarian texts, there is a more accepting attitude toward suicide, the mode of presentation makes imitation more probable than in the German mass media. At the same time, the high rate of indirect and obscure wording, sometimes even overt denial in the Hungarian mass media, may show tendencies of hiding a basically accepting attitude, and may allude to the ambivalence and to the role of denying in the Hungarian language code of self-destruction (Kezdi,1991). In the German as well as the Hungarian material, suicides by spectacular methods are overrepresented. Showing therapeutic, preventive possibilities, or alternatives to the act is infrequent. This alludes to the fact that the possibilities of the media in suicidal news, from the point of view of protective, preventive concerns, are not at all exhausted. In Germany the consultations of the German Suicide Prevention Society and media experts seems to provide an opportunity for forming a common stance concerning representatives in the mass media, psychiatry, and suicidology, about practical questions without essentially limiting the journalists' freedom. One example of such concerted action was stopping the epidemic of underground suicides in Vienna previously mentioned, which involved consultations with Austrian experts.

In the second part of our study concerning the changes of attitudes toward suicide in Hungary, the most important findings are shown. Comparing data from the two eras (1981 versus 1991–1993), it can be seen that the spectacular and heroic character of the presentations, the moral evaluation, as well as the extreme formulations, have become less frequent; in contrast to an increase in psychiatric and criminal labeling, openness and directness of formulations, presenting statistics, mentioning preventive and alternative possibilities, as well as attempts to understand the suicidal act better. However, alcohol and drugs cannot be found among the motives, and depression is very rarely mentioned.

Media reports of the two suicide "heroes" from the two eras started suicidal waves, in the presentations of the Beauty Queen's suicide in 1986 and the taxi driver's spectacular self-immolation in 1992. Relatively few differences can be found. However, in 1992 the depictions were characterized by more psychiatric labeling, as well as by some negative consequences. Also, the suicide was considered a tragedy less frequently than in 1986. Corresponding with these facts, the taxi driver's suicide imitation wave lasted for only 3 weeks, in contrast with that of the Beauty Queen's which was long-lasting. It is probable that the repeatedly publicized romantic and heroic presentations about her suicide increased the suicide rate over time.

Our analysis of the suicide reports in the electronic media in a two-week period in 1993 led to certain general conclusions. The vast majority of suicide reports on TV occurred in foreign films, the cultural evaluation and attitudes on TV and on the radio are much more "international," and less Hungarian-culture-specific than reports presented in the printed media.

The goal of the second part of our research was to investigate public attitudes concerning suicide as reflected in the mass media during a period of change in the Hungarian political system. In view of the structural suicidogenic conditions in society, the influence of the political-social transition from a totalitarian to a democratic society can be considered controversial (downswing in the economy, rapid increase of unemployment; but in contrast: new community ties and perspectives, strengthening of religiosity, more openness, freedom in society). Our results suggest that the way of thinking about suicide in the press indicates a changing trend during this period. On the basis of our content analysis, these changes seem to be positive from the point of view of the social learning theory of suicide imitation—because of potential decreasing model-effects. On the one hand, some political-social-cultural changes can impact on suicide rates directly; on the other hand, new values and attitudes in the mass media may have on indirect influence on suicidal behavior as well. Our findings suggest that the cultural and social changes covaries with the decrease of suicide rate in Hungary starting in 1988 (compared with continuous increase since 1956). There appears to be an indirect connection among these sociocultural phenomena. Further research is needed to explore and better understand these complex relations.

The media are only one feature of the social environment in which suicidal behavior can be learned, however, the media may reflect essential attitudes in the culture and their changes. The differences between the suicide rates in Germany and in Hungary correspond with differences in the cultural attitudes which are reflected in the newspaper headlines as well. According to the German psychiatrist Asmus Finzen, mass communication can do a lot for the society's psychohygiene and the prevention of suicides as well. Although mass media is only one element in the sociocultural environment—a drop in the ocean—it can be a reflection of the whole.

REFERENCES

Bandura, A. (1986). *Social foundation of thought and action: A social cognitive theory.* Englewood Cliffs, NJ: Prentice-Hall.

Berman, A. L. (1988). Fictional depiction of suicide in television films and imitation effects. *American Journal of Psychiatry, 145,* 982–986.

Biblarz, A., Biblarz, D.N., Pilgrim, M., & Baldree, B. F. (1991). Media influence on attitudes toward suicide. *Suicide and Life-Threatening Behavior, 21*(4), 374–384.

Blumer, H. (1969). Suggestions for the study of mass-media effects. In H. Blumer (Ed.), *Symbolic interactionism: Perspective and method.* Englewood Cliffs, NJ: Prentice-Hall.

Boldt, M. (1988). The meaning of suicide: Implications for research. *Crisis, 9*(2), 93–108.

Boncz, I., Pallag, L., & Fodor, J. (1985). A study on the hypnotic suggestibility of persons attempting suicide: Some therapeutic considerations. In D. Waxman (Ed.), *Modern trends in hypnosis.* New York: Plenum Publishing Corporation.

Bourgeois, M. (1969). Suicides by fire in the Bonze Manner. *Annales Medico-Psychologiques, 2,* 116–127.

Diehl, L. (1992). Einfluss der Suggestion auf Suizid. *Suizidprophylaxe, 19,* 115–121.

Etzendorfer, E., & Sonneck, G. (1990). *Suizidprävention: Minimierung medial bedingter imitationseffekte.* Paper presented at the Congress of German Society for Suicide Prevention, Günzburg.

Fekete, S., & Macsai, E. (1990). Hungarian suicidal models—past and present. In G. Ferrari, M. Bellini, & P. Cvepat (Eds.), *Suicidal behaviour and risk factors* (pp. 149–156). Bologna: Monduzzi Editore.

Fekete, S., & Schmidtke, A. (1992). Attitudes towards suicidal behavior in the mass media—analysis of newspaper headlines in Germany and Hungary. 4th European Symposium on Suicidal Behaviour, Odense, Abstract Vol. 40.

Gappmair, B.(1980). *Suizidberichterstattung in der Presse.* Dissertation. Salzburg.

Gould, M., Wallenstein, S., & Davidson, L. (1989). Suicide clusters: A critical review. *Suicide and Life-Threatening Behavior, 19*(1), 17–29.

Jonas, K. (1991). Modeling and suicide: A test of the Werther effect hypothesis. Unpublished manuscript, University of Tübingen.

Kezdi, B. (1989). Negation and suicide. In I. Munnich & B. Kolozsi (Eds.), *The complex investigation of deviant behavior in Hungary* (pp. 61–72). Budapest: Institut for Social Sciences.

Lester, D. (1987). *Suicide as a learned behavior.* Springfield, IL: Charles C Thomas.

Motto, J. (1970). Newspaper influence on suicide: A controlled study. *Archives of General Psychiatry, 23*(2), 143–148.

Niedermaier, C. (1985). *Das Suizid in der Presse. Bewertung, Darstellung und Wirkung des Suizids und der Suizidberichterstattung in der deutschsprachigen Presse von 1975 bis 1984*. Unpublished manuscript, Laudenbach.

Pell, B., & Watters, D. (1982). Newspaper policies on suicide stories. *Canada Mental Health, 30*(4), 8–9.

Phillips, D. (1974). The influence of suggestion on suicide. *American Sociological Review, 94*, 340–354.

Phillips, D. (1990). Suicide and the media: research and policy implication. In René F. W. Diekstra (Ed.), *Preventive strategies on suicide: A World Health Organization state of the art publication* (pp. 1–26).

Platt, S. (1993). The social transmission of suicide:is there a modeling effect? *Crisis, 14*(1), 23–32.

Riaunet, J., Stiles, T. C., Rygnested, T., & Bjerke, T. (1991). Mass media reports of suicide and suicide attempts and the rate of parasuicide. In B. Jerke & T. Stiles (Eds.), *Suicide attempts in the nordic countries* (pp. 157–165), Tapir Forlag.

Schmidtke, A., & Hafner, H. (1989). Public attitudes towards and effects of the mass media on suicidal and deliberate self-harm behavior. In *Suicide and its prevention* (pp. 313–328) Leiden: Brill.

Sonneck, G., Etzensdorfer, E., & Nagel-Kuess, S. (1993). Imitation effect in suicidal behavior: Subway suicide in Vienna. In K. Böhme (Ed.), *Suicidal behavior: The state of the art* (pp. 66–665). Regensburg: Roderer.

Stack, S. (1992). The effect of the media on suicide: The great depression. *Suicide and Life-Threatening Behavior, 22*(2), 255–266.

Taiminen, T. (1992). Projective identification and suicide contagion. *Acta Psychiatrica Scandinavica, 85*, 449–453.

Tantalo, M., & Marchiori, C. (1981). La reppresintazione de suicido della stampa quotidiana. *Rivista Italiana di Medicina Legale, 3*, 405–449.

Welz, R. (1992). Medien und Suizid: Zum Stand der Forschung. *Suizidprophylaxe, 19*, 7–16.

Chapter 12

Monitoring Repeated Suicidal Behavior: Methodological Problems

Unni Bille-Brahe, Gert Jessen, and Børge Jensen

This chapter presents some data and discusses methodological problems in determining the extent to which persons who attempt suicide are likely to have subsequent suicidal behavior. An important issue in understanding the impact of suicide attempts is the issue of the recidivism rate for attempters. [Ed.]

INTRODUCTION

Through the years, many studies have shown that a substantial number of all suicide attempters make more than one attempt at taking their own life, some even developing what we could call a chronic suicidal behavior. The numbers and percentages reported vary, however, a great deal, and for several reasons it is rather problematic to compare the results from the various studies. This is partly due to the fact that the methods of monitoring suicide attempts may differ considerably, and partly since the methods and concepts used are often not sufficiently described. The result is that the "true" magnitude of recidivism is rather obscure.

This is, of course, unfortunate per se, but even more so when we consider how often theories and recommendations as to prediction and assessment, high-risk factors and effects of treatments are founded on studies where recidivism constitutes the dependent variable. The problem is, however, not unique when research within suicidology is concerned; most areas within medicine at large struggle with similar problems.

At the core of the methodological problems, especially as far as recidivism is concerned, is also the banal, but nevertheless apparently common difficulty in discriminating between "events" and "persons" (Søgaard Nielsen et al., 1992). The object of this chapter is, however, restricted to a discussion on how to monitor repeaters and to calculate the frequency of recidivism.

MONITORING REPEATERS

Basicly, recidivism can be monitored by:

A. asking people (e.g., asking patients after an index attempt);
B. follow-up studies of patients admitted during a certain period of time;
C. studies following a number of individual patients from the time of an index attempt and over a period of time.

Generally, in most studies, the method used will be made clear as far as discrimination between A on the one hand, and B or C on the other is concerned. When it comes to discrimination between B and C, however, many studies fail to make clear whether in fact B or C has been used, or to give the details necessary to let the reader discern for himself.

To be able to compare results from various studies, we have, of course, to know which of the methods have been used, but we *also* need to know:

1. the length of the registration period;
2. the length of the period each individual has been followed;
3. whether the index attempt was a first-ever attempt or there had been one (or more) previous attempt(s);
4. whether figures on repeated attempts include all self-destructive acts—that is, acts with lethal *and* non-lethal outcome;
5. whether the sample under study is a special subgroup or it is representative of the population of suicide attempters.

In the following, results from follow-up studies carried out at Odense University will be used to illustrate the importance of these questions.

SAMPLE FROM A DANISH STUDY

In Denmark, suicide attempts resulting in treatment by the health care system are registered in a geographically delimited representative region (the county of Funen). The study is part of a European multicenter study, initiated by WHO in the late 1980s (WHO/Euro: Multicentre Study on Parasuicide) in which the Unit for Suicidological Research at Odense University Hospital, participates together with 16 research centers representing 14 European countries (Platt et al., 1992). The registration of suicide attempts in Funen County started April 1, 1989, and in the following, results based on analyses of data from the three first years of monitoring are presented.

Table 12.1 gives an overview of the frequencies of attempted suicide in the years 1989–1991. The figures include all attempts whether the patient was admitted to a hospital bed, went home after being treated in the emergency ward, or was treated by the local GP only.

It can be seen from the table, that both the number of attempts per year and the number of persons involved have decreased during the period of registration (by 22% and 16%, respectively), and that the ratio events/persons have been slightly decreasing over the years (1,32; 1,27; 1,23).

The figures shown in Table 12.1 do not, however, tell us anything about the actual proportions of one-timers and repeaters—for example, they do not show whether the index attempts happened to be a "first ever" or not.

In our study, the registration schedule comprised a question regarding previous suicide attempt (cf. method A). However, although the information given on the registration schedule could be supplemented by the

TABLE 12.1   Number and Rates of Attempted Suicide 1989–1991: Events and Persons

Attempts	Events		Persons		Repeated
	N	Rates[1]	N	Rates[1]	(in % of all)
1989*	1019	268	773	203	24%
1990**	836	219	659	172	21%
1991***	792	206	646	168	18%

*April 1, 1989–March 31, 1990.
**April 1, 1990–March 31, 1991.
***April 1, 1991–March 31, 1992.
[1]Rates per 100,000 inhabitants 15 years or older.

staff going through available case files and so on, we only succeeded in getting answers to the question of previous suicide attempts in half the cases.

Furthermore, control analyses indicated that the reliability of the data was questionable. From Table 12.2 we can see that too many of those who were asked at their second, third, and so forth, attempt within the year, and therefore should answer to the question about previous suicide attempts with a "yes," in actual fact reported *no*. When pooling all data from the three years, it turned out, that when we cross-checked our material, approximately 10 percent of the repeaters apparently had not wanted to admit to the previous suicidal acts. The retrospective study indicated by method A may then not be sufficiently valid, at least not to be relied upon as the only source of information.

Method B may formally be described as prospective, but in actual fact, most studies of this type are carried out by collecting data retrospectively by going through records and case files. In Table 12.3 is shown a rather common way of presenting results from such studies. The figures show all attempts taking place within a (calendar) year.

This type of calculation indicates a recidivism percentage of 18, 16, and 15, respectively, within each of the three years.

The obvious shortcoming of this type of presentations is, of course, that within each year the follow-up period for the individual suicide attempters varies from 1 to 365 days. Furthermore, only repeated suicidal acts with a non-fatal income are included, that is, persons making one (or more) repeated non-fatal acts during the period before the act with the fatal outcome, are left out—and finally, we are still left with the problem of repetitions in prior and following year(s). Accordingly, the figures underestimate the problem of recidivism.

Turning finally to method C, Table 12.4 shows results from an individual follow-up study of suicidal behavior. Here a number of suicide

TABLE 12.2   Previous Suicide Attempt Reported by One-Timers and Repeaters in the Follow-up Study

	One-timers			Repeaters			All
	Yes	No	Unknown	Yes	No	Unknown	Attempters
1989	158	148	326	64	22	55	773
1990	178	197	182	61	22	19	659
1991	141	100	310	42	9	45	646

TABLE 12.3   Suicide Attempters by Number of Attempts per Year

Repeaters in All	Persons N	1 attempt %	2–3 attempts %	4–5 attempts %	6+ attempts %	%
1989	773	82	15	2	1	18
1990	659	84	14	1.5	0.7	16
1991	646	85	14	0.9	0.4	15

attempters have been followed individually for a period of two years after an index attempt committed in the period April 1, 1989–March 31, 1990. The following material are based upon 773 persons.

To counter the question of underestimation, the figures include attempts with fatal *and* non-fatal outcomes. The implication of this is, on the other hand, that not all persons under study are followed for a full two-year period. When the follow-up study is carried out for a limited time period, for example, two years, the number of fatal events will probably be too small to seriously invalidate the result, but if the study is carried out over a longer period of time and therefore a greater number of completed suicides might be expected, calculation based on probability theories have to be employed if one wants to estimate the effects of such drop-outs.

During the two years, 232 of the 773 attempters (29 percent) repeated the suicidal act at least once; for 24 persons (3 percent) the last repeated act proved fatal. In all, the 773 suicide attempters made 1,267 suicidal acts. Of all repeated acts 98 percent were non-fatal, while 2 percent had a fatal outcome.

As can be seen from Table 12.5., the mortality by suicide apparently was highest among those who repeated the suicidal act once or twice within the two-year follow-up period; twenty-one out of the 24 attempts with fatal outcome (87 percent) were a first- or second-time recidivist.

TABLE 12.4   Repeated Suicidal Behavior During a Two-Year Follow-Up Period After the Index Attempt

N = 773 Persons	Index Attempt Only	1–2 Sui.Act	3–4 Rep. Sui.Act	4+ Rep. Sui.Act	Repeaters in All	Cases with Fatal Outcome
Within the first year	74%	20%	4%	2%	26%	2.7%
Within the two years	71%	22%	4%	3%	29%	3.1%

TABLE 12.5 Outcome After a Two-Year Follow-Up of Suicide Attempters

	Index Attempt Only	1–2 Rep. Sui.Acts	2+ Rep. Sui.Acts	All Attempters
Still alive	501 (93%)	153 (85%)	48 (92%)	702 (91%)
Dead from suicide	0 (—)	21 (12%)	3 (6%)	24 (3%)
Dead from other causes	40 (7%)	6 (3%)	1 (2%)	47 (6%)
Total	541 (100)	180 (100)	52 (100)	773 (100)

The results hitherto presented in Table 12.3–12.5, have been based on the somewhat dubious assumption that the index attempt was a "first ever" attempt. However, as mentioned earlier, reliable information on previous suicidal behavior is not easy to get hold of. In our study, the question whether the index attempt in actual fact was a "first ever" or a repetition after one or more previous attempts could only be unambiguously answered for half of the patients included in the two-year follow-up study (392 attempters).

It can be seen from Table 12.6 that the index attempt was a "first ever" act for less than half of the sample (43%). Two-hundred-twenty-two of the suicide attempters (57%) had made one or more suicidal acts before the attempt that included them in the study. However, of the 170 "first evers," 48 persons made one or more repeats during the follow-up period. That means that of 392 suicide attempters in the sample, 270 persons had attempted suicide more than once, that is, the recidivism frequency was 69 percent.

TABLE 12.6 Repeated Suicidal Acts in the Two-Year Follow-Up Period, and Previous Attempts (In Brackets % of Total Sample)

N = 392	Index Attempt	1–2 Rep. Sui.Acts	3–4 Rep. Sui.Acts	4+ Rep. Sui.Acts	Attempters in All
No previous attempts	122 (31%)	40 (10%)	5 (1,3%)	3 (0,8%)	170 (43%)
One previous attempt	66 (17%)	24 (6%)	3 (0,8%)	0 (—)	93 (24%)
Several previous attempts	58 (15%)	40 (10%)	15 (4,0%)	16 (4,0%)	129 (33%)
Total	246 (63%)	104 (26%)	23 (6%)	19 (5%)	392 (100)

DISCUSSION

The tables presented on p. 161 illustrate clearly that the results from studies on recidivism differ depending on the method used. In our material the various methods yield proportions of repeaters varying from 16 to 67 percent. Most likely the variation would have been even greater if the material had been divided in subgroups consisting of, for instance, patients admitted or not admitted as in-patients (Kreitman et al., 1988) or of various groups distributed by the choice of method (Platt et al., 1988).

The ratio of events to persons is often used as an approximate estimate of the rate of recidivism. A comparison of such estimates presuppose that the periods under study are of the same length (e.g., within one calendar year). Platt and associates (1988) found in their comparative study on parasuicide in Edinburgh and Oxford repetition percentages within each calendar year close to those from our study (24–19 percent). It should be noted, however, that the size of the ratio is dependent among other things of whether or not the material comprises patients with extraordinarily many attempts. For instance, in our material from 1991 one person accounted for 14 of the 796 attempts registered that year. It should also be noted that some attempters may repeat the attempt some time during the *following* years.

Using method A, and basing calculation of recidivism on information regarding previous suicidal behavior, forms part of many studies (Bancroft et al., 1977, Kreitman et al., 1988, Morgan et al., 1975). Usually the information is obtained in connection with an index attempt via interviews, sometimes through archive material or in a combination of the two methods, and we are, in short, talking about *retrospective* studies. Missing values might then easily be a problem. In our material, unambiguous answers to the question of previous suicide attempts could (in spite of the research team checking the material by going through files, etc.) be found for only half the attempters registered. Preliminary analyses indicated that these do not constitute a representative sample of our total population of suicide attempters; for instance, missing values were less likely to be found among attempters admitted to a hospital bed for treatment, and among attempters with a history of psychiatric disease. Probably there is also a greater likelihood of having answers from those who repeatedly have been in contact with the health system, be it because of a suicide attempt or for some other reason (Kessel et al., 1966).

Results from our study also indicate that not all people like to admit that they previously have tried to commit suicide. About 10 percent of those we *knew* had made at least one previous attempt, denied the fact. In their study, Bancroft and associates (1977) found that 36 percent of a group of interviewed suicide attempters had made a previous attempt—but after checking the figures, they calculated that the frequency of recidivism was underestimated by approximately 13 percent. In a Danish interview study from 1980, 66 percent of the attempters reported previous suicide attempts; however, the material in that study consisted of attempters admitted to a hospital bed (Bille-Brahe et al., 1982).

The importance of the question of previous suicide attempts is, of course, evident, see, for example, the study by Hassanyeh and colleagues (1989), who show that the only items in which repeaters and non-repeaters significantly differed were past history of deliberate self-harm in the repeaters. One way to solve the problem is, of course, to complete follow-up studies only on first-timers (Blumenthal et al., 1989, Siani et al., 1979).

As pointed out by Kreitman and Casey (1988), the discrimination between those who have made more than one suicide attempt (repeaters), and those who have not (first evers) should be followed by a study of subsequent suicidal behavior. However, whether or not information about previous suicidal behavior is employed (Goldacre et al., 1985), the main problem when conducting follow-up studies concerns the length of the time under study—and the discrimination between method B and method C. A related issue is the question of the the proportion of drop-outs. The feasibility of tracing patients depends upon, among other things, the local registration of patients, the census system, and on the local pattern of geographic mobility.

When the design is a comparative study concurrently carried out on two or more groups, the problems are of minor, if of any importance, as long as the groups are followed over the same period of time (Brent et al., 1993, Bronisch & Hecht, 1992). However, when only one group of persons is under study, it is of vital importance that the time period each individual can be followed is of more or less the same length. It has been argued, that as far as recidivism is concerned, the problem is of minor importance if the (average) follow-up period is very short, for example, 6 months, as most fatal and non-fatal repetitions take place shortly after, and usually within the first year after the initial attempt (Kreitman & Casey, 1988, Nielsen et al., 1989).

There is a problem, however, concerning the correspondence between the registration period and the follow-up period. For example: suicide attempters admitted to a hospital during one year are registered, and a "follow-up study" carried out 6 months later. The average follow-up period is then nine months, a length of time that should cover the high-risk period after the initial attempt. However, only some of the patients have been followed for this average period of time—some have been followed for 18 months, others for only 6 months. The problem grows more and more complex the longer the registration period. Thus the length of the registration period (e.g., the period during which the potential subjects enter the study) is pertinent: the longer the registration period, the longer the follow-up period has to be (Dahlgren, 1977; Zonda, 1991). A follow-up study of patients admitted to a hospital during, say, a ten-year period, requires, if one wants to follow all patients over a similar length of time, another ten years to complete the study. One has to be aware that the problem of tracing the patients increases with the length of the follow-up period, thus making the description of the drop-out more difficult.

Some studies exist, however, where the individual follow-up periods vary from one day to several years. In such studies, the follow-up period is usually given as some "average" or "mean" follow-up period (Brauns & Berzewski, 1988, Klasen et al., 1989, Sellar et al., 1990).

Also of importance is the length of time between ending the registration and beginning the follow-up. If the follow-up starts immediately after the registration has been completed, the difficulties mentioned above will be even more disturbing (Kotila et al., 1988). In the sample described above, the average follow-up period would then be somewhat shorter, namely 6 months, but the individual follow-up period would vary from 1 to 365 days. In some studies, data for the follow-up study have been collected at the end of or soon after the registration is completed, and the individual follow-up periods therefore vary from 1 day to 10 years (Fisker et al., 1993). In short, whenever an "on the average" length of the follow-up is reported, be it 6 months, 3.6 years or 11.6 years, caution is recommended when evaluating and comparing results from follow-up studies.

In a five-year follow-up study on Danish suicide attempters (Nielsen et al., 1990), it was shown that of 207 patients admitted to the hospital during a six-month period in 1980/1981, 27 percent made at least one more (non-fatal) attempt during the five years after the index attempt. The results are rather close to the results from our study as they were presented in Table 12.4 (p. 160). However, the figures on repeated attempts reported by Nielsen and associates only include the non-fatal repeated suicidal acts. Adding acts with a fatal outcome (in all 24 or 11,6%), the proportion of repeaters increased to 38 percent.

The difference between the two studies in the frequency of fatal suicidal acts may be explained by the fact that the material in the study of Nielsen and colleagues consists of cases where there had been indications for admission, while our study also includes cases that have been assessed as not so serious (for instance, cases where the attempter could go home after being treated in the emergency ward).

Taking into consideration the frequency of previous suicide attempts, the authors conclude that, of the 207 patients, 138 had made previous suicide attempt(s) and/or repeated the suicidal act during the follow-up period—that is, 67 percent were repeaters. In spite of the fact that the material in Nielsen and colleagues' study presumably represented a higher risk group, the frequency of recidivism is identical with our results ten years later.

CONCLUSION

In this chapter we have tried to show that in studies on recidivism, the choice of method may affect the results to a considerable degree. In our sample various methods are employed on the same material with the result that the percentage of repeaters varies from 15–18 to 67 percent. Reviewing only a small part of the literature, it becomes clear that results concerning the magnitude of repeated suicide attempts very often are impossible to compare. One should be particularly aware that in many studies on repeated suicidal behavior the frequency of recidivism is underrated, and thereby the seriousness of the problem tends to be underestimated.

REFERENCES

Bancroft, J., & Marsack, P. (1977). The repetitiveness of self-poisoning and self-injury. *British Journal of Psychiatry, 131,* 394–399.

Bille-Brahe, U., Kolmos, L., Hansen, W., Parnas, W., & Wang, A.,G. (1982). *Suicide attempts in Funen, 1980–81.* (Report No. DDA-401). Odense: Danish Data Archives.

Blumenthal, S., Bell, V., Neumann, N. U., Schüttler, R., & Vogel, R. (1989). Mortality and rate of suicide of first admission psychiatric patients. *Psychopathology, 22,* 50–56.

Brauns, M. L., & Berzewski, H. (1988). Follow-up study of patients with attempted suicide. *International Journal of Social Psychiatry, 34*(4), 285–291.

Brent, D. A., Kolko, D. J., Wartella, M. E., Boylan, M. B., Moritz, G., Baugher, M., & Zelenak, J. P. (1993). Adolescent psychiatric inpatients' risk of suicide attempt at 6-month follow-up. *Journal of the American Academy of Child and Adolescent Psychiatry, 32*(1), 95–105.

Bronisch, T., & Hecht, H. (1992). Prospective long-term follow-up of depressed patients with and without suicide attempts. *European Archives of Psychiatry and Clinical Neurosciences, 242,* 13–19.

Dahlgren, K. G. (1977). Attempted suicide—35 years afterward. *Suicide and Life Threatening Behavior, 7*(2), 75–79.

Fisker, N. J., & Klint Andersen, P. (1993). Dødsfald efter tidligere bevidst selvforgiftning—et tiårs materiale fra en intensivafdeling. (English summary). *Ugeskr Læger, 155*(24), 1857–1861.

Goldacre, M., & Hawton, K. (1985). Repetition of self-poisoning and subsequent death. *British Journal of Psychiatry, 146,* 395–398.

Hassanyeh, F., O'Brian, G., Holton, A. R., Hurren, K., & Watt, L. (1989). Repeat self-harm: An 18 month follow-up. *Acta Psychiatrica Scandinavica, 79,* 265–267.

Kessel, N., & McCulloch, W. (1966). Repeated acts of selfpoisoning and self-injury. *Proceedings of the Royal Society of Medicine, 59,* 9–12.

Klasen, H. J., Tempel, G. L., van der Hekert, J., & Savër, F. W. (1989). Attempted suicide by means of burns. *Burns, 15*(7), 88–92.

Kotila, L., & Lönnqvist, J. (1988). Adolescent suicide attempts: sex differences predicting suicide. *Acta Psychiatrica Scandinavica, 77,* 264–270.

Kreitman, N., & Casey, P. (1988). Repetition of parasuicide. *British Journal of Psychiatry, 153,* 792–800.

Morgan, H. G., Burn-Cox, C. J., Pocock, H., & Pottle, S. (1975). Deliberate self-harm: Clinical and socio-economic characteristics of 368 patients. *British Journal of Psychiatry, 127,* 564–574.

Nielsen, B., Wang, A. G., & Bille-Brahe, U. (1990). Attempted suicide in Denmark. IV. A five-year follow-up. *Acta Psychiatrica Scandinavica, 81,* 250–254.

Platt, S., Bille-Brahe, U., Kerkhof, A., Schmidtke, A., Bjerke, T., Crepet, P., De Leo, D., Haring, C., Lønnqvist, J., Michel, K., Phillipe, A., Pommereau, X., Querejeta, I., Salander-Renberg, E., Temesvary, B., Wasserman, D., & Sampaio Faria, J. (1992). Parasuicide in Europe: The WHO/Euro multicentre study on parasuicide. I. Introduction and preliminary analysis for 1989. *Acta Psychiatrica Scandinavica, 85,* 97–104.

Platt, S., Hawton, K., Kreitman, N., Fagg, J., & Foster, J. (1988). Recent clinical and epidemiological trends in parasuicide in Edinburgh and Oxford: A tale of two cities. *Psychological Medicine, 18,* 405–418.

Sellar, C., Hawton, K., & Goldacre, M. J. (1990). Selfpoisoning in adolescents. Hospital admissions and deaths in the Oxford region 1980–85. *British Journal of Psychiatry, 156,* 866–870.

Siani, R., Garzotto, N., Zimmermann Tansella, C., & Tansella, M. (1979). Predictive scales for parasuicide repetition. *Acta Psychiatrica Scandinavica, 59,* 17–23.

Søgaard Nielsen, A., Nielsen, B., & Bille-Brahe, U. (1992). Selvforgiftninger og præparatvalg. Bør undersøgelser baseres på henvendelser eller patienter. *Nord Journal of Psychiatry, 46*(3), 195–199.

Zonda, T. (1991). A longitudinal follow-up study of 583 attempted suicides, based on Hungarian material. *Crisis, 12*(1), 48–57.

Part IV

The Impact of Suicide and Society

Chapter 13

The Impact of Suicide on Society

Robert Kastenbaum

This chapter considers the impact of suicide on society within the broader perspective of the death system. The impact of suicide is shown to be mediated by our basic ideas concerning death and the particular nature of death by suicide within the system. [Ed.]

The professional staff of a large mental hospital decided that it was time to devote one of its regular conference hours to the discussion of suicide. A doctoral student at a local university was known to have some interest in this topic. Would he be willing to lead the discussion? Yes, of course, he would. The appointed day arrived, and so did the discussion leader. He was met by several very anxious people. "There will be no meeting today," he was told. "We cannot talk about . . . about *that*." But why could they not talk about . . . *that*? "Haven't you heard?" The staff could not possibly discuss suicide because the director of the hospital had just taken his own life. This incident provided an early lesson in the impact of suicide on society for that young man,[1] and a source of continuing instruction for us all.

---

1. Brian L. Mishara, director of the Montreal conference and editor of this book.

First, we learn something about one of society's most entrenched lines of defense, the mental hospital. Institutionalization is not an especially successful technique for preventing suicide, even among the garrison who serve in this outpost. In fact, psychiatrists are at greater risk for suicide than the population at large whether they are employed in an institution or the community (Esposito, Consiglio, & Petrone, 1987). As a line of defense, institutionalization is also a cumbersome and expensive enterprise that falls short of preventing self-destructive actions even during the hospital stay. In fact, "suicide epidemics" (Talminin et al., 1992) are sometimes generated within the institution itself.

Second, we learn something about the anxiety of society at large. It is this anxiety that has kept the mental hospital with us so long despite its limitations and defects. It is this anxiety that the mental hospital holds in check by stereotyping, distancing, compartmentalizing, concealing, and silencing. The agonized spirit, the disordered mind, and the impulsive action must be removed from the mainstream of communal life.

Michel Foucault (1965) has demonstrated that places of confinement have been with us since the rise of cities. These places were nearly always set off from the primary zones of social interaction. Even today, many a state hospital in the United States impersonates a medieval fortress as it deteriorates majestically on its once forbidding hilltop. Foucault also reports that society has repeatedly changed its mind about what kind of person should be "put away" (e.g., lepers, epileptics, insane, impoverished, etc.). What has not changed that much is the anxiety and the fantasy: the anxiety occasioned by encountering people whom we perceive as different from ourselves, and the fantasy that this anxiety can be controlled by physical and symbolic distancing.

One does not need the history books, however, to see that this process is still active. I served part of a clinical internship in a fortress-like building that had been built to house tuberculosis patients back in the days when "consumption" (tuberculosis) was the most terrifying of diseases. The building had since been restocked with mental patients who were thought to pose risks to themselves and the community. All these people had once been well enough integrated into the community to serve in the armed forces, and many had experienced combat. The most articulate of these men considered themselves to be captives in a prison. This idea was not entirely delusional, considering the locked doors and unremitting confinement. Those particular individuals are no longer threats to society. They have grown old or perished. But what is to be done with the empty beds inside the fortress? Why not restock the building with people who are infected with HIV and possible risks for infecting others? This proposal was made; fortunately it was rejected. However, if nature really does abhor a vacuum, then society seems to abhor vacant beds in its fortresses on the hill. Proposals to raze such fortresses to the ground tend to be put on indefinite hold: who knows when there may be some other people who have to be put away—for their own good, of course?

And so, the fears, the faces, and the diagnoses change, but the beat goes on. Society feels that it can sleep a little better at night if there is a solid wall between itself and its more unpredictable neighbors.

Silence is the interpersonal manifestation of this wall. "We cannot talk about . . . about *that!*" And so, what is society to think? The commander of the fortress committed treason. He chose death over the uncertainties and sorrows of life. If such an impressive person is vulnerable to suicide, then how can we ordinary people cope with our despair? And if his companions in the garrison enforce the rule of silence, then how can we be expected to examine our own anxieties in open discourse? In fact, why should we take mental health experts seriously when they invite us to "talk about it"?

The ordinary citizen may be in a predicament after observing this failure of the experts. How should one respond to suicide? Perhaps it would be best to maintain that nothing happened. Yes, that's it! Nothing happened, therefore there is nothing that needs to be said about the nothing that did not happen. It follows logically (?) that if we are careful not to think and not to talk about it, then this nothing that did not happen perhaps will not happen again. Tortured logic is more comforting than no logic at all! And it is infinitely preferable to recognizing that the danger may arise as much from the inside as the outside—that society perhaps has more to fear from its own destructive impulses than from those unfortunates who have been stricken by leprosy, tuberculosis, madness, or AIDS. And yet, we cannot turn away from this recognition: *We will never understand the impact of suicide on society by limiting ourselves to the impact of suicide on society.*

SUICIDE AND THE DEATH SYSTEM

On this day in the United States about 80 people will take their own lives—but physicians will be certifying about 6,000 deaths. We must consider the suicidal deaths within the contexts of all the deaths. It would be naive to assume that society's response to suicide is independent of its orientation toward death in general. It would also be naive to assume a simple and predictable relationship between an act known as suicide and an outcome known as death. Had the mental hospital director died suddenly of heart disease, stroke, or accident, the staff would still have experienced an emotional impact and would still have had to adjust their responsibilities. In any particular situation the response to a suicidal death may be weighted more heavily toward the act or the outcome. It is not unusual for the act—the self-destructure gesture—to have more impact on society than the outcome as such.

The impact of suicide on society is most usefully considered within a broader perspective. Every society has a *death system* that encompasses all of the society's physical, relational, and symbolic interactions with mortality (Kastenbaum, 1991). Through identifying the components and functions of the death system, we improve our chances of understanding the rules by which the system operates, and therefore also better improve our chances of introducing constructive changes. Suicidal thoughts and actions can be seen not as isolated and incomprehensible events, but as options within a society's overall death system of coming to terms with life and death.

Consider first the major *components* of the death system. Begin with *people*. Some people are officially enrolled in the death system, for example, funeral directors, coroners, and pest exterminators. Many others work for death without portfolio. This list includes life (i.e., death) insurance representatives, attorneys who busy themselves with trusts, wills, and estates, florists, gun manufacturers, butchers, and on and on. Most people are involved indirectly in the death system on a daily basis and occasionally find themselves right in the middle of the action. And absolutely everybody is a potential and eventual recruit into the death system.

Animals are also part of the death system. The can of pet food we offer to our furry little friends is itself filled with animal products; the faithful hunting dog helps its master to bag his limit of ducks; the image of a white shark has sold millions of dollars in movie tickets. Researchers who "sacrifice" animals in their laboratories during the work day may come home to romp with their pets. Broken relationships between humans and their animal companions result in the execution of tens of thousands of former household pets each day at the hands of highly stressed workers in animal shelters. Whether or not this is "mercy killing," it is surely killing. Perhaps the ambivalence or double-edged sword of the death system is seen most clearly in its relationship to animals.

Other components include *places*, *times*, and *objects* that have become identified with death. The cemetery, the memorial anniversary, and the smoking gun are obvious examples of each. What tests our powers of observation is the continual process of transformation in which "innocent" places, times, and objects become associated with particular meanings of death, or through which traditional meanings may be altered. For example, the golden arches of a fast food restaurant in California became so intensely associated with a mass murder that the parent company decided to tear it down and convert the space into a memorial park. Memorial Days in the

United States continue to be marked on the calendar, but the winds of change have long since swept away much of its meaning to the general populace. And yet a wall engraved with the names of those who died in Vietnam continues to have a profound effect.

This brings us to *symbols*. Words, gestures, images, and every communicational device available to society can represent death-related thoughts, feelings, and actions. For example, Dr. Jack Kevorkian (1991) recently coined the term *"medicide"* to denote an action that others have variously called "euthanasia," "assisted suicide," "deliverance," or "murder." (Parenthetically, from the standpoint of word origins, "medicide," actually refers to the killing of doctors, not the doctor's snuffing of patients.) All these terms refer to the same action, but society's interpretation of this action will be influenced by which of the terms wins most widespread acceptance. Years ago, The Euthanasia Education Society changed its name to Concern for Dying in order to avoid being misinterpreted. Compassion in Dying is the name selected by a new Seattle-based group (Ostrom, 1993) that supports the legalization of assisted suicide. Members of both groups are well aware that the public responds to names and symbols as well as actions and therefore emphasize concern and compassion rather than actions with lethal consequences.

CONFLICTING SYMBOLS AND INTERPRETATIONS

How society should respond to suicide is an issue that has stimulated the generation and conflict of symbols from the earliest times. This conflict is still very much with us. For example, the suicide prevention movement in the United States found its crusading banner in a phrase popularized by Norman Farberow and Edwin S. Shneidman (1961): *"the cry for help."* The image of a cry for help suggests a person in danger who has an urgent desire for rescue. It also implies other images that have strong impact—such as a person who is drowning and must have a helping hand immediately. A society that accepts the cry-for-help image will have the impulse to prevent the death of its companion in jeopardy, and will regret those occasions when it had failed to recognize the danger or to respond effectively.

By contrast, the image of a *"balance sheet"* is receiving increasing attention by activists and the media, although the idea has been around since at least 1919 when German psychiatrist Alfred Hoche (cited by Choron, 1972) recognized that some people take their lives after a process of calm, logical deliberation. This image has strong roots in Euro-American society. If "time is money," then perhaps one should not invest further in a life that is no longer profitable. This image also seems compatible with *disengage-*

ment theory, still perhaps the best known theory in the field of social gerontology. Disengagement theory (1961) asserts that as people grow older, both the individual and society engage in a pattern of mutual withdrawal. This process establishes a greater distance between the older person and society in general, and reduces the elder's sense of obligation. The disengagement process is characterized as inevitable and universal. "Balance-sheet suicide" might then be considered a natural continuation of this process. When the burden of age and loss exceeds one's attenuated connection to society, wouldn't it be logical to make that final entry in and that final exit from the ledger book?

The cry for help and the balance sheet symbolizations of suicide differ radically from earlier images in which suicide was portrayed as a crime against society and a sin against God (1991). The individual is said to have no right to dispose of his/her own life. Perhaps the most influential statement is among the earliest. Augustine of Hippo (later St. Augustine) argued in the fifth century that "Christians have no authority for committing suicide in any circumstances whatever. It is not without significance, that in no passage of the holy canonical books there can be found either divine precept or permission to take away our own life, whether for the sake of entering on the enjoyment of immortality, or of shunning, or ridding ourselves of anything whatever. Nay, the law, rightly, interpreted, even prohibits suicide, where it says, 'Thou shalt not kill'" (Augustine, ca. 400).

Augustine's argument was not only forceful, but forced by circumstance. He knew that many Christians had in fact sought martyrdom in imitation of Jesus and "for the sake of entering on the enjoyment of immortality." For centuries there had been a suicidal-like tendency within Christianity that Augustine and other spiritual leaders attempted to discourage. This was not an easy task, however, because the holy books had provided striking examples of approved self-destructive and sacrificial actions. Augustine therefore had to prohibit suicide while at the same time defending such events as Samson's combined suicide and murder of his foes and Jephthah's compliance with God's command that he kill his daughter as a consequence of victory of battle. Many others since Augustine have attempted to find a basis for denying the right of suicide to individuals on the basis of religious or societal principles, while at the same time approving of other forms of killing.

The earlier images still retain some potency, although suicide has been largely decriminalized in the United States and many other nations, and is more likely to be regarded as a cry for help than an expression of sinful impulses. How we respond to suicide obviously owes something to the symbolic constructions that our society has made available to us and the choices we make among these interpretations.

FUNCTIONS OF THE DEATH SYSTEM

Now we come to the *functions* of the death system. All societies rely on their death systems to perform certain critical functions. There are many ways in which these functions can be performed, but the essential tasks and challenges exist in all societies. The death system attempts to carry out seven major functions (Kastenbaum, 1991):

- To protect society from the threat of death by warnings and predictions
- To prevent death
- To care for the dying
- To dispose of the dead
- To ensure social consolidation after death
- To make sense of death
- *To kill.*

Obviously, if society's warning and prediction systems were more efficient, there would be less need to prevent death in those who are already stricken, or to care for the dying, dispose of the dead, and so on. Just as obviously, however, no society can succeed completely in meeting these challenges, although all must try. Anthropologists have observed that the viability of a society is closely related to its continued ability to mediate its members' physical and symbolic relationships to death. A society that abandons its funeral rituals and its care of the dead appears well on the way to dissolution. And a society that has no operative rules and customs regarding suicide—*but* who has ever heard of such a society!

Three points about these functions are worth keeping in mind. First, the functions of the death system are interrelated. Second, they are subject to the society's prevailing traditions and customs. Third, they are subject to change over time. Here is an example. A widow in her sixties had seen her husband die a painful and lingering death with chronic obstructive pulmonary disease. He seldom complained. In fact, he seldom said anything to anybody. But his distress seemed to have been intensified by one useless invasive procedure after another. She had heard about an alternative approach known as hospice or palliative care. In a quiet and deferential manner, she asked their physician if it might be time to emphasize comfort and symptom relief rather than subject her husband to further invasive procedures. The doctor told her to mind her own business. His business was to do everything possible to keep his patient alive.

The widow-to-be lost this brief skirmish of cure versus care. Her response was to light up even more cigarettes. Now her own lung disease was becoming impossible to ignore. She could not bear the thought of suffering as her husband did, nor did she wants to be squashed again by the doctor. What was left for her? Suicide presented itself as the least unacceptable alternative.

This episode featured the culturally endorsed roles of the physician as an authority figure, and the wife as an obedient auxiliary whose own ideas and wishes did not count for much. It also resonated with the current tension in our value system between the priorities of curing and caring. Each of these priorities, in turn, can be understood within a larger cultural and historical context. Do we still live at the dawning of a scientific-industrial epoch that licenses unlimited aggressive actions to bring the world into conformance with our ambitions? If so, then perhaps the physician represented society well in his insistence on firing every round in every cannon at Enemy Death. Or do we perhaps live in what have some have called postindustrial or postmodern society, a society the highest priority is accorded to communication, understanding, and a renewed harmony with planet Earth? If the truth lies in this corner, then perhaps death is simply a limiting condition that one should accept along with the gift of life. To use the commercial analogy, it is just part of the cost of doing business. Within this perspective, a person would not be thought politically incorrect in preferring support and comfort to relentless and invasive treatment.

Interestingly, there is some evidence to suggest that both health care professionals and the general public may be divided within themselves with respect to aggressive medical procedures. Respondents to a series of hypothetical situations favored intensive treatment for a demented aged patient with life-threatening gastrointestinal bleeding—but only if that person were a stranger to them. If a person in that condition belonged to their own family—or happened to be themselves—they were inclined to oppose intensive treatment as being inappropriate and overly aggressive (Darzins et al., 1993). Physicians, for example, were more than twice as likely to recommend palliative rather than intensive care when the situation involved themselves as when it did a person not previously known to them. Our attitudes obviously have much to do with our relationship to the person whose life and death are at stake.

WHY IS SOCIETY OPPOSED TO SUICIDE—SOMETIMES?

There are many possible relationships between a society's overall death system and its response to suicide. Several will be touched on here. It may be useful first to acknowledge that directionality and causality tend to be fig leaves of our imagination. Do we ever see suicide operating as an independent effect on society? Or society operating as an independent effect on the individual? I think not. What we do encounter is a continuous, complex, and multilevel interaction between social influence and individual behavior. If we are interested in real people in real societies (as distinguished from theoretical models), then we must respect the interconnectedness and the ongoingness, and we must exercise caution in pursuing discrete "causes" and "effects."

Society is passionately opposed to suicide: sometimes. This opposition and its exceptions derive from society's basic conceptions of life and death. Here are some reasons why.

First reason: Killers don't like competition. We touch here on a function of the death system that often escapes notice. Warning, predicting, and preventing death, caring for the dying, and helping the bereaved to reintegrate themselves into society are the functions that usually receive the most attention. With respect to suicide, for example, we attempt to identify people who may be at particular risk, introduce effective interventions, and, when these efforts have failed, try to provide support to those who have been bereaved.

Death by suicide often intensifies the felt need to *explain*, which we have already noted as another function of the death system. The need to make sense of death includes coming up with a satisfying explanation of why this death occurred and occurred in this particular manner. It also includes explaining death in general. Death in the particular and death in the universal often arouse different feelings and motivations and require different cognitive frames. What does society want from both facets of the explanation? Society needs a story that it can live with, a story that strengthens its ability to believe in itself and keep going despite the loss of individual after individual.

Anxiety increases when there is no ready explanation. This is the case with many suicides, as, for example, the unexpected demise of the hospital director that has already been mentioned. Suicide is likely to stimulate an urgent effort either to agree on a quick and simple explanation, or agree to compartmentalize and deny (the nothing that nothing needs to be said about).

It is one thing, however, to seek the individual's reason for suicide and another to discover why society is often so dead-set against self-destruction. *This is where killing comes in.* All societies engage in a give-and-take between the forces of life and death. In ancient times, fertility was ensured not only by sacrifices to the gods, but also often by symbolically sacrificing the gods themselves, along with the ritual murder of humans and animals. Monarchs, commanders, and priests have long asserted their authority by claiming power over both life and death. "I will feed you, I will protect you, I will lead you to glory, I will see that the gods look favorably upon you. But if you disobey or displease me—or if I just happen to be in the mood for a little bloodshed—why, then, I will have you killed!"

The emergence of constitutional law altered the terms of this arrangement, but not the arrangement itself. Whether expressed through the caprices of an absolute tyrant or through the deliberations of an obsessive legal system, the state reserves to itself the power to inflict death. We do not want to ignore some remarkable changes that have been occurring in many nations, notably the eradication of the death penalty. This voluntary restraint upon society's death-dealing powers deserves further attention in other forums. In the larger picture, however, society still tends to reserve for itself the right to take a life, whether by due process, war, or denial of the resources needed for survival.

I am suggesting that suicide is always a potential threat to society's monopoly on killing. And I am suggesting that suicide becomes a more salient threat when society believes that it is is under serious attack by divisive and rebellious forces. Consider any society of your choice. How confident is this society of its continued viability? How secure is its establishment? How faithfully does the populace honor its institutions and traditional values? If, upon reflection, this society appears to be in trouble, than its leadership will probably feel especially threatened by conspicuous acts of suicide, unless these acts are of the altruistic kind (i.e., a person seems to have given his/her life "for the cause").

The perceived threat will be intensified when suicide is accompanied by supportive symbols and rhetoric. It is possible to overlook the occasional suicide. The establishment, however, cannot feel comfortable when individual acts of self-destruction are presented as examples of an alternative point of view, each death challenging the official rhetoric as well as the state monopoly on killing. This was true when the Romans were embarrassed and infuriated by the insistence of Christians for martydom, and it is true today when people who still have life in them invite a Kevorkian to arrange for the extinction of that life. If doctors win the death franchise, then all the state really has left is taxation.

Suicide is feared and resented because it transfers power from society to the individual. It is true that suicidal individuals do not retain the stolen power. They demonstrate, however, the vulnerability of the regime. It is not the death that disturbs. It is the affront, the threat, the act of assertion, the act of defiance, the act of self-empowerment. Often the corpse that incites a growl of fear and rage from society would have brought only a shrug to the massive shoulders of society had the death certificate specified illness or accident rather than suicide.

In most instances, the death of old people is barely acknowledged. As director of a hospital for aged men and women I saw how little society at large cared about how they lived and died. State officials—those with the most legal responsiblty for the hospital—cared least. I saw these dynamics in situation after situation, as when touring other geriatric facilities to evaluate their custodial and therapeutic programs. Some staff members cared—a lot! State officials, the community at large, and even elderly peer advocacy organizations cared little.

The *suicide* of old people is a different matter. Suicide does not make an aged man or woman any "deader" than pneumonia or, for that matter, the loss of the will to live. But again, it is the act of self-empowerment that upsets society's equanimity. This position was articulated again recently in *Setting Limits*, an influential book by Daniel Callahan (1987). Health care in old age is where the limits are to be set. When a person has reached his or her "natural" life span, then society should no longer waste its costly health care resources on that person. As it turns out, the "natural" life span is whatever Callahan says that it is.

The most revealing part of this argument comes when the author acknowledges that some people might think of suicide as an escape. Escape from what? Escape from a situation in which they had lived too long, were experiencing too much suffering and disability, and were now—with Callahan's assistance—being denied resources from the society to which they had contributed for so many years. *But suicide must be denied to these people as well.* Why not suicide when ravaged by age and abandoned by society? Because to sanction suicide would be to establish "a special benefit for the aged." Suicide—a special benefit! Callahan explains that if we made an exception for old people by countenancing their suicide, why, we all would want this concession whenever our lives seem flat, weary, stale, and unprofitable. By implication, society's monopoly over killing would come to an end, seriously compromising the power of the group over the individual.

The second reason also offers much to dislike. *Suicide of the other person leads to a sympathetic vibration within ourselves.* This is true for society as well as the individual. In anger, in frustration, in disappointment, in despair, in confusion there is often an impulse to put an end to what pains us. This sense of relief can be achieved, or so it may seem, either by obliterating the situation or obliterating our capacity for experiencing the situation. Suicide is only one of several options. It may be possible, for example, to redefine the situation through political or religious rhetoric or through outright fantasy and therefore alleviate the felt distress. On the other hand, it may be more in keeping with the social organization's *modus operandi* to lash out and attack some convenient external target. This type of response, of course, brings us back to society as a licensed killer.

The suicide option is explored and tested by organizations more often than we might imagine. Some clinicians have become very skillful in identifying increased suicidal risk of individuals. *We need to develop parallel skills in identifying increased suicidal risk within groups and organizations.* Let us invite organizational consultants to share their observations and insights with suicidologists. We will quickly improve our sensitivity to self-destructive patterns within athletic teams, performing ensembles, educational programs, private corporations, public agencies, military units, and both national and international governing bodies. It is possible that the self-destructive patterns that can be discerned in some individuals also will reveal themselves on an organizational level, but that remains to be determined by systematic research.

Human organizations from the micro to the macro level are capable of committing themselves to a deliberate self-destructive course of action. Close analysis of failures in sports and business, for example, will sometimes reveal that the pattern of collapse has involved a suicidal intent. It would be understandable if we should decide to resist this unfamiliar idea for a while. It would be more useful, however, to undertake careful and open-minded observations of organizational processes, especially their patterns of communication. We will see that organizations as well as individuals frequently are tempted to exercise the suicidal option.

How often and under what circumstances society itself becomes suicidal is one of the monster questions of our times, even though it has seldom received direct attention. This is a monster we dare not arouse within the limits of the present discussion. Our point for now is simply that the vulnerability, the temptation, do exist.

This temptation can be intensified when individual acts of suicide occur while an organization is struggling to maintain its esteem and integrity. Not all acts of suicide are equally threatening, just as not all deaths are perceived as equal losses. Society lets us know when it feels alarmed by its own suicidal tendencies. One way society has for doing this is to come down hard on individual suicides that have particular resonance, for example, the impact of the suicide of Pierre Beregovy, the recently ousted premier of France, on the Socialist Party in France, which was already suffering from a defeat in the elections. Perhaps either the individual or the group can set the example for the other.

Third reason: Society—you study, lament, and attack suicide because this activity provides a marvelous distraction. Suicide offers an almost perfect diversion from death. The pattern expresses itself more or less like this:

- Neither individuals nor society willingly contemplate death. When such contemplation is forced upon us by circumstances, we tend to muck around for a little while with received clichés and images until we find our escape in action or fantasy.

- It is more convenient and less anxiety-provoking to keep death "out there" as an external force or enemy, rather than to live with the realization that death is ever our intimate companion.
- Preliterate societies typically sought external causes for death, especially the deaths of their most important people. Tracking down and killing the suspected sorcerer or assailant provided an excellent diversion and good exercise as well.
- Twentieth-century industrialized societies have continued to demonstrate their own versions of this thought process. We see this in the conspiracy theories that follow so often upon the death of an important person. And we see it in the observations made by Englishman Geoffrey Gorer (1965). He detected what he called a "pornography of death" in the prevailing social customs and media.

Gorer described a parallel between the ways in which society has decided to communicate to itself about death and sex. His observations were made about thirty years ago, at a time when hospice care and the death awareness movement were in their infancy, while sexuality had just burst exuberantly from its long period of restraint, so exuberantly that one might have thought sex had just then been invented.

Gorer made the subtle observation that society was being highly selective and rather perverse in its choices within the realms of both sex and death. There was plenty of kinky and sensationalistic sex and plenty of violent death. And he might have added, as one can still notice today, there was plenty of kinky sex together with violent death. He notes that "In both types of fantasy, the emotions which are typically concomitant of the acts— love or grief—are paid little or no attention, while the sensations are enhanced as much as a customary poverty of language permits." In other words, *a process of depersonalization and decontextualization has accompanied contemporary society's flirtations with both sex and death*. Bodies are displayed graphically and provocatively and bodies do things to bodies. Instead of being integral parts of the lives of real people, sex and death become items of their own that have some power to command attention and, therefore, sell products.

Suicide was never the prime example of the pornography of death, although vivid and bloody examples would qualify. Furthermore, suicidology as a field of education, research, and service has not embraced pornography. Nevertheless, suicide has recommended itself as a focus for concern precisely because it is *not* everyday, inevitable, "natural" death.

We can face deaths without having to face death. The traditional fantasy is still playing itself out: if we could only prevent suicide, why, then, we would really have Old Man Death up a tree, wouldn't we?

Think of how society welcomed suicidologists at the same time that it was still repulsing attempts to comfort people dying "natural deaths" or experiencing grief. Think of how much attention suicidology has given over the years to antecedents and circumstances of the act, and how little attention to its outcome, death. While you are at it, think of the entire death awareness movement: how often and in what depth is attention actually given to death (Kastenbaum, 1993)? Even philosophers have distracted themselves from the basic proposition that "Man is mortal" and have preferred instead to dabble in medical and legislative decision-making. There are certainly necessary and sufficient reasons to engage in suicide prevention, intervention, and postvention. But the drive that leads to a concentration on suicide also draws upon that relentless engine of death anxiety and that robust fantasy that we can restrict mortality to the role of misfortune or misjudgment.

To rephrase the answer, then: society invites us to attack suicide as a diversion from the anxiety-provoking personal confrontation with death.

There are exceptions to society's aversion to suicide: when the right kind of people commit the right kind of suicides. The right kind of suicides is the kind that can be interpreted as supporting a culture's self-image. An act of suicide that seems to be a confession of error or malfeasance may be seized upon eagerly as proof that truth, power, and virtue reside in the status quo. This is part of the larger domain of deeds and communications made in the immediate anticipation of death. History gives us many examples of people whose last words were either widely disseminated, firmly suppressed, or invented by others in order to conform to the needs of the regime. Often it is not even the act of suicide that arouses society, but what the act of suicide seems to be saying about society.

The impact of suicide on society is mediated by our basic ideas of death. We are returning now to that function of the death system which is to help us "make sense" of a particular death and of death in general. Although it is beyond the scope of this chapter to examine ideas of death in any detail (Kastenbaum, 1992), it is possible to remind us of the diversity of ideas within our society.

The following examples are drawn from the early phase of a study in progress. The respondents represent a society within a society. These are people who are united in belief rather than in age, gender, race, ethnicity, national origin, or socioeconomic level. They are active in a movement that society seems to have designated as New Age. The problem with this designation, as we have quickly learned, is that the respondents themselves reject this term. They refer to themselves as having a spiritual orientation toward life, but are not inclined to favor any particular descriptive term for the movement as a whole. While recognizing that any one term might not do justice to all the beliefs and behavior patterns that comprise this pattern, we do think it useful to have a term available to distinguish them from the population in general. For sake of convenience, then, we will be referring to the Aquarian orientation. The term "Aquarian" was brought to prominence by Marilyn Ferguson in a book published in 1980 and revised in 1987. *The Aquarian Conspiracy* has remained a popular text for the movement we are tempted to but will not call New Age.

The beliefs that unite "Aquarians" are rooted in concepts of life and death, which, in turn, are consequential for their response to suicide. The Aquarian movement offers a variety of guides for living. These guides usually involve diet, exercise, meditation, and techniques for self-development. There is a broad spectrum of specific ideas and practices under the Aquarian tent. An outsider might regard some of these ideas and practices as sensible and welcome, and other ideas as dubious or extreme. The lifestyle involves some detachment from traditional cultural institutions. This can be seen clearly in attitudes toward health and religion. Health and vitality are strong positive values, but alternative methods are preferred to those of the medical establishment. Similarly, there is a religious resonance to much of Aquarian rhetoric, but many adherents do not participate in mainstream church-going and rituals. The movement has found ways to become financially self-supporting, even lucrative. In their personal interactions, Aquarians tend to be open, pleasant, and optimistic. One might occasionally feel taken aback by their unremitting enthusiasm, but one seldom if ever feels indifference or menace.

What Aquarian society presents, then, is something rather distinctive in today's mass society. Here are friendly, well-behaved, non-threatening people who have significantly reduced their allegiance to major social institutions. They are neither rebellious nor violent. By and large, they do not engage in confrontational activities, nor do they seek financial support from the public treasury. No doubt many people have been attracted to this movement because interpersonal relationships tend to be more supportive and relaxed. One person put it this way: "I walked away from the ugliness, the noise, the everybody stabbing everybody else in the back, the whole big crazy lost machine."

Now—where does death come in? Unlike society at large, this satellite society is eager to speak of death, and does speak of death: easily, frequently, and almost merrily. We have started to listen to these voices. In the first pilot phase of an ongoing study, Marilyn Wilson, a graduate stu-

dent at Arizona State University, invited participants in a Whole Life Expo-
sition (San Francisco, April 1993) to express their thoughts on death. Here
are some representative examples:

- "It's a transition from one state to another. And it's just part of our
  lifecycle, part of our growth, just another stage of growth for us in
  another realm. I do think we live more than one life and we come
  back to whatever it is we have to learn and we pick our parents cause
  we have lessons to learn. . . . Once we arrive here, when that dimen-
  sional door is shut, we don't remember that and, in one way, if that
  door was not shut, how could we live our lives? Because we live each
  life as though it's the only one. And once we're released from our
  bodies, we are in the infinite and we are all-knowing . . ."
- "Death is just the death of the body and the soul lives on in the 4th
  dimension . . . just a different way of being."
- "Death is a change of clothes."
- "Death is your soul leaving your body, and I don't believe in spiritual death. I believe in spiritual life. And when it chooses the spirit
  will come back and recycle."

For all respondents, death was not the total annihilation that some
people fear and others, in a moment of panic or despair, may desire. Death
was not the prospect of punishment and torment. Death was not failure.
Death was not ending, nor outcome. Death was not a philosophical problem. Death, in fact, was not death, at least not in the ordinary definition as
the cessation of life.

This satellite society rejects the physicalistic conception of death that
has become dominant with the rise of science and technology. It also dis-
misses religious dogma that insists on a day of reckoning, damnation, and
other after-life anxieties. Continuity, transition, and spiritual development
through numerous incarnations are among the major beliefs, reflecting
more of an Eastern than a Western tradition. The optimism—even light-
heartedness—that often accompanies Aquarian attitudes toward death
differs from the sober, resigned, even fatalistic tone that often is expressed
in the Eastern tradition.

The prevailing conceptions of death have been mediating our attitudes toward suicide. Is it possible to maintain traditional attitudes toward
suicide if the foundation conception of death has changed? To phrase the
question a little differently: what would be the impact of suicide on a society
that considers death to be just a door, a transition, a passing event that
occurs within a long progression toward spiritual actualization?

Several respondents in the first pilot study provided some hints. For example, one woman had already offered a standard Aquarian response to the question, what is death? "Death to me is just a transition from one plane to another. We never die. The soul lives on forever. Death is nothing but a transfer.... I do, of course, believe in reincarnation. We live many life times." She then brought up the subject of the Branch Davidian tragedy near Waco, Texas, in which almost all members of a religious cult died as a result of suicide or assault. "But those children knew before they were born that they were not going to live very long, and they came here to accomplish something, to pay some karmic debt. They did it, and they probably will reincarnate real quickly into a new karmic life." The Aquarian version of reincarnation, then, leads to a radically different interpretation of a situation that had a powerfully disturbing impact on mainstream Americans.

A follow-up study now in progress explores Aquarian concepts and attitudes in more depth. We are finding that the response just cited was by no means unusual. There seems to be a strong inclination to regard suicide and other potentially disturbing deaths as an acceptable part of an overall plan. Parents of a suicided person, for example, naturally will feel sad, but they should realize that this person will soon be back to continue his/her spiritual journey.

Should this view become prevalent or normative, what implications might it have for suicide prevention? The questions go well beyond suicide, of course. For example, are we to *grieve* no longer? Since death is only transition, "a changing of clothes," does this mean that we try to persuade the bereaved that they actually have suffered no loss? Does it really matter how many precautions we take against death by suicide, accident, homicide, and disease since, once again, death is a form of adventure, liberation, and fulfillment?

The Aquarian movement has not emphasized suicide or integrated this topic into its ongoing discourse on life and death. We hope to learn more about this movement's implications for suicide prevention and postvention as our study proceeds. But there is no reason to limit our attention to this movement, interesting as it is. To assess the impact of suicide on society in the years to come we will need to develop a more comprehensive understanding of society's changing concepts of life and death. Improved understanding might help us to develop a viable alternative to both frames of reference that have been touched on here. Perhaps we do not want to continue in the prevailing mode of avoiding personal confrontations with death ... "We cannot talk about ... about *that*." And perhaps we do not want to substitute the fantasy that death is not death. These could remain the most popular choices, however, unless we are willing to re-examine society's—and our own—basic conceptions of life and death.

REFERENCES

Augustine of Hippo. (c. 400/1948). The City of God (Chapters XX to XXVII). In W.
   J. Oates (Ed.), *Basic writings of Saint Augustine. Volume Two* (pp. 27–34). New
   York: Random House.

Callahan, D. (1987). *Setting limits.* New York: Simon & Schuster.

Choron, J. (1972). *Suicide.* New York: Charles Scribners' Sons.

Darzins, P., Molloy, D. W., & Harrison, C. (1993). Treatment for life-threatening
   illness. *New England Journal of Medicine, 329,* 736.

Esposito, G., Consiglio, S., & Petrone. A. (1987). *Suicidal behavior: A literature review
   1970–1985.* Foggia, Italy: Centro Ricerche Interdisciplinari sul Suicidio.

Farberow, N. L., & Shneidman, E. S. (Eds.). (1961). *The cry for help.* New York:
   McGraw-Hill.

Ferguson, M. (1987). *The aquarian conspiracy. (Revised edition).* Los Angeles: J. P.
   Tarcher.

Foucault, M. (1965). *Madness and civilization: A history of insanity in the age of reason.* New York: Random House.

Gorer, G. (1965). *Death, grief, and mourning in Great Britain.* London: Doubleday.

Kastenbaum, R. (1991). *Death, society, & human experience (Fourth edition).* New York:
   Macmillan/Merrill.

Kastenbaum, R. (1992). *The psychology of death. (Revised edition).* New York: Springer.

Kastenbaum, R. (1993). Reconstructing death in postmodern society. *Omega, Journal of Death and Dying, 27,* 75–90.

Kevorkian, J. (1991). *Prescription: medicide.* New York: Prometheus.

Ostrom. C. M. (1993). Seattle group aids in suicide. *The Seattle Times* (August 30).

Taiminin, T., Salmenpera, T., & Lehtinen, K. (1992). A suicide epidemic in a psychiatric hospital. *Suicide & Life-Threatening Behavior, 22,* 350–363.

Chapter 14

The Impact of Suicide across Cultures: More Than a Fairy Tale

Michel Tousignant

Variations across cultures in the effects of suicide are reviewed and discussed in this chapter, which highlights the complexity in developing an understanding of the role and effects of suicide within different social contexts. [Ed.]

Durkheim was not particularly compassionate toward the individual trag-edies of suicide victims. For him, their psychological vagrancies were a white noise of little concern in the search of the social mechanics leading some members of a culture to quit voluntarily before the game was over. Nor did he pay attention to the consequences of suicide on society, being interested exclusively by the overpowering influence of the group on indi-viduals. His thesis was pessimistic and conservative. The sharp rise of suicide rates all over Europe during the nineteenth century prophesied the wane of the liberal and capitalistic enterprise. Individuals needed the guid-ance of stringent norms to avoid the chaos and confusion of their instincts. "Les suicides," rooted a strong tradition of morality where deviancy her-alded the doom of civilization. In his essay on the sociology of sociologists, C. Wright Mills showed how experts of social psychopathology of his time were, in the main, nostalgic for the small-town virtues of their birthplaces, a myth from which they could never sever themselves after being confronted with the intellectually confusing metropolis.

This influence is still very much alive in suicidology. The most recent literature is still paying its dues to the old master. Rising suicide rates alarm journalists, politicians, and thinkers alike and feed all the paranoia about the wrongs of society.

The cross-cultural research on suicide is slowly breaking this widely shared consensus. Suicide may not be, after all, an apocalyptic messenger, a reason to despair of social life. If rising rates of suicide are probably mirroring deep social changes, these are not to be peremptorily condemned. Suicide is too uncritically perceived as the symptom of a sick society. We propose here an alternative route, to think of suicide as a moment in a process, perhaps a liminal point of transition to a new equilibrium in the life of a culture. We have taken the risk to assemble a still fragmentary argumentation to defend a less gloomy view of suicide. By focusing on what happens after, rather than falling in the snag of social autopsies, we hint that the high and painful price of suicide may bring back some unforeseen dividends.

THE BAD AND GOOD INTENTIONS OF SUICIDE

The anthropological literature includes multiple examples of suicide as the starting point of a long social scenario. The sprouting terminology by which various types of suicide are designed mainly refers to the consequences intended by the victim. One example is the *atonement* suicide, by which one wishes to spare himself and his family public condemnation. The immolation precludes accusations and has some overtones of a purification ritual. The general model is the Japanese *seppuku*, now almost unknown, where the victim apologizes to the community for his misdeed and saves the honor of his family (DeVos, 1968). Hollan (1990) quotes a few examples across many tribes of Austranesia-speaking Oceania. Nearer to us, numerous cases were recently reported of Italian businessmen and politicians choosing death rather than the ordeal of the "clean hands" inquiry.

The self-immolaton of a few buddhist monks in opposition to the Diem repression in South Vietnam conformed to a quite different logic. This sacrifice was a radical form of nonviolent resistance, intended to save deaths and, for that reason, a paradoxical testimony to the sacred value of life. There was great care taken not to spread the habit to angered and frustrated young followers. The gift of these lives, not at all in the Buddhist tradition and rather inspired by Gandhi and Dr. Martin Luther King Jr., was generally well accepted by the population, and was reminiscent of the early Christian martyrs (Hope, 1967).

Revenge or *indignant* suicides are far more widespread than atonement suicides. The intent here is to ask for some kind of reparation which is not without stirring some guilt and discomfort among survivors. One good description comes from Tobi, an isolated island of the Trust Territory of Melanesia administratively dependent on Palau (Black, 1985). Emigration and epidemics have recently shrunk the population to around 60 citizens. Consequently, any suicide is a threat to social survival. Before the recent epidemics of revenge suicide, there had been modern stories of voluntary death and disappearances which were never considered as true suicides. In one instance, two frustrated lovers embarked on a frail canoe in quest of a more hospitable land, 400 miles north across open sea. Vague rumors years after spread the good news that they had reached safe haven and had borne twelve children. A man who had intended to poison a rival in a love affair, in the end poisoned himself while intoxicated, and the incident was officially classified as an accident. Finally, a man cut from his provision of taro, because of his wife's allergy to the staple and the recent illness of his sister who was cultivating it for him, felt wounded in his manly pride, and starved himself to death instead of relying on imported rice as men of his condition would reluctantly accept to do. Other similar cases were reported among the Tobi community of Palau (Rubinstein, 1983). The refusal of considering these deaths as suicides testify either to a very strict definition, or to the denial of the challenge to social solidarity implicit in suicide. We should not overstate the case though, as actions under the influence of alcohol, as well as self-starvation and disappearance, are also showing the cracks of our Western notion of suicide.

Alfredo's story ended up more embarrassing. Separated from his wife and living with his children, he was involved in a romance with a young non-married woman, a coveted treasure in such a small population. Having been publicly scolded by his lover's mother, he cut his arm, gathered his children, told them of his impending plan to die, and then fled into the forest. The reaction that followed and the attempts to understand and influence his behavior were quite revealing of the cultural response to a suicidal act. From an ethnopsychological point of view, the threat was viewed as the consequence of shame into which a helpless man, lacking adult kin to correct a serious public insult and the spreading gossip, was thrown in. A search was immediately organized to prevent the feared aftermath of such a state. It was indeed believed that those who were subjected to such a shame became like ghosts and lost all control. As ghosts, they were freed from social ties and entered a *liminal* state where common sense was lost. Then, either the victim got lost forever, ran amok, or committed suicide, in which case the shame would spread to his children, igniting a kind of social brush fire. In this case, Alfredo was finally found and retrieved from a tree where he had readied a rope for his hanging. Back to the village the elders tried to bring him to reason with him. Soon after, Alfredo repeated mock attempts, including a canoe trip during a dark night, but nobody cared this time. The community felt that it had to prove that he was not merely manipulating everyone.

What would have been the consequences on the community of the completion of Alfredo's plan? Though answers can only be guesses, there is no doubt that the reaction would have bordered catastrophe. If Alfredo's behavior was at times peculiar, for he wanted his presence felt in every public event of importance, it was by no way so weird as to excuse an aberrant death and clean the community from the ensuing guilt. The local magistrate, also the son of the young woman's mother, had a strong political interest in avoiding this suicide as he led the search. At least, we can conclude that all the energy spent during that dramatic day expressed the torment that could have resulted from this ghostly death.

The wandering spirit theme applied to suicide victims means that they belong neither to the dead nor the living. Also, among the Munda and Oraon of India, the corpse will be secluded in a secret location because the spirit keeps coming back and thus threatens those who come to pay their respects to the dead. The victim's name is also taken away in the lineage chain and it is prohibited to name a child after a relative who has committed suicide.

The elaborate work of Counts (1980, 1984, 1985, 1991) among the Lusi-Kaliai of New Guinea, more sociological in perspective, amply illustrates a phenomenon widely described in various analyses of suicide in the Southwest Pacific; that is the revenge motive, first coined *samsonite* suicide by Jeffries in 1952. Counts' contribution has been to demonstrate how powerless persons, in this case mostly younger women mistreated by their husbands or forced into unwanted marriage, did attempt by their suicidal threats to change the attitudes of their environment or, by killing themselves, to bring shame to their persecutors and to press their parents and kin to seek justice for their wretched situation.

The suicide of Agnes, a 16-year-old single girl, following a long series of events where guilt is shared by many actors, is the key illustration. First, Victor, a local boy, returned to the village with a young woman met at his patrol post where he worked. His mother, Gloria, angry at her son because she wanted him to marry locally, enticed Agnes, who already had some attraction for Victor, to elope with him without consulting Agnes' parents. The plan worked out but a feud arose between both families. Then Agnes was called a whore by Gloria, and the young couple moved in with

Agnes' parents. A while after, Victor returned alone to his post and it was learned that negotiations were going on to arrange his marriage to Rose, Agnes' kin. Agnes, feeling deeply rejected and becoming the object of vicious gossip, shared her suicide plans with a few confidents and was discovered soon after hanging from a tree on the road to the village gardens. Her father, upon learning the terrible news, went into a fit and cried out his anger on the plaza at those who "had killed" his daughter "with talk." Victor's parents paid an indemnity following the local tradition but they still feared to be the target of witchcraft, and they left the village for good.

Years after, the village was still upset by this desparate act which threatened further violence. A man who wanted to divorce his wife after a rough fight was persuaded otherwise by his father who didn't want a woman's blood on his head. There was also another incident with Rose. A young man had eloped with her as she was on the point of being offered to a man she didn't love. This time, the village leaders held a public meeting and heeded the true lovers' opinion by declaring that from now on, "the time of telling young people that they should marry is over." As we can see, Agnes' ghost was still hovering over the village and had paved the path for romantic marriage. But she was not elevated to a state of sainthood either, and her sad fate was recalled to misbehaving girls to show where promiscuity would lead them.

As in Tobi culture, the victim in Kaliai is said to be half-human, half-spirit and this belief presses its ashamed, angry kin to avenge the death. The ghost remains aware of what is going on in the community and is said to enjoy the revenge. That it will appear to avenge the death stirs a great fear among the kin. Also, they can hire a sorcerer to fulfill this wish. Apart from the shame, the victim's parents may feel guilty for not foreseeing the warning signs conforming to some kind of cultural pattern. Victims usually inform significant others of the intent, destroying private possessions and providing clues about the culprit. Almost as a matter of fact, husbands are requested to amend their behavior when their spouses attempt suicide, and to pay compensations to kin in case of death. Even this remittance is not always sufficient to appease his in-laws, who resort to witchcraft anyway. Sometimes kinsmen administer the medicine themselves and, in one instance, they cut the husband into pieces as he happened to travel to his ex-wife's birthplace.

The multiplication of revenge scenarios are not limited to the Lusi-Kaliai. They also extend to the Maring from Papua, New Guinea (Healy, 1979). Some women will go as far as killing one of their children along with them, thus begetting even more wrath among their kinsmen and depriving the husband of new kinship alliances. Contrary to the Kaliai scene, the revenge is accomplished before death, and not upon the ghost's visitation.

So is it with the Gainj, a nearby tribe (Johnson, 1981). The arrival of Europeans in their territory displaced the locus of aggressivity from inter-tribal warfare to the domestic scene. Psychological wars of sexes became rampant and required men to strive for one-upmanship. Violence was sometimes applied too liberally by challenged husbands, and some women noticeably hanged themselves nearby a public road with little discretion as to their intent to humiliate their partner for eternity. Husbands were ridiculed for failing to control their wives, jeopardizing their reproductive powers and having to return the dowry. These spectacular hangings later acted as a strong deterrent on husbands when women tried to correct their conduct.

The *indignant* suicide encountered in the Toraja highlands of Indonesia failed to explode into a feud between lineages (Hollan, 1990). Without doubt, the victims felt hurt but the rage was not outwardly directed. Those who killed themselves did it after being refused a favor to which they felt entitled. In this society where gifts are expected to flow according to a well-established code and love and concern are expressed, the parents' refusal to pay for high school education, or to yield to more capricious demands like pocket money, could lead a teenager to despair and impulsive suicide. This act, traditionally regarded as shameful and prohibiting entrance to the land of the dead, was nevertheless met with empathy by the community. And Hollan refused to consider these suicides as a sign of anomie in a period of acculturation. To the contrary, the message of those victims was to widen the field of exchanges to the new obligations of modern life, in this case higher education and consumerism. These numerous youth suicides had quite an impact on the relations between generations. They brought a strong tool of manipulation into the hands of teenagers and caused some confused parents to abdicate all their control over them.

Moving to Truk Island, in the trust territory of Micronesia, the same theme of revenge recurs but again, with important variations. The tedious work of Hezel (1985) and his team over an extended period, his intimate knowledge of the culture and of its people, his fine analysis of the discourse, and the opportunity to accumulate data about a few cases over many years led to a unique corpus in anthropological research. Suicide had always been known in this society of 40,000, apparently reaching peaks on a few occasions in recent history. Consequently, informants were not totally astonished by a significant increase in the rates after 1974. This wave, alarming to any Westerner and amounting to ten times the rate of United States in the 15–30-years of age category, struck especially hard among teenaged males. The average age of the victims in the general population was only nineteen. The social dynamic leading to and following suicide replicated familiar themes observed elsewhere in this area: the victim was thought to have experienced a lot of anger mixed with some shame and frustration.

The conflict, as among the Toraja, was mainly contained within the nuclear unit, between a son and his parents. Out of a series of 159 suicides, 96 were closely investigated and survivors regularly referred to a state of anger lacking cultural modes of expression as the triggering agent. Any hint of revenge was stongly denied and survivors showed genuine affects of grief and love at the funeral, rather than those mixed feelings of shame met elsewhere. If any anger was attributed to the helpless victim, it was described as introverted and lacking teeth. In the local ethnopsychological vocabulary, the state of the victim was one of *amwunumwun*, in which a person chose to withdraw to signal that one's feelings were hurt by those who were very dear to him. The provoking events were seemingly trivial requests, or family disputes in which the victim was not even involved. The preparation for death was usually discrete and orderly, at the same time expressing the hope that the departure would contribute to reconcile the dead child with his family or otherwise bring peace where fighting was present. This proved that the image of a lost treasure is more efficient than that of a brooding child. Two other examples in this series included an adoptive son killing himself on the commemorative day of his "brother's" death by suicide in order to secure the eternal love of the family.

The report did not document in detail the success of the reconciliation strategy. On the other hand, it depicted the young victims as subordinate and so worried by the family values in that period of rapid acculturation that they were perceived as some sort of modern saints, inviting more to imitation than to prevention. We witness less a culture disintegrated by anomie than vulnerable to its inner contradictions and in search of a new equilibrium; a city of martyrs little reminiscent of Durkheim's harsh sentence on his period.

In this same study, there were 15 cases where the victims also tried to maintain the integrity of the family, but in a very different context. They were guilty of a quite shameful act like cursing a brother-in-law or being involved in a sexual relationship with a taint of incest. Their goal was said to save the family from the damage to its reputation rather than a personal act of atonement for a highly transgressive conduct.

A report from the Sara Nar of Chad was a welcome contribution given the lack of data from Black Africa (Brown, 1983). The study covered a population of 20,000 where four suicides had been yearly observed over a period of three years by a close follow-up on every death, a proof that high rates can be found in small remote locations with the necessary effort. The fact that wakes and funerals shared an important portion of social life and that suicide was not kept secret facilitated the operation. Suicide victims were described as brave persons who were hurt by painful statements on their reputation. Though the Nar culture called for vengeance in the case of a bloody death such as suicide, there was, in fact, little hope that kinsmen would react to such a wish. Their felt duty was to organize a ritual cleansing because the violent death had contaminated the whole village. There was no special status attached to the victim's soul. One example clearly illustrated, though, some potential danger among survivors. A husband was taken into protective custody by the village chief for fear of suicide after his wife died from self-poisoning following repeated accusations by her siblings of having bewitched and caused the death of her male children.

SUICIDE AS A *FAIT DIVERS*

Some groups seem more immune to the social aftermath of suicide and to react with equanimity. Among the Old Tamils of the district of Vavuniya in Sri Lanka, the high rates of suicide, over 60 per 100,000 between 1970 and 1974, three times the rate of 1955, were not a cause of great alarm (Daniel, 1989). Soldiers of the local liberation group also used to wear a cyanide capsule around their necks to avoid being captured alive and the practice didn't stir any opposition. A similar case can be made in Latin America. Before the middle of this century, Métraux (1973) was told by missionaries during his field trip that the Matako of Argentine had a rather free and relaxed attitude toward suicide. Schoolboys were prone to consume the lethal fruit of the sachasandia (*Capparis salicifolia Griseb*) at an epidemic rate. Dances charged with sexual symbolism were the precipitators for these contagious deaths and the church quickly imposed a ban on these celebrations in order to prevent suicide. One story mentioned that the corpse of a self-poisoned girl was indifferently left naked in the street for dogs to lick and children to throw stones at.

In some islands of Melanesia, suicide became trivialized and selected as the theme of popular songs aired on local stations and on tee-shirt messages (Hezel, 1985; Rubinstein, 1983). For example, an 11-year-old boy, saved *in extremis*, candidly confessed that he wanted to "try out" hanging.

CLUSTER SUICIDE

One big threat of suicide lies in its contagion, and there is some ground to support this fear. The proof of contagion is difficult to make in a large nation, but small populations offer more solid ground to investigate some basic questions. Were the victims related or close enough to each other to suggest a direct influence of the first on the second? Was the time lag short enough? In the case of the second victim, are we in a position to argue that the shock following the first death weighed at least as much as his own problems in the decision? On the level of semantics, there is a need to differentiate between the terms *collective imitation*, and *contagion* under the generic term of *cluster suicide*. The expression "collective suicide" should be restricted to simultaneous deaths; imitation to a succession of suicides using the same means, especially if these are peculiar or rare; and cluster or contagion to a series of suicides among people with close relationships, as with friends and kin, and within a short span of time. Cluster suicide has been documented in a few reports. A rather impressive series was found in a Plains Indian community in the 1980s (Bechtold, 1988). Nine suicides occurred within eight weeks. All the victims were teenaged or young adult males and had died by hanging. Taking exception of the first suicide, eight of our nine cases had either a friend, a first cousin, or a girlfriend's sibling among the rest of the cluster who had committed suicide a few days or a few weeks before. This sad example illustrates a domino-like process started by one single suicide. Because of the tight dependence among members of small cultural groups, this example shows the urgency to intervene with the survivors.

Smaller series of suicides and attempts, not above three but each time occurring within a few days and involving closely connected persons, were also reported from the Truk islands (Hezel, 1985). Rubinstein (1983) added more examples of small series of interconnected persons in a study covering several Micronesian islands. In one community, Ebeye, where suicide had been nonexistent between 1955 and 1965, the suicide of a prominent family's son, caught in a love affair with two women from both of whom he had just begotten a child, begun a series of 25 suicides over the next 12 years. Many victims, as well as some attempters, had a vision of a boat filled with the past victims inviting them to join in. It is difficult here to conclude to a direct contagion effect because of the long time span. It is clear, though, that the first cases produced a seductive action on the next.

Other imitation series have been recorded even in complex industrialized societies. In France, eight students, apparently unknown to each other, committed suicide to protest the ordeals of the Biafran war in Nigeria. The struggle had been widely reported in popular magazines using vivid pictures to show the price paid by children. Was it international solidarity, the model of far-away Vietnamese monks, or the pains of one's own life projected onto an African tragedy that built this series? Biographical and clinical data are badly needed to assess the respective influence of each factor in such a series.

Two contemporary events in Japan are worth introducing, though they bear no real similarity with the cluster or contagion phenomenon; they have more to do with imitation. In one instance, the high-rise project of Takashimadaira in Tokyo became the rallying site of 20 suicides a year thanks partly to the media which had coined it "the Mecca of suicide" (Pinguet, 1984). The second site was Jukai, or the ocean of trees, a thick forest devoid of roads or trails at the foot of Mount Fuji and made famous by a novel in 1960. A young woman had left her husband to join her lover, but was compulsively attracted to this forest and lost herself in it. Since then, around October, a park patrol has discovered each year around 30 corpses in the area, killed by frost or famine, and badly mutilated by wild animals. The scarce clues indicated that the majority of victims were young women and not mainly careless weekend wanderers.

Again, the evidence is too scarce to conclude it was a contagion. These sites are more likely consecrated locations adding to a personal drama and the coloration of a pilgrim, as if a goddess of suicide, such as existed among the Mayas, presided over the final act. They offer some kind of prefabricated scenario to would-be victims. Yet, these facts demonstrate again the definite influence of media and literature in raising suicide to the level of a mythical performance. Following are some examples where actors were more famous.

SUICIDE AS A PUBLIC PERFORMANCE

No other suicide in this century has had such an international impact as the death of Yukio Mishima, the great Japanese novelist who died on November 25, 1970. After leading a desperate crusade for a return to feudal and militaristic values, he staged a suicide that could not be kept silent for long. Mishima managed to slip into the military command quarters of Ichigaya in central Tokyo, to kidnap an army chief, and to order one thousand soldiers to assemble on a parade court. Then, he challenged their courage in a confused speech from a balcony and committed *seppuku* in an adjoining room, after which an acolyte cut off his head. The news was immediately flashed around the world. The Western nations were generally less shocked than Japan and the Orient, because of the outdated perception that this was again a living example of folkloric Japan. Mishima's quasi-parody—his personal problems were widely publicized and recalled again at that occasion by the diagnosis of acting Prime Minister Sate—nevertheless had the effect of an earthquake. It brought to the surface the remnants of militaristic dreams crushed by the defeat of 1945 and painfully repressed until then. On the other hand, as pointed out by Pinguet, the time was ripe for a public exorcism of the old devils, to which Mishima had paradoxically contributed by destroying with him his obsolete project.

As foreseers and transformers of values, famous writers around the world are scrutinized because their lives may be living prophecy. As they more often terminate their lives by suicide, their deaths have always had a chilling effect on their environment. For their readership, they sometimes break the hope of a better world or lessen the credibility of a collective enterprise that they were heralding, as in the case of Mishima. The list of well-known writers who have committed suicide is quite long. We will just refer to two more examples. The death of the French novelist Henri de Montherlant during the 1970s, though less disturbing, embodied the possibility of a long-term plan. At the beginning of his literary career, de Montherlant had announced that he would end his life if ever severely handicapped by the ills of old age. Almost half a century later, he kept faithful to his promise after becoming blind. In Québec, Hubert Aquin was at the peak of his literary career and recognized by many as the most brilliant writer of his generation when he shot himself after a long series of professional and personal problems. Despite this peculiar biography, his death may have slowed the independence movement of which he was a great inspiration for his generation.

CONCLUSION

The cultural reports of suicide have brought a refreshing perspective to current ideas. Suicide cannot be simplistically regarded as the marker of a waning civilization, the opportunity for an autopsy of anything that could have gone wrong in a given society. Suicide is not only a dependent variable, to borrow the epidemiological terminology; it is but one moment in a larger process of societal change. Epidemics of suicide are certainly tragedies wherever they happen, to be analyzed and prevented at any rate. Yet, suicide is not only a social disease. Its impact on the wider society may contribute in the longrun to heal the wounds of rapid social change. The victims personify dilemmas experienced by the group. Their stories, by being integrated into the lore of a culture, help us to find new avenues of solution. But this is more than a fairy tale. As we have seen, the code of marriage, the authoritarian conduct of parents and husbands, the terrorism of in-laws, are efficiently counteracted by this passive but not innocent form of protest.

We unfortunately know little about the psyche of survivors. Wherever they live, they are certainly deeply affected by the loss of kin and friends as witnessed by the clusters of suicide. Because anthropologists have not usually been trained to detail the grief reactions of their informants, and also because it would not always be easy to find the appropriate tools for doing so, the exploration of differential reactions of the survivors is virtually virgin territory. We can only remind that the cross-cultural analysis of grief only very recently has become a focus of attention. The lesson we have learned for the future is that it would be difficult to isolate these reactions from an understanding of the culture and the social change process.

REFERENCES

Bechtold, D. W. (1988). Cluster suicide in American Indian adolescents. *American Indian and Alaska Native Mental Health Research, 1*(3), 26–35.
Black, P. W. (1985). Ghosts, gossip, and suicide: Meaning and action in Tobian folk psychology. In G. M. White & J. Kirkpatrick (Eds.), *Person, self, and experience* (pp. 245–300). Berkeley and Los Angeles: University of California Press.
Brown, E. P. (1981). The ultimate withdrawal: Suicide among the Sara Nar. *Archives Européennes de Sociologie, 22*, 199–228.
Counts, D. A. (1976/1977). The good death in Kaliai: Preparation for death in Western New Britain. *Omega, Journal of Death and Dying, 7*(4), 367–372.
Counts, D. A. (1980). Fighting back is not the way: Suicide and the women of Kaliai. *American Ethnologist, 7*, 332–351.
Counts, D. A. (1984). Revenge suicide by Lusi women: An expression of power. In D. O'Brien & S. Tiffany (Eds.), *Rethinking women's roles: Perspectives from the Pacific* (pp. 71–93). Berkeley: University of California Press.
Counts, D. A. (1987). Female suicide and wife abuse: A cross-cultural perspective. *Suicide and Life Threatening Behavior, 17*(3), 194–204.
Counts, D. A., & Counts, D. R. (1991). Loss and anger: Death and the expression of grief in Kaliai. In D. A. Counts & D. R. Counts (Eds.), *Coping with the final tragedy: Cultural variation in dying and grieving* (pp. 191–212). Amityville, NY: Baywood.
Daniel, E. V. (1989). The semiosis of suicide in Sri Lanka. In B. Lee & G. Urban (Eds.), *Semiotics, self, and society* (pp. 69–100). Berlin: Mouton and Gruyter.
DeVos, G. A. (1968). Suicide in cross perspective. In H. L. P., Resnik (Ed.), *Suicidal behaviors, diagnosis and management* (pp. 105–134). Boston: Little, Brown.
Healy, C. (1979). Women and suicide in New Guinea. *Social Analysis, 2*, 89–106.
Hezel, F. X. (1984). The cultural patterns in Trukese suicide. *Ethnology, 23*(3), 193–206.
Hollan, D. (1990). Indignant suicide in the Pacific: An example from the Toraja highlands of Indonesia. *Culture, Medicine, and Psychiatry, 14*(3), 365–380.
Hope, M. (1967). The reluctant way: Self-immolation in Vietnam. *Antioch Review, 27*, 144–163.
Iga, M. (1986). *The thorn in the chrysanthemum.* Berkeley and Los Angeles: University of California Press.
Jeffreys, M. D. W. (1952). Samsonic suicide or suicide revenge among Africans. *African Studies, 11*, 118–122.

Johnson, P. L. (1981). When dying is better than living: Female suicide among the Gainj of Papua New Guinea. *Ethnology, 20*(4), 325–334.

Métraux, A. (1973). Suicide among the Matako of the Argentine Gvan Chaco. *America Indigena, 3*, 200–209.

Pinguet, M. (1984). *La mort volontaire au Japon.* Paris: Gallimard.

Rubinstein, D. H. (1983). Epidemic suicide among Micronesian adolescents. *Social Science and Medicine, 10*, 657–665.

Saran, A. B. (1974). *Murder and suicide among the Munda and the Oraon.* Delhi: National.

Chapter 15

Public Option, Private Choice: Impact of Culture on Suicide

Michael J. Kral and Ronald J. Dyck

This chapter presents a social information processing approach to understanding the complex relationship between society, the cognitive processes involved in suicide, and suicidal behavior. [Ed.]

The traditional view in suicidology has been that suicide results from an accumulation of states within the individual that lead to voluntary self-destruction. These states of unbearable distress have been described as resulting from numerous factors attributed to both personal and social causes including the effects of poor social integration and normlessness (Durkheim, 1897/1951), hatred and aggression toward others turned against the self (Freud, 1917/1957), sudden interpersonal loss or ambivalence in one's interpersonal attachments (Menninger, 1938), and motivation to escape from intolerable stress (Baechler, 1979; Baumeister, 1990; Maris, 1992; Menninger, 1938; Shneidman, 1985). Many other "background" risk factors have been identified that are often specific to a particular temporal, cultural, or even data-gathering context such as being male, aboriginal or white, adolescent or elderly, alcoholic, unattached and living alone, being diagnosed with a major mood disorder, and having a history of suicidal behavior or ideation.

Shneidman (1985) summarized the major findings regarding suicide into two necessary and sufficient causes for the act to occur, expanded more recently by Kral (1994). The first is unbearable *perturbation*, being at an individually defined level of despair, agony, upset, hopelessness, helplessness, or what he has termed "psychache" (Shneidman, 1993). The perturbation, being subjective, can be brought on by any number of risk factors. When the level of perturbation exceeds an individual's threshold of tolerance, the person becomes motivated to do something about this unpleasant state. The second feature of suicide is *lethality*, which refers to the conscious decision to end one's life. Rather than referring to the dangerousness of the choice of method to end one's life, as the term is often used, lethality is actually much broader than that. It is simply the choice of suicidal death as the plan of action.

Although in suicidology and related mental health disciplines we have learned much about perturbation, and it is indeed the understanding, treatment, and prevention of perturbation which is at the center of these related disciplines, we have learned little about how people come to *choose suicide*. Most of the work in suicidology has been spent either on investigating the risk factors themselves, as if they somehow follow a linear and logical path toward suicide, or else on the treatment of people once they have become "suicidal". We know next to nothing about lethality. In this chapter we examine the social context of suicide, following the thesis that lethality for the individual is shaped by views within a particular culture about choices regarding unbearable perturbation. Suicide, then, is viewed as an idea (see Kral, 1994).

THE SITUATED SELF

The argument that lethality could be a culturally situated concept that becomes part of an individual's repertoire of choices must begin with an understanding of how ideas are spread throughout society and incorporated into a person's sense of self. The notion of the self being formed by and within a social context is certainly far from new. Gabriel Tarde (1898), for example, described as a fundamental "social law" an individual's repetition of similarities that are seen in the wider community. He saw these imitations based on cultural norms to form a basis of who we come to be, of how we define ourselves and our options. These ideas, attitudes, and behaviors then further strengthen the norm until highly visible and valued others begin new styles of thinking and behaving. Early American sociology and social psychology viewed ideas about self and others as adopted by individuals from the wider culture, and thus contextual in their origin and spread (Collier, Minton, & Reynolds, 1991). Tarde and others called on us some time ago to consider reversing our usual thinking about cause and effect regarding the individual and society.

Such earlier notions are currently being rediscovered and/or expanded upon. Some, for example, argue that imitation is as fundamental to being human as is language (Yando, Seitz, & Zigler, 1978). Furthermore, many current approaches to the development of the self rely heavily if not exclusively on the impact of social influence (Geertz, 1984; Juhasz, 1983; Markus & Cross, 1990; Paicheler, 1988). Hewitt (1991) provided a detailed analysis of how the self is located and developed within a larger community. He outlined a theory proposed by G.H. Mead (1934) on the formation of identity:

> Social identity refers to a sense of self that is built up over time as the person participates in social life and identifies with others. Its frame of reference is not the immediate situation and its role, but rather a *community*, the set of real or imaginary others with whom the person feels a sense of similarity and common purpose. To have a social identity is to identify with some set of people with whom one feels an affinity, in whose company one feels comfortable, and whose ideas and beliefs are similar to one's own. (p. 127, italics in original)

Bruner (1993) suggested further that rather than viewing culture as something we "acquire," in a simple sense, culture becomes *a way of knowing* that "situates and amplifies cognitive life" (p. 516). It is thus that our thinking and our sense of who we are cannot be separated from the social contexts in which we are continually participating.

Our emotional life can also be construed in this way.[1] Averill (1986) presented the view of how emotional experience and expression is essentially an "internal representation of social norms or rules" (p. 100). These internal representations would be based on how we categorize ourselves along similar emotional dimensions we see in others. Normative expecta-

---

1. It may not be neccessary to assume that emotion and cognition are independent processes, and Heelas (1986) indicates that some cultures do not appear to make this distinction. However, as an important Western concept, there is some controversy regarding the panhuman universality of emotions (e.g., Frijda's [1986] functional approach to emotions as "action-readiness" or Ekman's [1989] work on "basic" emotions) versus emotions as socially constructed (see Lutz & White, 1986).

tions of sex-role stereotypes, for example, have been related to differences in intensity of both positive and negative emotional experience among women and men (Grossman & Wood, 1993). Turner (1991) noted that this self-categorization opens up the likelihood of being influenced in one's attitudes about oneself and one's choices regarding action: "In so far as we categorize ourselves as similar to others in the same situation (in relevant respects), it is natural and logical to think that we should tend to respond in the same way" (p. 161).

What does it mean, then, to say that the self is "culturally situated"? An explicit assumption in this chapter is that culture is more than the expression of shared meaning systems; we advocate an approach suggesting that the psychology of the individual is shaped significantly by culture. The field of cognitive anthropology is active in trying to understand the mechanisms of this process. Central to this endeavor is the concept of *culture schemas*,[2] the shared meanings held by people that generally guide their lives (D'Andrade, 1992). A schema can be viewed as an internally coherent representation of the self, of others, or of acts. The range of one's self-categories would make up one's self-schema, for example. Rule and Bisanz (1987) have referred to a schema as the "social knowledge structure" an individual has "about the relevant tactics used to achieve various goals" (p. 185). The cognitive schemas derived from culture are, according to Quinn and Holland (1987), the sources of what is perceived by individuals to be "right" and "inevitable" (p. 13). These authors point out that cultural schemas or models are "used to perform a variety of cognitive tasks. Sometimes these cultural models serve to set goals for action, sometimes to plan the attainment of said goals, sometimes to direct the actualization of these goals, sometimes to make sense of the actions and fathom the goals of others, and sometimes to produce verbalizations that may play various parts in all these projects as well as in the subsequent interpretation of what has happened" (pp. 6–7).

Cultural schemas allow us to organize our worlds according to prototypical event sequences (e.g., grocery shopping—may involve having a list, pushing a cart through aisles, paying at the checkout), propositions, images, metaphors, narratives, and simplified metonymous (part-whole) relations (Casson, 1983; Quinn & Holland, 1987). In her study of emotion among the Ifaluk people of the Western Pacific, Lutz (1987) identified a number of cultural schemas linking events, emotions, and actions, including their cultural schema for suicide. She found, for example, that a rule

---

2. "Schemas" was selected as the plural form instead of schemata, given its wide use in the literature.

violation (event) could lead to justifiable anger (emotion) which could lead to suicide (action), or that being observed in failure (event) could lead to shame/embarrassment (emotion) which could lead to suicide (action). Kleinman (1988) also identified cultural factors which influence decisions regarding suicide, such as the emphasis on individual rights versus family responsibility; and that suicidal behavior in many societies appears to be related to factors such as "traditional use of suicide as a sanctioned idiom of distress and its place in cultural mythology" (p. 44). Suicide may thus be seen as a cultural schema with "directive force" (D'Andrade, 1984), essentially as a goal-schema linking the action of suicidal behavior or suicide itself with culturally reasoned motivation. If lethality, the idea of suicide, can be viewed as a type of social norm or schema that one can incorporate into one's sense of self, including one's emotional self and one's perceived available choices for action, then we must examine how the "idea of suicide" might be the essential, single, and only *direct* "cause" of suicide. Perturbation, although necessary, can only ever be indirect in its relation to suicide, acting as a motivator or catalyst (Kral, 1994).

THE IDEA OF SUICIDE

It has long been observed that the idea of suicide in society can produce deaths. Durkheim (1897/1951) wrote that "there is always and normally, in every society, a collective disposition taking the form of suicide . . . perhaps no other phenomenon is more readily contagious" (p.132). Accounts of suicide occurring in clusters or waves within communities are numerous throughout recorded history (see Colt, 1991). A famous example that has become known as "the Werther effect" is the rash of suicides among young men in Germany following the publication of Goethe's novel in 1774 about the hero's suicide following an unrequited love (Phillips, 1974). Suicide appearing in clusters continue to be described, including youth suicide clusters in Japan (Takahashi, 1993) or in some Amerindian communities (Davidson, 1989). An individual's method of suicide is also highly related to the "popular" methods that vary widely across communities or cultures (La Fontaine, 1975). For example, the spread of methods by burning, poisoning, hanging, and gunshot has been described (Gould, Wallenstein, & Davidson, 1989), and there is evidence that restricting access to popular methods will deter some—perhaps many—from killing themselves (Carrington & Moyer, 1994; Clarke & Lester, 1989; Lester & Leenaars, 1993). Much has also been written about a media effect on suicide, and a recent review found that suicides do appear to increase significantly following news stories about suicide (Phillips, Carstensen, & Paight, 1989). This effect appears to be strongest for 15–19-year-old males (Hafner & Schmidke,

1989) and when high-profile "models" are the suicides so described (Stack, 1992). Interestingly, a similar approach has recently been applied to alcoholism in terms of both cultural/attitudinal etiology (Vaillant, 1986) and prevention (Room, 1990).

What sort of self-concept might allow suicide to become part of one's range of options? What is needed if we are to answer this question is the beginning of an approach that addresses the concept of vulnerability not to the final act of suicide, nor to the detailed planning of method, nor even to parasuicidal behavior, but to the *idea* of suicide in the first place. Understanding how one comes to hold that suicide is within an acceptable range of options might be one starting place. Rogers and DeShon (1992) have found that acceptance of suicide as an option to end perturbation is one clearly independent factor in a widely used scale of attitudes toward suicide. Futhermore, Diekstra and Kerkoff (1993) have found that general acceptability of suicide is directly related to a higher likelihood of suicidal behavior in the same individuals. Biblarz, Brown, Noonan, Biblarz, Pilgrim, and Baldree (1991) provide evidence that young people with some known general risk factors for perturbation view suicide as more acceptable than those with fewer risk factors. These investigators also found that the presence of risk factors was related to viewing suicide as even *more* acceptable following exposure to film media about suicide. Thus there is some evidence that a vulnerability to social influence regarding suicide may be related to being in a state of perturbation. There is also increasing evidence that negative affect is related to cognitive inflexibility, that is, to being less open to alternative choices (Isen, Niedenthal, & Cantor, 1992). It may be that a person in a state of perturbation will be highly prone to experience fewer and more negative options regarding "what to do" about that state, and left vulnerable to ideas that most directly "fit" with current maladaptive views of self- and escape-focused defenses such as the idea of suicide. It is important to note, however, that Shneidman (1985, 1993) argues that perturbation is only indirectly related to but conceptually distinct from lethality; emotional perturbation is not a cause of death. Lethality appears to be directly related to holding the attitude that suicide is an acceptable option under some circumstances. This, followed by thinking through details of a method and rehearsing it in one's head (Litman, 1970), can make for a deadly combination.

THE CHOICE OF SUICIDE

Transforming the rather broad, philosophical notion of suicide as cultural experience or cultural idea to an individual's choice between behavioral alternatives is indeed challenging. The suicide research literature has not been particularly useful, to date, as it has tended to emphasize the search for specific predisposing and precipitating factors that contribute either directly or indirectly to fatal and nonfatal suicidal behavior. Thus, correlates of suicidal behavior related to the biological, psychological, and social areas have been delineated. More recently, there has been attention directed toward examining the role of cognitive factors in suicidal behaviors. Cognitive distortion, cognitive rigidity, attributional styles, and interpersonal problem-solving have received increased attention. Unfortunately, little emphasis has been devoted to addressing the process persons use in choosing suicidal behavior over other possible behaviors in a problem situation. Yet, understanding the decision-making process may help explain why some at-risk persons do not engage in suicidal behaviors while other low-risk persons actually do so. The purpose of this section, therefore, is to explore the process utilized in reaching and executing the suicide behavior choice.

The impetus to initiate closer examination of how persons make decisions about engaging in suicidal behavior derives from the findings that suicidal persons seem to have interpersonal cognitive problem-solving deficits (Mortensen, 1990). For example, Cohen-Sandler (1982) demonstrated that suicidal children were more deficient in generating alternate solutions to interpersonal problems than nonsuicidal children. Similarly, hospitalized children who were suicide ideators were found to be less likely to generate active cognitive coping strategies in comparison to nonsuicidal children (Asarnow, Carlson, & Guthrie, 1987). Others have found that suicide attempters have a decreased ability to cope with new life stressors due to their diminished ability to find viable alternatives to their problems (Goodstein, 1982), being worse in active problem-solving (Linehan, Camper, Chiles, Stosahl, & Shearin, 1987), and demonstrating more cognitive rigidity (Neuringer, 1964).

While it appears that problem-solving ability may be an important factor in explaining some suicidal behaviors, it does not provide answers regarding the process persons use in arriving at the decision to engage in suicidal behavior. Indeed, why do some poor problem solvers never exhibit suicidal behavior and some effective problem solvers turn to such behavior? To develop an answer, we shall examine problem solving within a social information processing framework.

A concept relevant to this framework is "information processing." A heuristic definition is provided by Massaro and Cowan (1993), who view information as "representations derived by a person from environmental stimulation or from processing that influences selections among alternative choices for belief or action," and information processing as "how the information is modified so that it eventually has its observed influence" (p. 384). Important to the approach presented here are the notions of choice, attitudes/beliefs, goals, and actions.

Although several models of social information processing are applicable to this discussion (Allen, Chinsky, Larcen, Lochman, & Selinger, 1976; Dodge, 1986; McFall, 1982; Rubin & Krasnor, 1986), one of particular relevance to suicide has been developed by Mortensen (1990). In a qualitative study, Mortensen attempted to specify the process undertaken by female suicide attempters in coming to a decision to engage in suicidal behavior. Out of her in-depth interviews together with objective data collection, Mortensen formulated a framework within which to understand the transition from suicide as societal idea to personal choice.

As in several other approaches, the starting point for Mortensen's framework is a *precipitating* or *stimulus event* which initiates the problem-solving process. Such an event activates an "event schema" which directs the search of the environment for needed information, influences what information will be given attention, and suggests the direction of possible responses to that information. In other words, how the precipitating event is perceived and interpreted will influence the problem-solving process through the activation of a certain schema at the expense of others.

The second stage proposed in the social information processing model involves *problem definition* and *goal specification*. Mortensen suggests that how the problem is defined will necessarily determine and/or limit the possible solutions to that problem. For example, if a person defines a set of events as a major life crisis where the goal for dealing with that crisis is death, then engaging in behavior that has a high likelihood of achieving that goal, such as attempting suicide, would be an obvious possible response.

The third stage involves a response search through the hierarchy of solutions elicited by the activated schema. If suicide is not part of the hierarchy of responses, then obviously it will not be considered as a possible solution. On the other hand, suicidal behavior can be located very high on the hierarchy of possible responses, which increases the likelihood that it will be chosen as the solution to the problem. Such placement of suicidal behavior within the activated schema may be the result of a learning history with that behavior. Observational learning has been proposed as an explanation as to how suicidal behavior becomes included in the hierarchy of responses (e.g., Diekstra, 1985). In fact, Diekstra has asserted that the best predictor of future suicidal behavior is a history of knowing of similar behavior by others (*models* that are either fictional or personal) or by the self.

Once the response has been chosen, Mortensen (1990) proposes that it is evaluated in terms of its expected result or outcome (the fourth stage). If the expected outcome is not what is desired, then it will be discarded and another possible solution in the hierarchy is selected and evaluated. For example, a person in crisis may have a response hierarchy elicited with suicide high in the repertoire of solutions. If, however, death is not the desired solution to the problem, and the selected response to the problem is suicidal behavior, and suicidal behavior is evaluated as resulting in *death*, then the individual may discard this response as a possible solution and select another behavior from the hierarchy. On the other hand, if manipulation of the environment is perceived as the expected result of suicidal behavior, and a *changed environment* is the goal, then suicidal behavior may be selected as the solution. That is, there would be a match between the goal and the perceived outcome of the selected solution. Note that such behavior may be selected only if other, more acceptable solutions were not available, or if these other solutions have been unsuccessful in achieving the goal in the past.

Last, implementation of the selected response occurs if the solution is judged to be acceptable. However, after initiation of the response, Mortensen suggests that the individual monitors the results in terms of goal achievement and problem resolution. If the problem is judged to be resolved, then the problem-solving process ends. If resolution of the problem is only partially achieved, the individual might accept this state of affairs as good enough and end the process, or the individual may try again. If there is no problem resolution as a result of the implemented action, then the individual may either try again with the same selected response, select a new strategy to achieve the same goal, or stop the problem resolution task altogether (Mortensen, 1990).

While it is beyond the scope of this section to analyze all the possible variables that might mediate the problem-solving process, it is important to mention several that have direct influence on the different stages of the model. Perceived self-efficacy, as defined by Bandura (1984), has to do with an individual's judgment of his/her confidence in and capability of executing given levels of performance. Thus, within the described social information processing model, self-efficacy can have a direct effect on problem solving in terms of the degree to which one searches for alternative solutions and the selection of one of those solutions. If a person has low self-efficacy, then some solutions, including the "healthy" ones, may be rejected because of a lack of confidence in his/her ability to actually carry out the necessary behavior.

Impulsivity has also been suggested as influencing problem-solving behavior. An impulsive person may be defined as rushing into a problem-*solving* mode before having given enough time to information gathering for the purpose of problem definition. Moreover, this person may not give adequate time for the search of the response hierarchy for an appropriate solution nor adequate time to evaluate the perceived outcomes of the selected behavior (Mortensen, 1990).

Intense affect, linked earlier in this chapter with cognitive inflexibility, may also mitigate health problem-solving behavior (Mortensen,

1990). Anger or profound grief, when combined with social influence/ contagion, may influence what hierarchies are available and the decision-making process (CDC Report, 1992; Holtzworth-Munroe, 1992; Mortensen, 1990).

Attitudes of persons toward various behaviors in the response hierarchies may have a major impact upon the acceptance or rejection of a solution to a particular problem. When suicidal behavior is one of the selections from the response hierarchy, a person's attitude toward suicide may influence the acceptance or rejection of response implementation. As stated earlier, social acceptability of suicide as a response to a problem or crisis may well affect the choice to engage in that selected behavior or to continue to evaluate other alternatives (see Linehan, 1973). It may be that a state of extreme perturbation will, for those who percieve suicide to be an acceptable option under such dire circumstances, readily access the "suicide schema" whereby it becomes one of a restricted range of options, if not the only perceived option.

One of the strengths of a social information processing approach to understanding the choice of suicide is its complexity. Appropriate and healthy choices in behavior to the problems encountered are, in the end, the result of complex cognitive processes. Thus, understanding this complexity and being able to identify specific areas of weakness or vulnerability along the decision pathway may prove to be a significant advance in developing more effective prevention and intervention strategies.

CULTURE AND MOTIVATION

In this chapter we have outlined an approach to the study and understanding of lethality, defined earlier as "the idea of suicide." How one comes to hold the idea that suicide is an option for oneself is very poorly understood, yet placing it within the study of how ideas are adopted by people in the first place may be a most heuristic direction. Allow us to briefly summarize our thinking thus far.

We accept the premise that the self is culturally situated, meaning that the very essence of who we are—our customs, beliefs, values, commitments, relationships, ideas, even identity—are deeply embedded within our culture. Although this notion may be completely obvious, anthropologists and sociologists are well aware of the difficulty of being cognizant of one's own cultural lens. Hutchins (1980) coined the term *transparency* to refer to this level of non-awareness: "Once learned, it becomes what one sees *with*, but seldom what one *sees*" (p. 12, italics in original). Effort is indeed required to begin to "see" this larger picture.

It is insufficient to argue that we are merely culturally situated or constituted, as noted by D'Andrade (1992). In order to postulate that culture is but one albeit important influence on the psychology of the person, the process by which this occurs needs to be understood. A second premise here is that lethality is a cultural schema. We must learn not only why but *how* certain individuals internalize this idea along the continuum decribed by Spiro (1987) ranging from an indifferent acquaintance to a highly salient conviction (D'Andrade, 1992). Thus, the acceptability of suicide, together with a plan and method, becomes a schema within the person's range of options.

It may be that the general acceptability of suicide, rather than a series of precipitating crises for the individual, is where we should begin in the study of lethality and the perception of choice. This broader level of general acceptability would fit, for example, with D'Andrade's (1992) concept of "top-level schemas," where "a person's most general interpretations of what is going on will function as important goals for that person" (p. 30). Acceptability of suicide as an option may function as a goal-schema for people of a particular culture, group, or disposition that is barely noticed—until a circumstance or series thereof make this schema salient and accessible.

Not everyone will adopt cultural schemas in the same way, and numerous factors surely influence the degree to which lethality might be seen as an option for someone. This is another area ripe for further investigation. Some evidence has been presented here suggesting that being in a state of perturbation (e.g., major mood disorder, "psychache") leaves certain individuals vulnerable to suggestions of suicide as an option. Perturbation has been shown to restrict the range of options people will select from, and suicide may be a highly salient, accessible schema—perhaps the only one— for those who have reached the point of unbearable upset and who have previously viewed suicide as a generally acceptable choice in their world. A person's particular learning history and self-efficacy have also been mentioned. The motivation for suicide, then, will come from two sources. The state of perturbation is an indirect source, while the direct link is the more general goal-schema of lethality together with a now specific plan and method—also selected from among several popular and available choices in the current culture. If people can be viewed as active problem-solvers according to the social information processing framework presented here, with response options selected from a heirarchy of alternative schemas and directed toward a particular goal, but with perhaps little if any awareness that one's experience and expression of emotions and choices regarding action are based on one's social, family, and cultural models, then we may have the beginning of a strategy for the study of how a person comes to choose self-inficted death.

REFERENCES

Allen, G. H., Chinsky, J. M., Larcen, G. J., Lochman, J. E., & Selinger, H. V. (1976). *Community psychology and the schools: A behaviorally oriented multilevel preventive approach.* Hillsdale, NJ: Lawrence Erlbaum.

Allport, F. H. (1924). *Social psychology.* Boston: Houghton Mifflin.

Asarnow, J. R., Carlson, G. A., & Guthrie, D. (1987). Coping strategies, self-preceptions, hopelessness, and perceived family environments in depressed and suicidal children. *Journal of Consulting and Clinical Psychology, 55,* 361–366.

Averill, J. R. (1986). The acquisition of emotions during adulthood. In R. Harre (Ed.), *The social construction of emotions.* New York: Basil Blackwell.

Baechler, J. (1979). *Suicides* (B. Cooper, Trans.) New York: Basic. (Original work published 1975)

Bandura, A. (1984). Automatic and conscious processing of social information. In R. S. Wyer, Jr., & T. K. Srull (Eds.), *Handbook of social cognition* (Vol. 3, pp. 1–43). Hillsdale, NJ: Lawrence Erlbaum.

Baumeister, R. F. (1990). Suicide as escape from self. *Psychological Review, 97,* 90–113.

Biblarz, A., Brown, R. M., Noonan Biblarz, D., Pilgrim, M., & Baldree, B. F. (1991). Media influence on attitudes toward suicide. *Suicide and Life-Threatening Behavior, 21,* 374–384.

Bruner, J. (1993). Do we "acquire" culture or vice versa? *Behavioral and Brain Sciences, 16,* 515–516.

Carrington, P. J., & Moyer, S. (1994). Gun control and suicide in Ontario. *American Journal of Psychiatry, 15,* 606–608.

Casson, R. W. (1983). Schemata in cognitive anthropology. *Annual Review of Anthropology, 12,* 429–462.

Centers for Disease Control (1992). *Youth suicide prevention programs: A resource guide.* Atlanta: Author.

Clarke, R. V., & Lester, D. (1989). *Suicide: Closing the exits.* New York: Springer Verlag.

Cohen-Sandler, R. (1982). *Interpersonal problem-solving skills of suicidal and nonsuicidal children: Assessment and treatment.* Unpublished doctoral dissertation, American University, Washington, DC.

Collier, G., Minton, H. L., & Reynolds, G. (1991). *Currents of thought in American social psychology.* New York: Oxford University Press.

Colt, G. H. (1991). *The enigma of suicide.* New York: Simon & Schuster.

D'Andrade, R. G. (1984). Cultural meaning systems. In R. A. Shweder & R. A. LeVine (Eds.), *Culture theory: Essays on mind, self, and emotion* (pp. 88–119). New York: Cambridge University Press.

D'Andrade, R. G. (1992). Schemas and motivation. In R. G. D'Andrade & C. Strauss (Eds.), *Human motives and cultural models* (pp. 23–44). New York: Cambridge University Press.

Davidson, L. E. (1989). Suicide clusters and youth. In C. R. Pfeffer (Ed.), *Suicide among youth: Perspectives on risk and prevention.* (pp. 83–99). Washington, DC: American Psychiatric Press.

Diekstra, R. F. W. (1985). Suicide and suicide attempts in the European Economic Community: An analysis of trends, with special emphasis upon trends among the young. *Suicide and Life-Threatening Behavior, 15,* 22–42.

Diekstra, R. F. W., & Kerkof, A. J. F. M. (1993, June). *Attitudes toward suicide: The development of a Suicide-Attitude Questionnaire (SUIATT).* Paper presented at the combined meetings of the International Association for Suicide Prevention, Canadian Association for Suicide Prevention, l'Association quebecoise de suicidologie, and Suicide-Action Montreal; Montreal.

Dodge, K. A. (1986). A social information processing model of social competence in children. In M. Permutter (Ed.), *Cognitive perspectives on children's social and behavioral development: The Minnesota Symposia on Child Psycholology* (Vol. 18, pp. 77–125). Hillsdale, NJ: Lawrence Erlbaum.

Durkheim, E. (1897/1951). *Suicide.* Glencoe, IL: Free Press.

Ekman, P. (1989). The argument and evidence about universals in facial expressions of emotion. In H. Wagner & A. Manstead (Eds.), *Handbook of psychophysiology: Emotion and social behavior* (pp. 143–164). New York: John Wiley.

Freud, S. (1917/1957). Mourning and melancholia. In J. Strachey (Ed. 2nd Trans.), *The standard edition of the complete psychological works of Sigmund Freud* (Vol. 14, pp. 237–258). London: Hogarth.

Frijda, N. H. (1986). *The emotions.* New York: Cambridge University Press.

Geertz, C. (1984). "From the native's point of view": On the nature of anthropological understanding. In R. A. Shweder & R. A. Levine (Eds.), *Culture theory: Essays on mind, self, and emotion* (pp. 123–136). New York: Cambridge University Press.

Goodstein, J. L. (1982). *Cognitive characteristics of suicide attempters.* Unpublished doctoral dissertation, Catholic University of America, Washington, DC.

Gould, M. S., Wallenstein, S., & Davidson, L. (1989). Suicide clusters: A critical review. *Suicide and Life-Threatening Behavior, 19,* 17–29.

Grossman, M., & Wood, W. (1993). Sex differences in intensity of emotional experience: A social role interpretation. *Journal of Personality and Social Psychology, 65,* 1010–1022.

Hafner, H., & Schmidtke, A. (1989). Do televised fictional suicide models produce suicides? In C. R. Pfeffer (Ed.), *Suicide among youth: Perspectives on risk and prevention* (pp. 117–141). Washington, DC: American Psychiatric Press.

Heelas, P. (1986). Emotion talk across cultures. In R. Harre (Ed.), *The social construction of emotions* (pp. 234–266). Oxford: Basil Blackwell.

Hewitt, J. P. (1991). *Self and society: A symbolic interactionist social psychology* (5th ed.). Boston: Allyn and Bacon.

Holtzworth-Munroe, A. (1992). Attributions and maritally violent men: The role of cognitions in marital violence. In J. Harvey, T. L. Orbuch, & A. L. Weber (Eds.), *Attributions, accounts, and close relationships* (pp. 165–175). New York: Springer-Verlag.

Hutchins, E. (1980). *Culture and inference: A Trobriand case study.* Cambridge, MA: Harvard University Press.

Isen, A. M., Niedenthal, P. M., & Cantor, N. (1992). An influence of positive affect on social categorization. *Motivation and Emotion, 16,* 65–78.

Juhasz, J. B. (1983). Social identity in the context of human and personal identity. In T. R. Sarbin & K. E. Scheibe (Eds.), *Studies in social identity* (pp. 289–318). New York: Praeger.

Kleinman, A. (1988). *Rethinking psychiatry: From cultural category to personal experience.* New York: Free Press.

Kral, M.J. (1994). Suicide as social logic. *Suicide and Life-Threatening Behavior, 24,* 245–255.

La Fontaine, J. (1975). Anthropology. In S. Perlin (Ed.), *A handbook for the study of suicide* (pp. 77–91). New York: Oxford University Press.

Lester, D., & Leenaars, A. A. (1993). Suicide in Canada before and after tightening firearm control laws. *Psychological Reports, 77,* 787–790.

Linehan, M. (1973). Suicide and attempted suicide: Study of perceived sex differences. *Perceptual and Motor Skills, 37,* 311–334.

Linehan, M. M., Camper, P., Chiles, J. A., Strossahl, K., & Shearin, E. (1987). Interpersonal problem solving and parasuicide. *Cognitive Therapy and Research, 11,* 1–12.

Litman, R. E. (1970). Suicide as acting out. In E. S. Shneidman, N. L. Farberow, & R. E. Litman (Eds.), *The psychology of suicide* (pp. 293–304). New York: Science House.

Lutz, C. (1987). Goals, events, and understanding in Ifaluk emotion theory. In D. Holland & N. Quinn (Eds.), *Cultural models in language and thought* (pp. 290–312). New York: Cambridge University Press.

Lutz, C., & White, G. M. (1986). The anthropology of emotions. *Annual Review of Anthropology, 15,* 405–436.

Maris, R. W. (1992). How are suicides different? In R. W. Maris, A. L. Berman, J. T. Matlsberger, & R. I. Yufit (Eds.), *Assessment and prediction of suicide* (pp. 65–87). New York: Guilford Press.

Markus, H., & Cross, S. (1990). The interpersonal self. In L. A. Pervin (Ed.), *Handbook of personality: Theory and research* (pp. 576–608). New York: Guilford Press.

Massaro, D. W., & Cowan, N. (1993). Information processing models: Microscopes of the mind. *Annual Review of Psychology, 44,* 383–425.

McFall, R. M. (1982). A review and reformulation of the concept of social skills. *Behavioral Assessment, 4,* 1–33.

Mead, G. H. (1934). *Mind, self, and society.* Chicago: University of Chicago Press.

Menninger, K. (1938). *Man against himself.* New York: Harcourt Brace.

Mortensen, P. M. (1990). *The development of a social information-processing model for examining adolescent parasuicide.* Unpublished doctoral dissertation, University of Alberta, Edmonton, AB, Canada.

Neuringer, C. (1964). Rigid thinking in suicidal individuals. *Journal of Consulting Psychology, 25,* 445–449.

Paicheler, G. (1988). *The psychology of social influence* (A. St. James-Emler & N. Emler, Trans.). New York: Cambridge University Press.

Phillips, D. P. (1974). The influence of suggestion on suicide: Substantive and theoretical implications of the Werther effect. *American Sociological Review, 39,* 340–354.

Phillips, D. P., Carstensen, L. L., & Paight, D. J. (1989). Effects of mass media news stories on suicide, with new evidence on the role of story content. In C. R. Pfeffer (Ed.), *Suicide among youth: Perspectives on risk and prevention* (pp. 101–116). Washington, DC: American Psychiatric Press.

Quinn, N., & Holland, D. (1987). Culture and cognition. In D. Holland & N. Quinn (Eds.), *Cultural models in language and thought* (pp. 3–40). New York: Canbridge University Press.

Rogers, J. R., & DeShon, R. P. (1992). A reliability investigation of the eight clinical scales of the Suicide Opinion Questionnaire. *Suicide and Life-Threatening Behavior, 22*, 428–441.

Room, R. (1990). Recent research on the effects of alcohol policy changes. *Journal of Primary Prevention, 11*, 83–94.

Rubin, K. H., & Krasnor, L. R. (1986). Social-cognitive and social behavioral perspectives on problem solving. In M. Permutter (Ed.), *Cognitive perspectives on children's social and behavioral development: The Minnesota Symposia on Child Psychology* (Vol. 18, pp. 11–68). Hillsdale, NJ: Lawrence Erlbaum.

Rule, B. G., & Bisanz, G. L. (1987). Goals and strategies of persuasion: A cognitive schema for understanding social events. In M. P. Zanna, J. M. Olson, & C. P. Herman (Eds.), *Social influence: The Ontario Symposium* (Vol. 5, pp. 185–206). Hillsdale, NJ: Lawrence Erlbaum.

Shneidman, E. S. (1985). *Definition of suicide.* New York: John Wiley.

Shneidman, E. S. (1993). Suicide as psychache. *Journal of Nervous and Mental Disease, 181*, 147–149.

Spiro, M. E. (1987). Collective representations and mental representations in religious symbol systems. In B. Kilborne & L. L. Langness (Eds.), *Culture and human nature: Theoretical papers of Melford E. Spiro* (pp. 161–184). Chicago: University of Chicago Press.

Stack, S. (1992). The effect of the media on suicide: The great depression. *Suicide and Life-Threatening Behavior, 22*, 255–267.

Takahashi, Y. (1993). Suicide prevention in Japan. In A. A. Leenaars (Ed.), *Suicidology: Essays in honor of Edwin S. Shneidman* (pp. 324–334). Northvale, NJ: Jason Aronson.

Tarde, G. (1898). *La logique sociale* (2nd ed.). Paris: Felix Alcan.

Turner, J. C. (1991). *Social influence.* Pacific Grove, CA: Brooks/Cole.

Vaillant, G. (1986). Cultural factors in the etiology of alcoholism: A prospective study. *Annals of the New York Academy of Sciences, 472*, 142–148.

Yando, R., Seitz, V., & Zigler, E. (1978). *Imitation: A developmental perspective.* Hillsdale, NJ: Lawrence Erlbaum.

Chapter 16

Suicide and Society

David Lester and Bijou Yang

There are many ways that suicide might impact upon a society, including the economic cost of suicide, the impact of deaths by suicide on life expectancy, as well as the questions of the function of a suicide for a society and the possibility that a society could have a "natural" suicide rate. [Ed.]

The relationship between suicide and society raises two issues, one of which is well-studied (the impact of society on suicide) and one of which has been ignored (the impact of suicide on society). This imbalance, of course, makes the issue of the impact of suicide on society all the more interesting, and so this chapter will begin by examining some ways in which suicide might have an impact on society.

THE IMPACT OF SUICIDE ON THE SOCIETY

The impact of suicide on society has rarely, if ever, been considered by scholars, yet suicide must be presumed to have an impact on the society for suicide has been made illegal (as in the United Kingdom prior to 1961 and in Canada prior to 1972), condemned as immoral and sinful, and been the focus of strenuous prevention efforts. Perhaps in these three areas, respectively, suicide is viewed as a negative comment on the state, upon organized religion, and on the competence of the mental health profession.

In each case suicide undermines the power of the social system (political, religious, and mental health).

Many communist nations in the past (including China, East Germany, Romania, and the USSR) refused to report suicide rates, possibly because they felt that suicide was an index of the misery experienced in those societies as a result of the communist dictatorships. Suicide also emphasizes the rights of the individual over those of the larger society, and many societies have asserted that the lives of its citizens belong to the state. Even the humanitarian trend in the Netherlands recently for providing a mechanism for citizens to apply for assisted suicide can also be seen as a way for the state to regain control over a person's decision to commit suicide.

Viewed as an index of misery, suicide serves to draw attention to the social ills affecting a group, whether it be youth, native Americans, and other aboriginal groups, or the elderly. In addition, suicide, like all deviant behaviors, serves to define normality for the society.

There have been occasional suggestions by others for the impact of suicide on society, and these will be reviewed in the following sections.

Population Longevity

Waigandt and Phelps (1990) noted that 51,147 people died from suicide and homicide in the U.S.A. in 1980. They calculated that this reduced the life expectancy of men by 0.705 years and of women by 0.261 years. A total of 1,305,805 person years per decade are irretrievably lost from suicide and homicide. Waigandt and Phelps did not calculate these figures separately for suicide.

The Centers for Disease Control (CDC, 1984) calculated that suicide accounted for 645,680 years of potential life lost in 1984, with seventy-one percent of the total attributable to suicide among white males. Homicide accounted for an additional 609,678 years of potential life lost.

Economic Impact

Epidemiological studies suggest that major depressive illness affects about two percent of the population of the U.S.A., and there are about 30,000 suicides each year. What economic cost do these behaviors involve for the nation? Stoudemire et al. (1986) made an effort to estimate this cost.

For those suffering from a major depressive illness, there are both direct costs and indirect costs. The direct costs include the cost of treatment (such as physician visits, hospitalization, pharmaceuticals, and travel costs when seeking care) while the indirect costs accrue from the loss of productivity of those who suffer a major depression. For those who commit suicide, the costs are mainly indirect.

Using data from studies conducted under the auspices of the National Institute of Mental Health, Stoudemire estimated that the number of cases of major depressive illness in a six-month period in 1980 was $4.8 million.

From other epidemiological studies, Stoudemire estimated that affective disorders accounted for about half a million hospital admissions in 1980, 7.4 million hospital days, and 13.3 million physician visits.

For inpatient care, the total cost came to $1.3 billion. For outpatient care, the cost was $0.6 billion. Other costs (including medication) came to $0.2 billion, giving a grand total of $2.1 billion.

The indirect costs of major depressive illnesses were based on an estimate of 5.7 million treated cases and 2.8 million untreated cases in 1980. Stoudemire estimated that these cases led to 127 million days lost involving treatment and 92 million days lost over and above the treatment days. Using data on the proportion of men and women in the labor force, Stoudemire estimated a loss of $10.0 billion in earnings.

Many persons with depressive illness commit suicide. Stoudemire estimated that about 60 percent of all suicides have a major depressive illness. In 1980, there were 26,869 suicides in the United States, and Stoudemire estimated that the suicides of those with major depressive illness (using sex-specific estimates of discounted lifetime earnings) involved an indirect cost of $4.2 billion.

Thus the total cost of major depressive illness in 1980 was estimated to be $2.1 billion for direct costs, $10 billion due to lost productivity, and $4.2 billion due to mortality from suicide. These costs add up to $16.3 billion.

It should be noted that the suicides of those with major depressive disorders eliminates the need for treatment for these individuals in future years and so results in savings in direct costs. Thus, the direct costs for treatment might be higher, for example, in 1980, if some of those suffering from a major depressive illness in earlier years had not committed suicide.

Stoudemire's estimate for the indirect cost as a result of the suicide of those with a major depressive illness was $4.2 billion. This was based on an estimate of 60 percent of suicides having a major depressive illness. From this, we can estimate that the indirect costs of all of the suicides through lost lifetime earnings would be $7 billion.

In addition, suicides also involve medical and legal costs in the efforts to revive suicides and to certify the deaths. These costs, however, are probably dwarfed by the social costs of economic production.

In addition to the behavior of suicide in which the person dies, there are many attempts at suicide each year where the individual survives. It is difficult to count the number of attempts at suicide each year because many attempters do not require medical attention and so do not come to the attention of the authorities. However, it has been estimated by Shneidman and Farberow (1961) that there at least eight suicide attempts for every completed suicide. Thus, if there are 30,000 completed suicides in one year, there may be upwards of 240,000 attempted suicides.

Many attempted suicides require medical care, and a good proportion of them receive psychological and psychiatric treatment. These attempters will be lost to the labor force during this period, incurring additional economic costs. It can be seen that the economic costs of suicide are considerable.

Looking just at suicides by those aged 15–24, Weinstein and Saturno (1989) estimated that each youth suicide results in the loss of 53 years of human life and $432,000 of economic productivity. The national cost of youth suicide in the U.S.A. in 1980 came to 276,000 years of life lost, 217,000 years of productive life lost (before the age of 65) and economic costs of $2.26 billion. Adding in the costs of nonfatal suicidal acts, the cost rose to $3.19 billion.

Suicide and Political Protest

Occasional suicides have an impact on society because of the political motivation behind the death. For example, the Buddhist monk, Thich Quang Duc, immolated himself in Saigon on June 11, 1963, as a protest against the regime of Ngo Dinh Diem in South Vietnam, following which other people immolated themselves in Vietnam, the U.S.A., and elsewhere to protest the political situation in Vietnam (Coleman, 1987). It is difficult to assess the impact of such acts, and they are quite rare.

Societal Approval of Suicide

Schelling (1978), an economist, has noted that people's behavior often depends upon how many other people are behaving in the same way. An activity becomes self-sustaining (and may increase in incidence) once the frequency of that activity increases beyond a certain level. If this idea is applied to national suicide rates, it can be hypothesized that a given suicide rate creates a certain amount of publicity about suicide and a particular likelihood that a person in the society knows someone who has committed suicide. Once the suicide rate reaches a critical level, the publicity and probability of knowing suicides increase to such an extent that the effect of suggestion (or imitation) makes the behavior self-sustaining and perhaps accelerates it and may also increase the society's tolerance for and approval of suicide.

Lester (1989) has conducted several tests of this hypothesis and showed that, both for nations of the world and for the states of America, those regions in 1970 with higher suicide rates experienced greater absolute increases in the suicide rate by 1980.

Celebrity Suicides Leading to Further Suicides

Related to this last point, Phillips (1974) and Stack (1990) have documented that suicides reported by the media, especially of celebrities, is followed in the next week by an increase in the suicide rate, especially among those similar in age and sex to the celebrity suicide. The existence of suicide clusters (Coleman, 1987) illustrates a similar suggestion effect. Thus it appears that a suicide stimulates, and perhaps creates, more suicides.

WHAT IS THE FUNCTION OF SUICIDE FOR SOCIETY?

In his discussion of crime, Durkheim (1982) argued that crime was necessary. It was linked to the basic conditions of social life. If one form of crime disappeared, other forms would develop to fill the void. If serious crimes were to be viewed sternly by society, they may be reduced in frequency. But the stern values would then lead people to view the hitherto minor crimes more seriously, making them now major crimes.

Durkheim also noted that not everyone in a society shares the same moral values, and so some people will always offend against the moral and legal rules of the society. Furthermore, some behaviors which were once labeled as criminal later prove to be important for the society. Today's traitors may be tomorrow's heroes; today's terrorists tomorrow's rulers.

What then might the social function of suicide be? To date, this question has not been addressed. Lester (1988b) has explored this question at the biological level, suggesting that suicide may function to remove the genes of defective people (those who are psychiatrically disturbed, for example) and those past child-bearing age from the society and may also serve to reduce the size of the population. DeCatanzaro (1981), looking at suicide from a sociobiological perspective, similarly suggested that suicide may be altruistic by benefiting others who share our genes. But we have little to suggest for the social function of suicide.

IS THERE A NATURAL SUICIDE RATE?

Durkheim (1982) noted that crime was normal in the sense that it was completely impossible for any society to be entirely free from crime. Crime served a function for society and could never not occur. This raises the question of whether suicide is normal in the sense that it is impossible for a society to be free from suicide.

Yang (1989; Lester and Yang, 1992) mathematically analyzed theories of the relationship between economic conditions (x) and the suicide rate (y) and concluded that all theories predict that the curve has a positive intercept on the y-axis during normal economic conditions and that, therefore, there is an inevitable non-zero suicide rate for every society, the "natural" suicide rate of the society.

Durkheim's (1897) theory of suicide implies a non-zero suicide rate for societies since he argued that suicide was more likely at both high and low levels of social integration and social regulation. A moderate level of social integration and social regulation would not necessarily result in an absence of suicide. Maris (1981) also suggested that no society could be free from suicide because of the inherent harshness of the human condition.

Yang and Lester (1991) tested this idea by examining several multiple regression analyses in which the suicide rates of the states of America in 1980 were regressed on several sets of socioeconomic variables. Setting the socioeconomic variables to zero (that is, for example, a zero divorce rate and a zero unemployment rate) still left the suicide rate as non-zero and positive. They concluded that if social conditions were made ideal from the point of view of producing a low suicide rate, the suicide rate of Americans would still be non-zero and positive.

WHAT IS THE IMPACT OF SOCIETY ON SUICIDE?

This is a less interesting question since it is the most well studied. Many studies have appeared which document an association between societal characteristics and the suicide rates of societies (Lester, 1992a). However, several issues are worth noting here.

Concrete versus Abstract Social Characteristics

Recently, two critiques of the sociological approach to the study of suicide have appeared (Moksony, 1990; Taylor, 1990) which are remarkably congruent. They both suggest that sociologists have failed to demonstrate the influence of the society on suicide. Taylor (1990) argued that Durkheim (1897), in his book on suicide, demonstrated associations between social variables (such as religious affiliation and marriage) and societal suicide rates. According to Taylor, Durkheim did not, however, mean to suggest that religious affiliation or marriage in themselves caused the differences in suicide rates. Rather, Durkheim used these associations to reveal a common underlying cause of suicide, which was the extent to which people are intergrated and regulated by the society. Durkheim was searching for underlying and unobservable mechanisms and causal processes.

Later sociologists have foresaken the task of searhcing for invisible but real forces acting upon individuals in a society and have pursued instead a more empirical study of the relationships between observable social phenomena and suicide. They then view suicide as caused by these external social factors.

Moksony (1990) critiqued recent ecological studies of suicide, particularly the spatial differences in suicide rates over the different areas of cities. The early studies of this by Cavan (1928) and Schmid (1928) attributed the spatial pattern of suicide in cities to their location in the ecological structure of the city. For example, those areas of the city with higher suicide rates tended to have an increased turnover in their population which Cavan saw as impeding the development of both a coherent system of norms and values governing behavior and stable social relationships.

Moksony argued that recent studies, such as Maris's (1969), use aggregate data to describe relationships between various characteristics of the population in each area of the city to the suicide rate. These studies tend to explore the effects of the composition of the population in an area on the suicide rate rather than the area as an environment. For example, if areas have high numbers of migrants, then the suicide rate is predicted to be high because migrants have higher suicide rates. Cavan and Schmid, according to Moksony, would instead have treated the high proportion of migrants as a characteristic of the area and sought to show that this characteristic of the area impeded the development of a stable social life for everyone in the area, newcomers and old-timers alike.

Moksony felt that his characterization of modern ecological studies was correct because the investigators often cast their studies as a preliminary step leading to a study in which the individuals would be directly observed. For example, if areas with many socially deviant individuals have higher suicide rates, the next step is usually to study suicidal behavior in the socially deviant and non-deviant people without regard to where they live (McCulloch & Philip, 1972).

Both Taylor and Moksony have made the point, then, that sociologists have not studied the effect of society on suicide rates. Rather, soci-

ologists have studied the imapct of social variables as causal agents in themselves on the suicide rate of individuals in the society. Is there any research
which might satisfy Taylor and Moksony?

Lester (1988a) suggested that social variables could be subjected to a
factor analysis in order to identify factors, or clusters, of related variables.
The factor scores can then be correlated with the suicide rates. Lester found
that a cluster of variables including divorce rates, rates of interstate migra-
tion, and church attendance correlated most strongly with the suicide rates
of the states of the U.S.A. Lester's study does not imply that any of these
three variables is more important than the other two in this association. It
also does not imply that these three social variables cause the state suicide
rates. Rather the study implies that there is a broader social characteristic,
manifested perhaps in the states' divorce rates, migrant composition, and
religious patterns, which is associated with suicide rates. This higher order
characteristic, whatever it may be called (though low social integration
seems a good possibility) seems close to satisfying Taylor's and Moksony's
requirement for a societal or areal effect.

More detailed analysis of the data in the study above (Lester, 1992b)
has shown that the higher order characteristic (perhaps indicating low
social integration) is associated with the suicide rate of males and females,
whites and blacks, those of all ages, and those of all marital statuses. Thus,
the association has generality and, in particular, despite the fact that one
of the variables loading on the factor is the divorce rate, is found for those
of each marital status.

Angyal (1941, 1965), a personality theorist, argued for a holistic position both for the consideration of the individual mind and for the society
in which the individual lives. For the person, he discussed possibilities for
the system principle, the pattern that organizes all of the component processes of the person's mind. Similarly, for the society, he argued that the
individual valences and demand qualities present in the society that impact upon the individual are organized into axiomatic values, which are
themselves organized into systems of axioms. These systems of axioms then
form a system princple for the society. Although he gave no examples of
possible societal system principles, the distinction between democracy and
totalitarianism can be seen as referring to a societal system princple, as
might a conservative versus a liberal government.

In Parsons' (1966) analysis of societies, he distinguished between
primitive, archaic, advanced intermediate, and modern societies. These
distinctions are really definitions of the system principles of different types
of society as they developed over the centuries (Lester, 1984).

If we could classify a sample of modern societies according to such
high level system principles and then compare the suicide rates of the

nations so classified, again we would have come close to satisfying the requirements of Taylor and Moksony of demonstrating a possible societal effect on suicide rates.

There is the suspicion that the issue raised by Taylor and Moksony may be a special case of the holistic/atomistic debate. Holistic theorists like to view the system (be it an individual mind or a society) as a whole, and they dislike analyzing the parts. However, a holistic analysis raises the question of the cause of the association. If we found, for example, that some broad characteristic of societies was associated with the suicide rate of those societies, then we would likely wonder how this association came about. The answer to such a question typically demands a non-holistic approach. From social integration, for example, we tend to move toward an examination of the various social customs that might affect social integration and eventually move to an examination of the impact of these customs on the individual. Then we will have laid ourselves open to the Taylor and Moksony criticisms.

For example, if we consider Eastern and Western European nations, which differ in democratic versus communist governments, it is hard not to consider specific differences in some features of the society, such as the freedom of the press, and difficult not to consider the impact of these characteristics on specific subgroups, such as the young and the old. However, even if research and theorizing often moves toward an atomistic analysis, it would be intellectually satisfying if we could first demonstrate a societal or areal effect.

THE IMPACT ON THE SOCIETY VERSUS
THE INDIVIDUAL

Lester and Yang (1991) noted that the social context of suicide can be examined from both the interpersonal and the cultural perspectives. An analogy here is economics where microeconomics is concerned with the behavior of individual economic units and macroeconomics with the economy as a whole. Lester and Yang suggested parallel terms for sociology, with macrosocionomics examining the imapct of the culture on the members of the society while microsocionomics examines the impact of individuals on one another.

They explored the impact of divorce on suicide. In the microsocionomic perspective, divorce has a dramatic impact on the individuals involved. A person who was living with a spouse is now without that partner. The loss often leads divorced people to attach themselves impulsively to other, often inappropriate, individuals. Divorced people sometimes find that former friends have taken the side of their ex-spouse and they often feel lonely. Divorced persons typically feel angry, depressed and anxious, and they are preoccupied with thoughts about the past and the future. From Durkheim's (1897) perspective, divorced people are less well socially integrated than those who are married.

To illustrate a macrosocionomic perspective, Lester and Yang compared those who get divorced in Ireland (where the divorce rate is very low) versus the USA (where the divorce rate is very high). How might the macrosocionomic variable of the divorce rate of the society affect the individual?

In Ireland where divorce is rare, the divorced person may feel stigma, and for a person to get divorced in such a society implies a low degree of social regulation. In contrast, in the U.S.A. where divorce is common, there is less stigma to being divorced, and divorce does not imply less social regulation in those divorcing.

Furthermore, as we noted in the previous section, the divorce rate of the society may also be an indicator of a more abstract characteristic of the society, a characteristic which may affect all members of the society. For example, societies with low levels of social integration, indicated by a high divorce rate among other variables, may have a high suicide rate in all groups of the society. Lester and Yang showed that, in the U.S.A. in 1980, states with high divorce rates had high suicide rates in the single, married and widowed as well as in the divorced.

TIME SERIES VERSUS REGIONAL STUDIES

It has been noted that societal variables which are associated with, and may therefore cause, societal suicide rates appear to differ for regional studies of suicide rates and for time-series studies of suicide rates. For example, while unemployment rates appear to be associated with the suicide rate in the U.S.A. over time (Yang & Lester, 1990), they do not appear to be associated with the suicide rates of the states (Lester, 1988a). This raises the possibility that different sociological theories may needed to account for the results of the two types of studies.

PREDICTING THE SMOOTHED TREND IN THE SUICIDE RATE VERSUS DEVIATIONS

In time-series studies of the societal suicide rate, the departure from the smoothed trend in the suicide rate is often viewed as "random noise" in the data. Thus, it of interest to ask whether theories which account for the smoothed-trend in the societal suicide rate over time might also account for these fluctuations. Yang and Lester (1990) found in the U.S.A. that the unemployment rate predicted both the smoothed trend in the suicide rate and the fluctuations from this trend. In contrast, the divorce rate predicted only the smoothed trend. Again, different sociological theories may be required to account for these two phenomena.

SUMMARY

In this brief essay, we have tried first to identify some ways in which suicide might impact upon a society. We noted the economic costs of suicide and the impact of suicide on life-expectancy, and we also mentioned the possible impact of political suicides on the society.

In discussing the effect of society on suicide, we have focussed on several issues which merit thought and research in the future. Can we identify and show the impact of broad societal characteristics on suicide? Are different theories required for the regional variation in suicide rates and for the variation of societal suicide rates over time. And in time-series studies, are different theories required for predicting the smoothed trend and for predicting fluctuations from this trend?

Finally, we asked two questions which we hope will stimulate sociologists and social psychiatrists. What is the social function of suicide for a society and could there be a natural (non-zero) suicide rate for societies?

REFERENCES

Angyal, A. (1941). *Foundations for a science of personality.* New York: Commonwealth Fund.

Angyal, A. (1965). *Neurosis and treatment.* New York: John Wiley.

Cavan, R. S. (1928). *Suicide.* Chicago: University of Chicago Press.

Centers for Disease Control (CDC) (1987). Premature mortality due to suicide and homicide. *Morbidity Mortality Weekly Report, 36*(32), 531–534.

Coleman, L. (1987). *Suicide clusters.* Boston: Faber & Faber.

DeCatanzaro, D. (1981). *Suicide and self-damaging behavior.* New York: Academic Press.

Durkheim, E. (1897). *Le suicide.* Paris: Felix Alcan.

Durkheim, E. (1982). *The rules of sociological method.* New York: Free Press.

Lester, D. (1984). Systems theories of personality: some Parsonian implications. *Psychology, 21*(1), 12–14.

Lester, D. (1988a). A regional analysis of suicide and homicide rates in the USA. *Social Psychiatry and Psychiatric Epidemiology, 23,* 202–205.

Lester, D. (1988b). *The biochemical basis of suicide.* Springfield, IL: Charles C Thomas.

Lester, D. (1989). *Suicide from a sociological perspective.* Springfield, IL: Charles C Thomas.

Lester, D. (1992a). *Why people kill themselves.* Springfield, IL: Charles C Thomas.

Lester, D. (1992b). Patterns of suicide and homicide in America. *Proceedings of the Pavese Society, 4,* 118–211.

Lester, D., & Yang, B. (1991). Microsocionomics versus macrosocionomics as a model for examining suicide. *Psychological Reports, 69,* 735–738.

Lester, D., & Yang, B. (1992). *The economy and suicide.* New York: AMS.

Maris, R. W. (1969). *Social forces in urban suicide.* Homewood, IL: Dorsey.

Maris, R. (1981). *Pathways to suicide.* Baltimore: Johns Hopkins University Press.

McCulloch, J. W., & Philip, A. E. (1972). *Suicidal behavior.* Elmsford, NY: Pergamon Press.

Moksony, F.(1990). Ecological analysis of suicide. In D. Lester (Ed.), *Understanding suicide* (pp. 121–138). Philadelphia: Charles Press.

Parsons, T. (1966). *Societies.* Englewood Cliffs, NJ: Prentice-Hall.

Phillips, D. P. (1974). The influence of suggestion on suicide. *American Sociological Review, 39,* 340–354.

Schelling, T. C. (1978). *Micromotives and macrobehavior.* New York: Norton.

Schmid, C. F. (1928). *Suicides in Seattle, 1914–1925.* Seattle: University of Washington Press.

Shneidman, E. S., & Farberow, N. L. (1961). *The cry for help.* New York: McGraw-Hill.

Stack, S. (1990). Media impacts on suicide. In D. Lester (Ed.), *Current concepts of suicide* (pp. 107–120). Philadelphia: Charles Press.

Stoudemire, A., Frank, R., Hedemark, N., Kamlet, M., & Blazer, D. (1986). The economic burden of depression. *General Hospital Psychiatry, 8,* 387–394.

Taylor, S. (1990). Suicide, Durkheim and sociology. In D. Lester (Ed.), *Understanding suicide* (pp. 225–236). Philadelphia: Charles Press.

Waigandt, A., & Phelps, L.(1990). The effects of homicides and suicides on the population longevity of the United States. *Journal of Traumatic Stress, 3,* 297–304.

Weinstein, M. C., & Saturno, P. J. (1989). Economic impact of youth suicides and suicide attempts. In M. L. Rosenberg & K. Baer (Eds.), *Report of the Secretary's Task Force on Youth Suicide, Volume 4* (pp. 82–93). Washington, DC: Department of Health.

Yang, B. (1989). *A real income hypothesis of suicide.* Paper presented at the meeting of the Eastern Economic Association meeting, Baltimore.

Yang, B., & Lester, D.(1990). Time-series analyses of the American suicide rate. *Social Psychiatry & Psychiatric Epidemiology, 25,* 274–275.

Yang, B., & Lester, D. (1991). Is there a natural suicide rate for a society? *Psychological Reports, 68,* 322.

Index